Freedom Walk

Freedom Walk

MISSISSIPPI OR BUST

Mary
Stanton

University Press of Mississippi
Jackson

www.upress.state.ms.us

Paperback Edition 2010

Library of Congress Cataloging-in-Publication Data

Stanton, Mary, 1946–
    Freedom walk : Mississippi or bust / Mary Stanton.
        p. cm.
Includes bibliographical references and index.
    ISBN 1-60473-540-6
1. Civil rights movements—Southern States—History—20th century. 2. African
Americans—Civil rights—Southern States—History—20th century. 3. Southern
States—Race relations—Case studies. 4. Alabama—Race relations—Case studies.
5. Mississippi—Race relations—Case studies. 6. Civil rights workers—Crimes
against—Southern States—Case studies. 7. Civil rights workers—Southern
States—Interviews. 8. Whites—Southern States—Interviews. I. Title.
E185.61 .S785 2003
305.8'00975—dc21   2002006909

British Library Cataloging-in-Publication Data available

For Dr. Sue Shirah-Sands, daughter, sister, wife, mother, educator, friend.
She stayed in Alabama and worked to make the dream come true.

Many a time a few simple words have helped further the welfare of the nation, no matter who uttered them; the voice itself, displaying its latent powers, sufficed to move the hearts of men.
—PETRARCH

Contents

Acknowledgments

Nobody writes a book alone, not a book worth reading. What brings life to narrative history are memories, recollections, *stories. Freedom Walk* is a collaboration involving the following people: Mary Hamilton Wesley (CORE), actress Madeleine Sherwood, Gadsden, Alabama, district attorney James Hedgspeth, former Birmingham, Alabama, district attorney Bill Baxley, Danny Lyon, SNCC photographer, Jerry Thornbery, Ed Chance (CORE), Neil Carew, National Public Radio, Alabama special investigator Bob Eddy, Anne Braden (SCEF), Benita Crow, Mendy Samstein (SNCC), Casey Hayden (SNCC and SDS), Mary King (SNCC), Sue Thrasher (SSOC), Dr. Bobs Tusa, University of Southern Mississippi, Joan Browning (SNCC), Jane Stembridge (SNCC), Dorothy Zellner (SNCC), Norm Conard, Jan Hillegas, Mississippi Freedom Information Service, Professor J. Angus Johnson, Hunter College, former Gadsden district attorney William W. Rayburn, Barbara Joye, Harlan Joye (SSOC and SLAM), Nelson Blackstock (SDS), Walter Tillow (SNCC), Robert Pardun (SNCC), James H. (JimHerb) Williams (SSOC and SCEF), Steve Max (SDS), Dr. Martin Morand, Atlanta ILGWU, Marshall Hawkins, Boston Unitarian Universalist Archives, and John M. Kelso, Jr., Freedom of Information–Privacy Acts Section, Office of Public and Congressional Affairs, U.S. Department of Justice.

The Freedom Walkers were Zev Aelony (CORE), Robert Gore (CORE), Eric Weinberger (CORE), Winston Lockett (CORE), Bill Hansen (SNCC), and Bob Zellner (SNCC).

I want especially to thank Ed Hamlett, SNCC campus traveler, a founder of SSOC, member of the SDS executive committee, and a lifelong social justice advocate; Sheila Michaels of SNCC and CORE; and Dr. Sue Shirah-Sands, without whom I would not have known where to begin.

I am also indebted to the following institutions for their help with my research: Birmingham Public Library; Chattanooga Public Library; the library of Woodstock, New York; New York City Public Library, Research Division; the Schomberg Center for the Study of Black Culture, New York City; Gadsden, Alabama, Public Library; Museum of Television and Radio, New York City; Library of the Interchurch Center, New York City; Broome County Library, Binghamton, New York; Broome County Historical Society, Binghamton, New York; Columbia University Oral History Project, New York City; Methodist Archives, Drew University, Madison, New Jersey; Library of the General Seminary (Episcopalian), New York City; Rutgers University Library; and the library of Marymount College, New York City.

For help with the development of the manuscript and for their unfailing enthusiasm, deepest thanks are due Carolyn Jackson, Martha Hughes, Sally Hand, and Kathleen McSherry.

Introduction: Shadow History

On April 23, 1963, Bill Moore, a white mailman, was shot dead on a highway near Attalla, Alabama. He was walking to Jackson, Mississippi, from Chattanooga, Tennessee, to hand-deliver a plea for racial tolerance to Governor Ross Barnett. Floyd Simpson, a white Alabama grocer, was arrested and charged with Moore's murder.

One week later, Sam Shirah, a white college student, and nine activists from the Student Nonviolent Coordinating Committee (SNCC) and the Congress of Racial Equality (CORE) attempted to finish Moore's walk. They were beaten and jailed outside Gadsden, Alabama, in the first of five unsuccessful attempts to complete the postman's final delivery.

The names of these men have faded into shadow history, that storeroom of news-pushed-aside when more compelling events capture the spotlight. The battle of Birmingham and the March on Washington were the compelling events of the spring and summer of 1963. Children bitten by snarling police dogs, demonstrators scattered by fire hoses, thousands gathered peacefully at the Lincoln Memorial—*those* images absorbed the light, leaving one mailman, one assassin, and ten Freedom Walkers in the shadows.

It is presently fashionable to maintain that their time, the civil rights era, was a better one than our own—a time of high principles and stirred consciences. How we remember the past often indicates what matters most to us in the present. A careful study of the shadow history of the 1963 Freedom Walk, however, deflates such nostalgic notions by exposing the fallacy that it was easier to identify the good guys from the bad ones forty years ago.

Recalling a Dr. Martin Luther King, Jr., or even a George Wallace, one might be tempted to say, "I could *never* do what he did." Those men were larger than life, but Bill Moore, Floyd Simpson, and Sam Shirah were men of ordinary stature. They are important because of the great stir they created nearly four decades ago in a place Flannery O'Connor called "the Christ-haunted South."

Individually their stories might feed our fascination for the lost, the wrong-headed, and the expendable. Their personal calamities might even seduce us into agreeing with Boston's Richard Cardinal Cushing that "the greatest tragedy is not pain, but wasted pain."

Their public lives, however, make us question whether pain is ever really wasted. Often a perspective of decades is needed for recognition of the waves of change stirred by one troublemaker's ripples.

Bill Moore, the troublemaker whose ripple became the Freedom Walk, pursued the American dream with the passion of an outsider. Success, in a traditional sense, always eluded him. He was an economic failure, a loner, and an atheist in a society which distrusted all three.

Floyd Simpson, Moore's alleged murderer, was a self-identified Christian segregationist who believed that the United States Congress was being held hostage by godless communists whose civil rights bill would destroy the Southern Way of Life.

Sam Shirah, who continued Moore's walk, was determined to take America to task for refusing to honor the Constitution's promises. The son of a Methodist preacher, Shirah sincerely believed that if white Americans understood the inhumanity of segregation, they would force their representatives in Congress to eliminate it.

Early on in my research I thought that I might have uncovered an important motive for the seemingly senseless slaying of Bill Moore. When I learned that he was an *atheist* I wondered if his lack of religious conviction might in some way have contributed to his brutal murder in the Bible Belt.

When I shared my theory with a white friend who'd been raised near Meridian, Mississippi, she shook her head. "Mary," she said, "don't get distracted. For certain whites control was all that counted. It was no sin to kill an atheist, an integrationist, a communist, or a Jew. They were Satan's conspirators: enemies of the white Jesus and the white South. Religion *was* politics, understand? Integrationists were atheists, and atheists were communists, most likely Jews, and they all deserved to die."

She was right, of course. It's all very complicated—wrapped in shadows—consigned to shadow history where past and present, significance and insignificance reside in unrelenting tension. What happens, who it happens to, who wins, who loses, is at once valuable and useless information—all as mystifying and as baffling as the individual life.

The facts of this particular story have been carefully researched and reconstructed from accounts of people who knew Moore, Shirah, and Simpson (in some cases marched with them or in opposition to them), from newspapers and newsreels, from Bill Moore's insightful memoir, *The Mind in Chains*, and from their FBI files secured through the Freedom of Information Act. It is the space between the facts that often captures my imagination, and there, without violating any knowns, I speculate about some unknowns. I've set the lives of three white southern men against the backdrop of a turbulent and decisive year in American history. What they shared was a love of the South; what separated them were their convictions about who ought to be permitted to walk its highways.

Freedom Walk is the story of a long march—of five unsuccessful attempts to walk across Alabama to reach the governor's mansion in Jackson, Mississippi. In the pages that follow I've examined the life of a white man who ventured a freedom walk in the days when white activism was not fashionable. I've traced Bill Moore's influence as the movement gained momentum and more whites volunteered, and as men like Floyd Simpson tried to stop them.

Through the experience of Sam Shirah I've explored the irony of white activism complicating everything and ultimately proving a very mixed blessing for both races.

The singular and restless lives of William Moore, Floyd Simpson, and Samuel Shirah, Jr., bear witness to the distortions and oversimplifications that obscure our understanding of the recent past.

In 1963, the streams of religious renewal, racial unrest, and cold war politics were feeding a growing river of social paranoia. In the spring the river overflowed its banks; by summer it would flood. The paths of these three men converged in April as two were pressing hard to change, and one to maintain, an America that was already over. Be warned that this story has no Hollywood ending. Justice was never served. One might reasonably ask what three dead white men can teach contemporary Americans about the civil rights movement. Nothing simple.

Part I

The Postman's Walk

*Neither snow, nor rain, nor heat,
nor night stays these couriers
from the swift completion
of their appointed rounds.*
—HERODOTUS

Walker

The spring air was warm, almost hot, when Bill Moore arrived at the Greyhound bus station on Market Street in downtown Chattanooga. It was nearly three o'clock on a Sunday afternoon, April 21, 1963. Moore looked like a lot of the men who came through the terminal that day—tall, middle-aged, white, heavyset, a little down on his luck. He had on a jacket that had seen too many seasons and heels that were worn to forty-five-degree angles.

He wore a set of sandwich board signs, but even that was not unusual. Drifters often picked up a few dollars in Chattanooga by hiring themselves out as walking advertisements for restaurants, beauty parlors, tourist attractions, or first-run movies. Moore's signs, however, were handwritten, made of cardboard, and he wasn't selling anything. His front panel read, *"End Segregation In America, Eat At Joe's—Both Black and White,"* and on the back, *"Equal Rights For All (Mississippi or Bust)."*

Moore could hardly wait to start walking; he'd been sitting since nine-thirty the night before. The ride from Washington, D.C., was long and bumpy, and his head felt heavy from the gasoline fumes he had inhaled. He walked out to Market Street pulling a small shopping cart which served as his suitcase. Directly ahead was the Hotel Plaza, and to his left the shopping district. Behind him the railroad yards stretched out—that way felt right.

"Can you tell me how I get to 11 South?" he asked a man who was staring at him. The man stiffened.

"Keep going straight till you hit Broad," he said slowly, "then follow it all the way."

"Thanks." Moore smiled.

"Don't mention it."

Moore followed Eleventh Street past the Johnson Tire Company and out to Broad near the big Union Depot railroad station. An old Negro man limped toward him making eye contact as if he might speak. Moore stopped and the man shouted "No!" Lunging forward he tore the word "Black" right off Moore's front sign, leaving a gaping hole.

"*Hey!*" Moore dropped his shopping cart and tried to grab the man, but he was too agile.

"It's *colored*," the man shrieked. "*Colored people*. Ain't you never heard of the 'Sociation for 'Vancement for *Colored* People?"

The man was half Moore's size and twice his age. Moore could easily have picked him up and tossed him across the street. Instead he took a deep breath. "Sorry, mister."

The old man glared at him. "*Colored*," he growled, backing toward the bus station.[1]

Moore had expected *white* resistance, not this. But he wouldn't permit it to distract him; there was too much to do. He picked up his cart and continued to follow Broad Street's wide curve toward Lookout Mountain. To his left, side streets ran into a cheap rent district where pawn shops, grimy restaurants, and storefront churches crowded under a towering neon sign for the Grand Hotel. The hotel looked as if it rose right up from the center of the squalor.

An elderly white lady listing to one side from the weight of her shopping bags crossed in front of him. "What are you selling?" she demanded.

"Integration," he said.

"Damn fool," she mumbled, shaking her head as she negotiated her way across the Southern Railway tracks.

Beyond the tracks Moore entered a stretch of oil drums and storage tanks before passing a large armory. Pushing south to Moccasin Bend, where the winding Tennessee River turns back on itself and heads north, he entered the countryside.

It would have been hard to imagine William Moore, in his rumpled clothes, pulling a shopping cart and wearing hand-lettered signs, as someone who'd studied in London and Paris, attended graduate school at Johns Hopkins University, and published a book, and who had a steady job, a wife, and three teenagers who loved him—but he had, and he'd done, all those things.

Now Moore planned to walk all alone through Georgia, Alabama, and Mississippi, the Deep South, where resistance to race mixing was fiercest. His destination was Jackson, Mississippi, and he had to cross the Appalachian South to get there. The distance from Chattanooga to Jackson is roughly 350 miles. Moore would follow Highway 11 through lower Tennessee and across Georgia and Alabama. It was the easiest route for a man on foot, but probably the most dangerous. Route 11, known as the Birmingham Highway, hugged the southern tip of the Appalachian Mountains, a region of poor farmers, mill hands, and mountaineers who distrusted strangers.

Stretching between Chattanooga and Birmingham, the Sand Mountain area was home to devout men and women who recognized the Holy Spirit and trusted that the Bible meant what it said—even the Word that called the faithful to put their hands in fire, drink poison, take up serpents, and dance before the Lord.

Sand Mountain was also Klan country. In 1963 the United Empire of Tennessee, the Alabama Realm of the Invisible Empire, and the Georgia Knights claimed the area east of Chattanooga from the foot of Missionary Ridge to Rossville, Georgia. Hooded knights still gathered in Chattanooga to parade through the downtown with big blinking crosses made of lightbulbs strapped to the hoods of their cars.

"Our home will be closed to you on a trip of this nature," Moore's aunt Helen Cagle had written from Birmingham. "And I don't want your name or picture to appear in a paper in Mississippi in any such mess. You'll find out when you hit this section of the South that what you are doing is not a joke after all."[2]

A joke. Some, including Aunt Helen, would say that Moore's whole life had been a joke. She signed off "with love and a prayer to God that He will deliver you from this thing that has taken possession of you."

Aunt Helen and Uncle Charlie were Moore's closest relatives. He'd lived with Aunt Helen on his grandparents' farm in Mississippi—almost twenty-five years before. He figured that he just might stop to see them anyway. Aunt Helen had always been nervous. She was probably just upset about Martin Luther King's demonstrations in Birmingham.

"I'm recovering from surgery and my nerves can't take this kind of foolishness," she'd written. He obviously couldn't count on staying overnight like he'd planned, but he could visit a while.

Before she married Charlie Cagle, Aunt Helen, who was his father's sister, had lived in Russell, Mississippi. "I'm sure you understand our feelings on the subject," she wrote. "I'm sure I can't see how you can expect us to welcome you down here with the motive you have in mind. It's not that we don't love you, cause we do, but we certainly don't love what you stand for. When I was a young girl I did the best I could to help Mama and Daddy take care of you, and we tried to raise you right. And this is the thanks we all get. We just do not appreciate it at all. You do not seem to have any respect for Mama and Daddy's memory."[3]

Route 11 was deserted on this late Sunday afternoon. The WPA Tennessee guidebook that Moore had studied in the Baltimore library was accurate. "Tennessee line to Alabama line 23.6 miles. Roadbed graded dirt: condition poor in some places, Southern Railway parallels route throughout. Limited accommodations."

Once in a long while a pickup, flatbed truck, or broken-down sedan would rumble along the two-lane blacktop, but few people passed the big white man with his cardboard signs. Moore was determined to make it all the way to Jackson, Mississippi—*Mississippi or Bust*—just as his sign said. He'd planned his route carefully, beginning in Washington, D.C., where the Freedom Riders had started their journey in 1961, and connecting with U.S. 11 in Chattanooga, Tennessee, near the site of the 1962 Southern Peace Walk. He would pass through Birmingham where the Freedom Riders were nearly beaten to death, and follow 11 South straight through to the Mississippi state capital.

Moore's goal was to speak directly with Governor Ross Barnett about segregation. The governor's refusal to permit the integration of the University of Mississippi the previous year had triggered a riot that left two people dead. Moore would appeal to Barnett as white southerner to white southerner—as a mailman delivering a plea for tolerance right up to 300 East Capitol Street, the Governor's Mansion. Barnett had a reputation for making himself available to anyone who wanted to speak with him, and Moore was going to make a request.

The night before James Meredith, a black man, was scheduled to register at Ole Miss, Governor Barnett had waved a Confederate flag at a Mississippi-Kentucky football game in Jackson and shouted, "I love Mississippi! I love our customs!" Moore would remind him that there were *many* people in the Magnolia State and *many* customs.

Barnett might listen, or he might just call security and have Moore hauled away. Either way, there was an opportunity for publicity, and that's how his message would reach other white southerners. Moore had nearly been arrested in front of the White House just two days before when he'd tried to deliver a letter to the president explaining the purpose of his walk. A black reporter had interviewed him and taken his picture.

Moore's strategy was to cover forty miles a day for ten days. That would take him roughly four hundred miles. Two weeks was all the vacation leave he'd accrued at the Baltimore post office where he worked. He'd carefully packed his cart with a change of clothes, an extra pair of shoes, a blanket, his journal, and mimeographed copies of the letters he'd written to Governor Barnett and to President Kennedy. He planned to hand the letters out on the road as he walked.

But Moore's gait quickly deteriorated into a lumber as he continued on past small farmhouses with tin roofs and wooden porches. Everything glistened in crisp shades of green, yellow, and gold. Hills rolled gently into mountains, and clean puffball clouds raced swiftly between them. Moore loved the South.

Just beyond Moccasin Bend he spotted three empty crosses standing in an open field. They were supposed to represent hope—a reminder of the risen Christ who assured one of the thieves crucified with him that they'd be together in Paradise. They were familiar but unsettling symbols for Moore. Every few miles other signs warned him that Jesus was coming soon or asked if he'd talked with Jesus today. Some were hand-painted and hammered onto fence posts or trees; others were carved right into the posts. "Turn or Burn," "Where Will You Spend Eternity?," "The Lord is Coming—Be Ready."

Mountains rose on both sides of him as Moore ascended the slow relentless grade of Highway 11, lifting him high above the river, over Civil War battlefields, and up Lookout Mountain. The Army of the Confederacy, flush with their victory at Chickamauga, had crested Missionary Ridge exactly one hundred years before. They'd surrounded the Army of the

Cumberland, trapping it in Chattanooga. General Grant himself had been forced to cross the Tennessee River that winter to free his men, reclaim Chattanooga, and allow General Sherman to move on to Atlanta.

Moore pushed hard to maintain a decent pace. The clothesline straps on his signs were rubbing his shoulders raw and he was sweating, but he hoped the weather would stay warm, because he didn't relish walking in the cold or in the rain—not without an overcoat, which he didn't have, or an umbrella, which he'd forgotten. Although southeast Tennessee was alive with lavender-blue chicory and wild irises, southern weather could be fickle. Uncle Charlie used to say if you don't like the weather in Mississippi, wait ten minutes.

Moore's strained calf muscles cramped as he entered Tiftonia, Tennessee. He rested under a train trestle and tried to massage his spasms out. Checking the map, he confirmed that he was crossing from Hamilton County, Tennessee, into Dade County, Georgia. It was 6:20 P.M. He noted the time in his journal.

Lookout and Sand Mountains separate Dade County from the rest of Georgia. Until 1948 when a road was built across Lookout Mountain, Dade residents could not travel to any place in Georgia without first going through Tennessee or Alabama. Legend had it that Dade, calling itself "the Free State of Dade," had seceded from the Union before the rest of Georgia. The American flag flew over the State of Dade for the very first time after the outbreak of World War II, and in 1945 the county finally passed a resolution to join the Union.

Dade was a dangerous place for a man to protest segregation, yet Moore walked across it without incident. By Wildwood, Georgia, the brown farmland had turned to red clay, and dust blew into his sweaty face, leaving rusty streaks and trails that stained his handkerchief. By nine o'clock he was exhausted, although he'd completed only a little more than twenty miles. At that rate he'd never make Mississippi. He'd have to force himself to walk faster. Reaching Jackson was the whole point.

Moore called the *Chattanooga Times* before he made camp for the night. He'd mailed the editor a copy of his letter to Governor Barnett, and it was important to follow up. If his walk was going to make a difference, people had to know about it.

He found a pay phone outside a darkened filling station. The young man covering the city desk said he didn't know anything about a letter to

Barnett, but he listened as Moore described his encounter with the black man who tore at his sign.

"What I'm most concerned about," Moore said, "is that the Negroes will misunderstand me. See, I believe the South really *can* solve its own problems."

The reporter took the information, but didn't ask any questions.

At about 9:30 P.M., just outside Trenton, Georgia, Moore found an abandoned orange school bus that had run off the road. Most of its windows were knocked out, and the door was jammed open, but it was welcome shelter for the night. He climbed inside, and pulled his cart up after him. By flashlight he made an entry in his journal. *Crossed Georgia State line. No criticism of walk so far.*[4] It was true. The old black man had been angry, but not about the walk. Actually, Moore had passed so few people in seven hours that criticism was hardly the issue. He wrote a postcard to Rev. Irving Murray, who'd been so helpful to him back in Baltimore. Murray was pastor of the First Unitarian Church and chair of the Maryland chapter of the American Civil Liberties Union, the only organization that had endorsed his walk. Murray had given him a list of lawyers to contact in case he got arrested.

"Dear Dr. Murray," Moore wrote. "Everybody hospitable here. I am beginning to feel more secure now, but if anything ever happened I wonder if anybody would ever know. The road is a lonely place."[5]

Moore rested his head against the dusty hard-caned school bus seat. The hill country was dark and silent. The only sounds were the mournful buzzing of tree toads, a diesel whistle in the distance, and the occasional whimpering of some poor animal. He got up, rubbed his pulsating legs, and spread his blanket down the narrow bus aisle. As he lay staring up at the roof, his thoughts turned to the black reporter from *Jet* magazine who'd taken his picture on Saturday while he picketed in front of the White House. Moore had tried to give the guard a copy of the letter he'd written to President Kennedy explaining his purpose in walking to Jackson. He'd even joked that if the president had a message for Governor Barnett he'd be happy to take it to him, but the guard wasn't in the mood for joking. He told Moore to mail his letter like everybody else and move on. Moore did, but not before a small crowd had gathered. They were just curious tourists, but the reporter sensed a story. He read Moore's sign, *Mississippi or Bust.*

"You really going to Mississippi?" he asked.

Moore nodded.

"They'll kill you down there," the black man said.[6]

Student

Life without a friend is death without a witness.
—Spanish proverb

Marine corporal William Lewis Moore was honorably discharged from Camp Lejeune, North Carolina, on March 15, 1949, after serving for four years as an infantryman and a colonel's courier on the island of Guam.

Robert Moore, Bill's father, and his stepmother, Clara, were happy to have their son back home in Binghamton, New York—at least initially. For a time it seemed that the animosity surrounding his enlistment was forgotten. Bill was four years older, seasoned by military service, and Robert's hopes were rekindled. Maybe the boy *would* make something of himself.

By late spring, however, old tensions had resurfaced in the small house on Woodland Avenue. Bill had begun talking about going to college and working for the foreign service again—pipe dreams as far as Robert was concerned.

For most of the twelve million returning veterans the "service years" had been enough adventure for a lifetime, but for Bill Moore they were just the beginning. Through the Armed Forces Institute he'd completed one year of college, and he planned to finish a GI bill bachelor's degree and prepare himself for a professional career.

Moore was born on April 28, 1927, on the south side of Binghamton, New York, at the confluence of the Susquehanna and Chenango Rivers. His mother, Ruth Manning Moore, a Binghamton native, died of cancer two years later, and Robert sent Billy and his older sister, Louise, to rural Russell, Mississippi, to live with Robert's parents. Bill and Louise were raised on their grandparents' farm in Lauderdale County until 1937, when Robert remarried and sent for his ten-year-old son and twelve-year-old daughter.

While Robert and his children had shared letters, birthday cards, telephone calls, and occasional two-week vacations, living together proved to be a difficult adjustment. Clara Moore hadn't spent much time around children, and while she tolerated Louise, Billy was something else.

The boy asked too many questions, got too dirty, made too much noise. During his first term at Longfellow Elementary School he learned about the Children's Crusade, and the following day he ran away to find Jerusalem and join up.[1] His teacher wrote that "Billy is doing very poor work. I wonder if you have noticed how nervous he is. At times he twitches and jerks very noticeably. If he must repeat 5A it will do him good."[2]

Russell, Mississippi, was a crossroads consisting of a Baptist church, a gas station, and a general store/post office. The railroad passed through but didn't stop, and the temperature seldom dropped below sixty degrees year-round. It took Billy Moore a long time to adjust to Binghamton's towering stone buildings, whizzing traffic, and bitterly cold winters. It wasn't until he entered Central High School that he was able to focus enough to start pulling A's in English, Spanish, algebra, and history. These achievements made little impression on his father, however, since they weren't subjects that qualified a man for a job. Robert Moore insisted that his son withdraw from the college prep program he'd chosen and take commercial courses to prepare himself for the "real world."

Robert assured Billy that he would not pay for college. He'd never gone beyond high school himself and had done just fine. Robert managed an A & P supermarket on Broad Street in nearby Johnson City where Billy worked as a stock boy after school.

Billy Moore struggled until 1942, his sophomore year, before he experienced any real scholastic encouragement. When Gustaf Youngstrom, his history teacher, told him that he had "a fine mind," Billy could hardly believe his ears. That someone he admired could think well of him was astounding.

Professor Youngstrom

Gus Youngstrom, who'd once taught college philosophy, encouraged his students to question everything. In ancient history class he assigned Plato,

Aristotle, and the Greek tragedians. Bill read the words of Aeschylus: "Men must learn by suffering. . . . / Drop by drop in sleep upon the heart / Falls the laborious memory of pain, / Against one's will comes wisdom. . . ."

Youngstrom explained that the path to wisdom leads through pain, and that Jesus Christ and Mahatma Gandhi demonstrated that human suffering could be alleviated by "weeping with those who weep." Billy daydreamed about living a life of sacrifice and purpose like Jesus and Gandhi, a life that would be remembered by teachers like Mr. Youngstrom.

Youngstrom encouraged Moore to study the subjects that interested him—politics and languages. Since Moore was not used to unconditional support, he sometimes went overboard with his gratitude. On an ancient history exam he proposed that Aristotle, Alexander the Great's teacher, share credit for Alexander's achievements because he was the conqueror's inspiration.[3]

By 1944 the seventeen-year-old junior was spending every lunch period with Gus Youngstrom discussing politics, economics, literature, and philosophy. He could question anything his teacher said: the more he questioned, the more Youngstrom supported him.

Youngstrom was fascinated by phrenology, an interest he shared with his adoring student. Although phrenology had become a discredited science by the 1940s, it had once enjoyed immense popularity. It was the first American self-help movement which wasn't spiritually based. Phrenologists "read heads" to determine which personality traits were strongly developed and which required additional work. By charting the swellings and indentations on the surface of a person's skull, they claimed to be able to judge levels of traits like trustworthiness, self-esteem, memory, mathematical and musical ability, creativity, ingenuity, and respect for authority. People often got their "heads read" to discover their career aptitudes or their marital compatibility.

Youngstrom, modifying basic phrenological tenets, theorized that the thoughts and emotions of a person's lifetime could become stamped on his or her face. He believed that, with a combination of careful observation and skull examination, he could read a person's character.[4] Large, protruding eyes indicated a good memory; broad, square jaws, stubbornness; an arched nose, a desire to command; and a high vertical forehead, conscientiousness, sympathy, and kindness.

Youngstrom petitioned psychiatrists to permit him to test his theories in the treatment of seriously ill mental patients and prisoners, and he was often surprisingly successful in locating consulting work.

He believed that character could be improved if a person learned to exercise reason. Moore accepted his teacher's theory that the universe is governed by immutable laws of cause and effect and that people injure themselves by their own actions. Youngstrom taught him that a meaningful life required courage and determination, and that these traits could be cultivated.

"The world rides roughshod over sensitive natures," Youngstrom cautioned him. "You have to be strong to go your own way. You have the intelligence, Bill, what you need is the courage."[5]

Overcompensating in his quest for courage, Moore abruptly stopped trying to please his parents. When he said he wanted to become a teacher like Youngstrom, his father assured him that "if Mr. Youngstrom was all that brilliant he'd be more than a teacher," and threatened to get Youngstrom fired if Bill didn't stop hanging around with him outside of the classroom.[6]

In 1945, Moore's senior year, Youngstrom left Central High to study for a doctorate in philosophy at Syracuse University. Moore kept in touch with him through his wife, Mildred, a teacher in Central High's English department.

The War

Robert Moore absolutely refused to finance his son's college education, but he also refused to sign permission for Bill to enlist in the army. Moore felt trapped. In 1945 eight thousand Broome County, New York, residents were serving in the military, and everyone knew someone in basic training. Posters screaming *Avenge December 7*, *Uncle Sam Needs You*, and *Buy War Bonds* filled the storefronts of downtown Binghamton. The American Legion ran a rubber drive under the slogan *Choke the Japs With Your Girdles!*, and even Moore's stepmother, Clara, saved bacon fat for the butcher to recycle.

At Vestal Avenue's Art Theatre the *Movietone News* showed army patrols guarding American war plants. Gasoline and sugar were rationed, and

Binghamton's Blind Workers Association shipped six thousand pillowcases overseas.

For three years Moore followed Ernie Pyle's columns describing guys like himself from places like Binghamton, who were developing the kind of courage that Gus Youngstrom talked about. If he couldn't go to college, Bill Moore wanted to go to war.

In March 1945, right after his midyear graduation, he enlisted in the marines. It was too late to see action, but Bill was eighteen and his father couldn't keep him in Binghamton any longer.

Now, four years later, with all the Moores back under one roof, old tensions crackled in the air. To Robert's dismay, his son was still a dreamer and still in contact with Gus Youngstrom.

Moore's motor pool duties on Guam had left him time to correspond with his teacher, who'd left the Syracuse doctoral program after a year, taught sociology back in his home state of Kansas, and conducted character analysis research for a summer at a California psychiatric hospital before returning to Central's history department in 1948.

"The service is maturing you," Youngstrom had written. "That old attitude that you're special and while the jaws of fate might snap and crush others, they will always spare you, seems to be diminishing."[7]

Back to the Farm

In his last letter to Moore, Youngstrom had shared his plans to take early retirement and move back to Kansas. He and his wife, Mildred, planned to buy a farm. They dreamed of establishing a small-scale utopian community where Youngstrom could continue his character analysis research. Moore enthusiastically volunteered to help, since he knew a few things about farming.

Youngstrom didn't respond right away, and Moore received his final orders to ship out for a Mediterranean cruise. Before he sailed however, a telegram arrived from Mildred Youngstrom notifying him that Gus had been hospitalized for yellow jaundice. By the time Moore finished his cruise and returned to Binghamton, Youngstrom was recuperating from surgery.

"They don't operate for yellow jaundice," Clara told her stepson. "Something else must be wrong with him."

But when Moore visited, Youngstrom appeared to be improving, and Bill dismissed his stepmother's negativity. He applied to Harpur College (then a branch of Syracuse University), and returned to work at his father's A & P while he waited for his acceptance letter. Robert, completely disregarding his son's plans, badgered him to apply for an assistant manager position at the store. Exasperated, Moore accepted a job as a camp counselor in rural Massachusetts for the rest of the summer.

Soon after he arrived at the camp, Moore learned that Gus and Mildred had found their farm. Eccentric in some ways, with interests running the gamut from phrenology to utopian socialism, Youngstrom never intended to retreat from the world, but to follow Thoreau's advice to "simplify, simplify." He invited Moore to join him and Mildred once they got settled. Moore was elated. He knew that he often pushed himself on people, and sometimes his enthusiasms irritated even Youngstrom, but it was clear that they wanted him to work with them to build the commune. "I'll come," he wrote.

Late in August 1949, Moore bought a secondhand motorcycle and drove to Russell, Mississippi, to visit his grandparents. His aunt Helen and her husband, Charlie Cagle, drove from their home in Birmingham, Alabama, to see him. They were still his first family. In September, he continued on to Mexico for some sightseeing before entering his sophomore year at Harpur College.

Moore worked hard at school. He registered for economics, sociology, English, and political science, and maintained a high B average, determined to complete his degree before moving to Kansas. But in February 1950, one month into his second semester, he received a telegram from Mildred Youngstrom. After a hospital admission in Wichita and a series of conflicting diagnoses, Gus had died suddenly from what appeared to be pancreatic cancer.

Moore was devastated. Overnight both his best friend and his future had vanished. He got on his motorcycle and roared west. Sleeping on the side of the road, eating cold canned food—not caring much what it was—he pushed hard for Kansas. There he visited with Youngstrom's mother, met his brothers and sisters, and drove out to the family grave site where he camped for the night. Nothing could console him. When he returned to Harpur College he couldn't concentrate and barely completed the semester. A sense of hopelessness threatened to overwhelm him. He had to get away from Binghamton.

Europe

Moore learned that he could use his GI bill to study in Europe, and he applied for a year of concentrated study in economics at Southampton College, on the English Channel. In September 1950, as U.N. forces were landing in Korea, Moore arrived in England and rented a room at Rosyth Cottage on Oakley Road in Millbrook, a suburb of Southampton.

Moore's landlady and his fellow student boarders were warm, friendly, and always eager to engage him in conversation about Korea. After the Soviet Union tested its atomic bomb, the Brits were terrified that General MacArthur would use nuclear weapons again. To their surprise, Moore defended the egotistical general.

"I believed in 1951 that . . . if we had shown a little courage when the Chinese armies first hit us from ambush and from 'sanctuary,' if we had dropped a few of our most powerful bombs on her cities and blockaded her coast, we would have brought peace to Korea within a month," he wrote in his journal.

"It is insane to fight a war, yet remain afraid to win it."[8]

Moore believed that communism was an absurd but dangerous political philosophy. It reduced human motivation to economic forces and taught that the individual's class rank determined his values. Moore took issue with the communist preference for the welfare of the state over the welfare of the individual. He argued that just governments derive their authority from the consent of the governed, and wrote in his journal, "For a while I read the *Communist Daily Worker* pretty regularly. I had been anti-communist before, but that paper really woke me up to what a terrible tyranny over man's mind their philosophy and allegiance to Stalin had produced. For those who think, there is no greater antidote for communist propaganda than to read their newspaper."[9]

Dang, an Indonesian exchange student who was a fellow boarder at Rosyth Cottage, became Moore's closest friend. They took trips to London together on Moore's motorcycle and spent a semester break in Paris. Dang introduced Moore to the communist student fellowship where he enjoyed debating. Moore confided to his journal that "my arguments certainly were pure heresy to the Communists, like an atheist in a verbal contest with a Holy Roller; but the position of the Communist and the religious crusader is such that they never can afford to lose the opportunity to convert someone, and their faith is so dogmatic that practically no arguments will ever faze them.

"The communists had their stereotyped replies to my every question save one, 'What about Yugoslavia?' I asked. They could not answer because their minds could not conceive that a country could actually be so discontented with the 'workers paradise' that it would break away."[10]

Moore excelled at his course work, wrote for the school paper, and debated on the side of free trade and world government at the Southampton United Nations Association. Nine months later when his studies were completed, he tied his Marine Corps seabag to the back of his motorcycle, crossed the English Channel, and headed for the University of Madrid, where he began a month-long intensive Spanish language review course, paid for again with the GI bill.

In the fall he drove to Paris for a similar course in French at the Sorbonne and applied for employment with the United States Commission for the United Nations Educational, Scientific and Cultural Organization (UNESCO). He also registered with the Economic Cooperative Administration and with the American Embassy. When his French course ended he traveled to Geneva, Switzerland, and applied for positions with the United Nations and with the International Labor and Trade Organizations. But despite fluency in three languages he wasn't able to land even an entry-level job, although the International Trade Organization asked him to reapply in six months.

Moore was frustrated by his lack of success. What was wrong? he asked himself. The opportunities existed, but he wasn't getting them. Was he trying too hard? Was he too glib? Too desperate? Was it his nervous tic? He'd never been able to rid himself of the facial tic which had started when he went to live with his father, and it had gotten worse during his service years. Sometimes he jerked his neck in what Clara said was an irritating manner. Could that be it?

Or was it his qualifications? Had economics been the wrong major? Should he have studied political science or languages? Hoping he'd make a better candidate for international employment once he completed his degree, he returned to Binghamton and rented a small apartment near the Harpur College campus.

Moore graduated from Harpur in 1952 and immediately applied to Johns Hopkins University for graduate study in economics. He chose Hopkins for its proximity to Washington, D.C., where he planned to continue his job search.

Baltimore, 1952

Moore found part-time employment with the Baltimore post office, and while his mail route and graduate studies at Hopkins kept him busy, he had difficulty settling down. Unable to sleep, he began to reexperience the emotions that had overwhelmed him after Youngstrom's death.

In England Moore had enjoyed the company of other students, but in Baltimore he never tried to make friends. The Hopkins graduate students seemed cynical to him. Moore missed the enthusiasm and warmth that he'd found in Britain, and he was sorry he'd come home.

"I could neither live with people nor without them," he wrote in his journal. "A man needs to be needed and to be useful to others is a reason for living. My own reason for living was my daydream of future usefulness, and that daydream was wearing thin."[11]

Determined to locate a job that would take him back to Europe, Moore applied to the School of Advanced International Studies in Washington, D.C. He passed a civil service test for "junior management assistant" at the same time and was told that his name would be placed on a State Department appointment list if he passed a security clearance. His background would be searched for links to the Communist Party. Moore had a clean service record and a good education, and although his connection with the British Communist students worried him, he was sure that he'd be able to explain it satisfactorily.

A spirit of mistrust, however, was engulfing America. Even returning military prisoners of war were not above suspicion of collaborating with the Red Chinese. Senator Joseph McCarthy had been ferreting out "card-carrying Communists" in the State Department since 1950, and he maintained that American soldiers had died in the Korean War "for a tie" because Communist sympathizers working for the government had undermined the war effort.

The Internal Securities Act (McCarran Act) passed during the early months of the Korean War called for revocation of citizenship for Americans caught in the service of foreign governments and job loss for all "red sympathizers" on the federal payroll. Still, Moore was certain that he could survive a background check. The most subversive thing he'd done was fail to achieve his quota of tickets when he was on motor pool duty in Guam, and the marines had already disciplined him for that.

In late fall however, Moore's depression deepened. As much as he longed to move ahead with his career, he stopped attending classes at the School of International Studies, spent most of his time daydreaming, and became convinced that State Department personnel were observing him around the clock.

In November 1952, as President Dwight Eisenhower's inauguration approached, Moore began to believe that his security clearance was delayed because he was being considered for a position with the new administration.

But who could have recommended him? Who knew enough about Bill Moore to submit his name for high-level government work? Who had enough confidence in him to know that he would do a good job? It could only be Gus Youngstrom!

Suddenly Moore was elated. Yes, that *must be* it! Gus had served in the marines in the 1930s. He'd probably known General Eisenhower before the war! Perhaps he'd convinced the general that character analysis was an asset in counterintelligence work, and Eisenhower had recruited him for the RAND corporation, or for Los Alamos, or some other top-secret mission. Gus would probably have had to fake his own death to go into deep cover. That was it! And maybe now he wanted Bill Moore to work with him!

It made perfect sense. Gus must have been keeping tabs on him while he was in Europe. *That's* why he couldn't land a job—Gus had *prevented* the offering of any job because he was preparing a place for Moore in the State Department!

Years later Moore recalled the winter of 1952 as one of the happiest times of his life. If he believed that a conspiracy was spinning around him, he never felt conspired *against*.

"There is something to the theory that when a person's frame of mind is such that he faces life full of faith and optimism then happiness and goodness somehow follow as a matter of course. . . . When the world looks good to a man, it becomes good to him," he wrote in his journal.[12]

In his ecstasy Moore contacted Mildred Youngstrom, convinced that she'd known about Gus's plan all along. He was anxious to let her know that now he understood. "Is Mr. Y still alive? Love, Bill," he printed on a postcard in block letters. Then he packed up and headed back to Binghamton.

Moore dropped off his bags at his sister Louise's house in east Binghamton and went straight to Central High to find Mildred. He could not understand why she acted as if she didn't know what he was talking about. When he explained about President Eisenhower, she actually seemed frightened. Mildred called Louise, who called Robert and Clara. Moore soon found himself in Binghamton State Hospital welcoming the new year, 1953, on the overcrowded schizophrenia ward.

Outsider

You can't understand it. You would have to be born there.
—WILLIAM FAULKNER

"Hey, you, *you* nigger lover! Better watch yourself!"[1] Two young white men taunted Bill Moore from their flatbed pickup truck. It was six in the morning, Monday, April 22, 1963. Moore massaged his stiff neck and stretched the aching muscles of his back. The floor of the old school bus was as hard as a concrete slab.

He'd been reading the *Chattanooga Times* by flashlight as he waited for the sun to rise. The Mississippi Delta voter registration project was running into trouble in Greenwood. Moore was a member of the Baltimore chapter of the Congress of Racial Equality (CORE), one of the organizations helping to register the blacks in Greenwood. The Mississippi chapters of CORE, the NAACP, the Southern Christian Leadership Conference (SCLC), and the Student Nonviolent Coordinating Committee (SNCC) were conducting a joint voter education campaign organized by the Southern Regional Council, and white resistence was getting nastier. Last he'd heard, the white Leflore County supervisors had voted to withdraw from the federal programs that provided surplus milk, rice, and beans, supplies that the black poor depended on for survival. SNCC and CORE were running food and clothing drives to help them.

Before he left Baltimore, Moore had written to *Washington Post* columnist Drew Pearson about Jimmy Travis, the black Delta volunteer and former Freedom Rider who was shot outside Greenwood. Moore asked Pearson to let his readers know just how bad the plight in Greenwood was. He also asked the newsman to support his walk.

"I will be engaged in interstate travel and entitled to equal protection under the 14th Amendment," Moore wrote, "but I would feel better if I knew that if I was shot or beaten or arrested somebody would be informed of what it was all about."[2]

Although no whites had been killed in the southern freedom movement so far, a few Freedom Riders had come close to such a fate in 1961. Publicity, Moore believed, was minimal insurance in a world where anything might happen. The voices of the white Citizens' Councils, raging since the *Brown* v. *Board of Education* school desegregation decision nine years before, were growing angrier.

"I have a family and creditors who cannot afford any lengthy termination of my pay check," Moore explained. But Drew Pearson didn't extend support for him or for Jimmy Travis. The journalist never answered his letter.

Moore stuffed the *Chattanooga Times* back into his cart. It forced a large manilla envelope through a broken slat and onto the ground. His poster—a *New Masses* reprint of Art Young's line-drawn portrait of Jesus Christ on a wanted poster with the words "Wanted—agitator, carpenter by trade, revolutionary, consorter with criminals and prostitutes" written beneath it.[3]

He attached the drawing to the front of his cart with one of the binder clips he'd packed in case his signs fell apart, adjusted his sandwich boards, and headed south. By midmorning he was passing white-fenced dairy farms, stone houses with wide front porches, garages and tractor repair sheds, and small family cemeteries. The Southern Railway tracks to his left were constant companions.

Monday was another fine day. The roadside bloomed with white dogwood, pale pink laurel, and rhododendron. Near Morganville, Georgia, a billboard reading "See Rock City, The World's Eighth Wonder" encouraged him to turn around and go back to Tennessee. "It Would Be a Pity," the sign teased, "To Miss Rock City." Within an hour three other markers cautioned him to "Get Right With God." Aunt Helen would have declared it an omen, and counseled him to turn back. Well, he'd already seen Rock City, but he couldn't recall if he'd ever been right with God. God never said one way or the other. It was impossible to get away from God, more specifically from *Jesus*, in the South. Even the Klan recruited chaplains!

At eight o'clock an old farmer read Moore's signs and asked him if he was a Christian. He didn't answer directly, but suggested that maybe they could convert each other. The farmer didn't think that was funny. "I already been converted," he mumbled, refusing to accept a copy of Moore's letter to Governor Barnett.[4]

In his Sunday school classes at the Russell Baptist Church, Moore had learned that Jesus loved children and hated Pharisees, that human souls were in constant peril, and that it was impossible to get into Heaven without walking with Jesus and staying away from alcohol. Everybody told him to try to be more like Jesus, although no one had ever explained exactly how that was done. He and his classmates had packed cartons of soap, washcloths, books, pencils, and Bibles for the African missions as they sang, "Jesus wants me for a sunbeam to shine for him each day. . . ." They were sunbeams all right—not a black face among them.

The black kids went to Sunday school someplace else. When Moore asked his teacher why they couldn't go to church together she explained that Ham, Noah's son, had seen Noah naked. So, Noah cursed Ham's son Canaan, and all his descendants turned black and became slaves. That made no sense, not even to a six-year-old boy who'd believe almost anything.

Who *was* God? Moore often asked himself. The angry old man who told Abraham to kill his son Isaac? The one who had all the firstborn of Egypt slaughtered, who commanded Joshua to spare no one? That was the God his grandparents believed in. Was he the God who gave Moses the Ten Commandments, then demanded that he kill all the poor Jews who'd built the Golden Calf?[5]

Moore didn't find much enlightenment when he moved up north, either. Few blacks lived in conservative Binghamton, New York, and none attended his parents' church. Robert and Clara used to take him to "Strawberry Festivals" and "Bring a Friend and Bring a Pie" dinners, hoping that he'd meet a nice girl. Moore hadn't met a nice girl, nor did he ever bring a friend or a pie, which reminded him that he was very hungry.

His stomach growled loudly as he entered Trenton, Georgia, the county seat of Dade. He walked through the town square and around a large Confederate memorial, before entering a small café on the south side. A large sign on the far wall warned him that "We reserve the right to refuse service to anyone."

It was eight-thirty. Moore set his signs on the chair beside him and ordered eggs, ham, and biscuits. The waitress asked if he wanted coffee and he shook his head. He never drank coffee. He asked for a glass of milk.

"You sure?" she asked. He nodded.

The waitress was almost Moore's height and nearly as big. When she brought his breakfast she asked what the signs were all about.

"I'm walking to Mississippi to talk to Governor Barnett."

He explained that he thought the governc had acted badly last year when he refused to allow James Meredith, a black man, to register for classes at Ole Miss. The governor had no right to keep a resident of Mississippi who'd passed his entrance exams out of a public college.

"Don't the niggers have their own schools?" the waitress asked matter of factly, shifting her substantial weight.

"Yes, but Meredith's a veteran," Moore argued. "He earned the right to use his GI bill."

The woman scratched her head with the tip of her pencil. "Why do *you* care?"

"I was raised in Russell," Moore said.

"Where's that at?"

"Just above Meridian. Two of my great-grandfathers fought for the Confederacy. I have a right to talk to the governor, don't you think?"

She looked into his broad, open face. He had big ears and light hazel eyes and might have passed for a younger brother of the vice president, Lyndon Johnson. "I suppose. But what's Meredith to you? He can get a diploma from any nigger school. You don't see whites calling out the army so's they can get into nigger college, do you?"

"The black schools are awful," Moore told her, mopping up the last of his runny eggs with the dusty biscuit.

"Well, Lord help us, whose fault is that? Look, sugar, you being from Meridian and all, you *know* about the niggers. If we paid our kitchen help what they was worth they'd *owe* us money."

Moore looked like he was waiting for her to finish. "Look," she continued, "I'm a Christian and I don't wish the niggers no harm, but you're dead wrong about this integration business."

"Why's that?"

She sighed again. "Would you like some sorry-ass nigger doctor operating on *you*?"

Moore didn't answer. Slowly he rubbed the back of his neck.

The waitress snapped his check off her pad. "Whites ain't never gonna accept what you're selling, honey. That's just the way it is."

He reached into his pocket for his wallet.

"Look here, you seem like a nice enough fella. Why don't you make your walk for somebody you *can* help—like them starvin' kids in China?"

Moore smiled as she put the check in front of him.

"I hope you make it."

"I'll be fine if the niggers don't get me," he teased.

She shook her head again. "No, sugar, I think it's the *whites* will get you."[6]

Moore left a copy of his letter on the table and gathered up his belongings. He walked on for a long while without seeing a soul, passing a motel, a hardware store, a gospel chapel, and one of the famous "See Rock City" signs painted on the black tin roof of a red barn. Just beyond Rising Fawn's Hanna Cemetery he stopped at a Western Union window in a filling station to send a telegram to the Birmingham Associated Press Bureau. He reported that his reception in the South had been "very courteous." That was pretty much true. He still believed that a white mailman walking through his native South to deliver a plea for racial tolerance to the governor was newsworthy.

If he could get some press attention he could reach other white southerners. Good people were all around in the South. Moore and his sister had grown up among them, but so many—like Grandma, like Aunt Helen and Uncle Charlie, like his own father—pretended that they didn't see how black people were denied anything much, didn't see how it was wrong, anyway, or how it concerned them.

After Rising Fawn the highway pitched uphill. It was only noon and there were just four miles left to the Alabama border. Moore handed copies of his letter to an old woman who smiled at him, to a young man who shrugged and handed it back, and to a farmer who tore it up. All moved away once they began to understand what he was saying. As he neared the Alabama border the road narrowed abruptly and the farms began to look shabbier. The split-rail fences were older, unpainted, and in disrepair. More and more barns were covered with advertisements for Crystal Caves and Sequoia Caverns.

Outside a small chapel a mangy dog slept in a hard-dirt yard. Cracked paint peeled from both sides of the steep ladder-like steps set between two windows which had been hand-painted in blue and gold to look like stained glass. At a small filling station he stopped to ask for a key to the washroom. The man pumping gas stared at his signs. "Toilet's plugged up," he said. "'Sides, I don't think I want your business anyway."[7]

Moore utilized the privacy of a clump of bush pines, then sat beside the road to rest his throbbing feet. He considered removing his shoes, but was afraid he wouldn't be able to get them on again. He was thirsty, too, so he hunted around in the cart until he found the bottle of Coke he'd bought up in Chattanooga.

"A blister is forming at my heel," he wrote in his journal. "A short while ago I heard a loud call from behind, 'nigger lover why don't you go back up north where you belong?' Soon rocks started whizzing down the hill at my back."[8]

As he drained the warm Coke a burly white man about his own age walked up to him. Even though it was hot, the man wore a brown leather cap and carried a blue denim jacket slung over one shoulder. "Fred" was embroidered on the pocket of his short-sleeve blue-and-white striped shirt, the kind filling station attendants wore. Moore stood up.

"What's doin', buddy?" Fred asked.

"Just heading to Mississippi," Moore said, and handed him a copy of his letter.

The man scanned it and nodded. "That's a long way. . . ."

"I know. And I hope the governor's in. I don't have an appointment."

Fred stared at "End Segregation In America, Eat At Joe's—Both Black and White." He said, "Ain't from around here, are you?"

"I grew up outside Meridian," Moore said.

"Then you oughta know stuff like 'at can put you in a worlda hurt. Got people here?"

Even though Aunt Helen and Uncle Charlie were less than a hundred miles away, Moore shook his head.

"No family?"

"My wife."

"Well, *she* oughta have more sense than to let you outa her sight! What's it you tryin' to do?"

Moore took a deep breath. He wanted to make himself clear. "See, segregation violates the Constitution, and Governor Barnett took an oath to uphold the Constitution. . . ."

"Whoa, preacher!" Fred held up both hands. "Slow down. Feelings on that run high 'round here. Less said the better. You best be careful, mister, hear?" And he hurried on without looking back.

A nice guy. But the real trouble was that there were too many nice guys like Fred who didn't want trouble.

Patient

Schizophrenia cannot be understood without understanding despair.
—R. D. Laing

By 1953 one-fifth of all the patients admitted to state psychiatric hospitals and one half of all chronic mental patients were classified as schizophrenics.[1] William Lewis Moore fit the broad profile of a male between twenty and thirty-five out of touch with reality who'd suffered a childhood trauma (the death of his mother), had an adversarial relationship with his father, and defended an irrational belief (namely, that a dead friend was recruiting him to work undercover for the president of the United States).

While Moore was certainly delusional, he did not suffer hallucinations, paranoia, speech distortions, or compulsive behavior, the other classic symptoms of schizophrenia. He was not moody, accusative, or irritable. Although he was grandiose, he never suspected anyone of conspiring *against* him, and he never believed he was anyone other than Bill Moore. Because of this, his family was assured that his illness was probably reactive, that some precipitating stress rather than an irreversible disease process was responsible for his break with reality. That made for a cautiously optimistic prognosis. With treatment the disease might be arrested before it became full-blown.

Today, a patient in Moore's condition might be briefly hospitalized and would receive medication and therapy on an outpatient basis. But in 1953 there were no antipsychotic drugs. Moore received the standard course of treatment—institutionalization, electroshock, Metrazol shock, and insulin shock therapy to induce convulsive seizures and coma. His convulsions normally lasted about sixty seconds, and coma up to sixty minutes, after which he remained in a stupor for about an hour.[2]

Shock therapies, introduced less than twenty years before Moore's hospitalization, were hailed as miracle cures. In 1937 *Time* magazine reported that insulin injections cured hundreds of schizophrenics in Vienna, and by 1942, seventy-five thousand Americans had received at least one type of shock therapy.[3] Reports of improvements and cures approached 70 percent by the mid-1950s, but later research would reveal that these figures were inflated in an attempt to make shock treatments appear to be more effective than "talking cures."[4]

Dr. List

Binghamton State Hospital provided Moore with all that midcentury psychiatry could offer. Psychoanalysts challenged his belief that Gus Youngstrom was still alive. His assigned psychiatrist, whom he identifies in his autobiography as "Dr. List," produced a copy of Youngstrom's death certificate and asked, "Why would any man leave his wife and pretend to be dead?"[5]

"Gus and Mildred sometimes lived apart," Moore explained. "He went to school in Syracuse for a year, out to Kansas a few times, and once even to California. Mildred understood how important his research was, and she didn't want to leave her job at Central High. . . ."

"Do you understand that Youngstrom is dead?" the doctor asked.[6]

Moore replied that he'd read in Drew Pearson's "Washington Merry-Go-Round" column that one of Mamie Eisenhower's friends had been telling the First Lady's fortune with a crystal ball for ten years. "Should Mrs. Eisenhower be put in a State Hospital because she believed her friend?" he asked.[7]

A more sophisticated patient might have realized that trying to stump his psychiatrist was not the quickest route to release. Although never belligerent, Moore insisted that he was right, and seemed unaware of the impression he made on the doctors who told him repeatedly that his certainty that Youngstrom was alive was a symptom of his illness.

"He [Dr.List] got me in a position where I either had to be right and prove it, or I was crazy," Moore wrote in the journal he would later publish as *A Mind in Chains*. "That seems hardly fair. Apply that reasoning to the rest of the world and you would have to put every man on earth in the insane asylum. . . . It does no good to yield on one point. They will insist that I yield and yield until I have no independent mind left. Better hold the line and never compromise. . . .[8] My only saving grace is what I call stubbornness, though others do not define it quite the way I do. I am not aggressive with people, I am mild and meek and anxious to please, but if people back me up too far I draw a line and I hold that line so that all the forces on earth cannot prevail against me. . . . That is my one saving grace. I should be a pitiful wretch without it."[9]

In 1961, Dr. Greer Williams, former director of information of the Joint Commission on Mental Illness and Health, wrote that schizophrenic patients "appear stupendously egotistical, unafraid of madness, cool in a battle of wits, impervious to insult, and they maintain a cheerful imperturbability reminiscent of a glacier in a bright spring sun."

"Most doctors," Williams observed, "including the majority of psychiatrists, regard schizophrenic patients as unpleasant to be around, and a waste of valuable time. . . ."[10] Was this how Dr. List felt about his irritating patient William Moore? Moore seems to have paid a high price for his stubbornness—especially if, as he suggests, he was actually arguing from principal. The young doctor prescribed a course of twelve electroshock treatments to induce seizures and seventy progressively higher doses of insulin to induce coma. Moore's mind became fuzzy, his vision blurred, and his short-term memory impaired. His heart pounded and he sweated profusely, even though his hands and feet were always cold. When he complained, he was assured that he was doing just fine.

Again, he retreated to his journal. "In the insane asylum to be satisfied [is]not considered normal," he wrote, "and to complain [is] to court trouble."[11]

Moore argued that his hospitalization violated his rights of free speech and free association, making him a prisoner rather than a patient. Ultimately, he stopped struggling and merely declined to cooperate. He retreated into books, renewing his interest in the works of Thoreau, Dostoyevsky, and Gandhi, which he'd read for the first time in Gus Youngstrom's classes. He became fascinated by A. J. Muste, a founder of the Fellowship of Reconciliation, who wrote that there's no way to peace; peace *is* the way.

Moore also began to pay more attention to his fellow inmates. Some were obviously very ill, but others seemed merely lost, confused, or dependent. Moore played cards, Ping-Pong, and Scrabble with them, finding what he called some "pretty good heads."

"My ward seems normal enough now that I'm used to it," he wrote. "The really bad patients no longer seem crazy, but merely eccentric. It is the patients in other wards that look crazy because I do not know them. . . . I still resent the idea of being imprisoned, though. . . .[12] The world is full of Christians who believe a man rose from the dead—where is their proof? I'm not saying anything that fantastic. I didn't say Gus rose from the dead, I'm just saying he didn't die!"[13]

Moore compared himself with Johnny, a frightened young man who'd been discharged and readmitted three times. Johnny was terrified that someone would flush him down the toilet, yet Dr. List wrote him the weekend passes he denied Moore.[14]

"The doctor has your best interests at heart," Robert Moore assured his son, "but he feels it's useless to try to reason with you. When you meet resistance you only try harder. He says he's at the end of his rope. He hates to see you just rot here, but he knows no way of changing you, and he thinks you think you have a message to give to the world."[15] Moore hadn't articulated a message yet, but he was working on one.

On a subsequent visit, Robert brought a letter that had been forwarded from Baltimore notifying Moore that he'd passed security clearance for the junior management assistant position. Such exquisite timing appealed to Moore's ironic sense of humor. When he'd been able to keep appointments for interviews he'd been rejected; now he'd qualified for a job he'd wanted all his life and couldn't leave the hospital.

With continued insulin therapy Moore became docile. His facial tic and the jerk in his neck gradually relaxed as he drifted into a dream-like state.

"I wasn't in a coma," he wrote, describing the sensation, "or unconscious, but I felt like I'd traveled into a new and different world. I felt like a man after he was dead. . . . I could only vaguely make out the others in the room. What they might be doing or thinking seemed insignificant and small. I was somewhere else. I became overwhelmed by what I felt were profound philosophical thoughts. I was possessed by the idea that the word impossible was a convention—that our life is but one form of life. . . . I felt disconnected from my body, severed from the world. . . . When one's mind leaves the body we all become equal. In the end everything resolves itself into the same thing. . . . Everything, stupidity, wisdom, sanity, insanity is relative."[16]

Moore's stubbornness had run its course by the spring of 1954. Perhaps the job appointment from the State Department convinced him that Youngstrom wasn't intervening after all, or maybe the insulin-induced twilight allowed him to weigh what was really important, or maybe he was just tired of struggling. "How easy it is to waste a life," he'd written.[17]

"I now believe that Gus Youngstrom is probably dead and therefore could not have been responsible for the strange happenings I gave him credit for. I thought you would like to know," Moore wrote to Dr. List on June 2, 1954.[18] List responded by granting him a weekend pass to visit his sister, Louise.

A New Beginning

Bill Moore was discharged from Binghamton State Hospital on August 13, 1954, with a "much improved" prognosis. After eighteen months of treatment the ex-marine and former defender of General MacArthur had become a pacifist. Perhaps the doctors considered this part of his general improvement, perhaps they were unaware of it, or perhaps they didn't consider it worth noting. What was critical to them was that Moore had finally affirmed that Gus Youngstrom was dead.

"Was I crazy?" Moore asked his journal. "Yes, I was crazy as fanatical Christians are crazy, though not quite so bad. I never preached an eternity of hell for those who disagreed with me."[19]

Much had happened during the year and a half that Moore had been away. Sir Edmund Hillary had climbed Mt. Everest, Joseph Stalin had died, and the Korean War had ended. In Binghamton, the Montgomery Ward department store on Main Street had expanded, the new Brandywine Highway had opened, and Donald Kramer was reelected mayor.

Moore moved into his sister Louise's home on Carey Street determined to get the three novels he'd written—two while he was in the Marine Corps and one during his hospitalization—published. He'd decided to make his living as a freelance writer. *December Diary* was his account of an unrequited love affair on Guam; *The Dream of Private Alvin Allan*, also set in the South Pacific, recounted the story of a young marine's yearning to be a hero; and *Blessed Are the Damned*, set in Italy, Greece, and Turkey, was based on his 1949 Mediterranean cruise. Moore hired a literary agent who assured him that since Korea and World War II were fresh in the minds of most Americans, military adventures, mysteries, and especially romances were in demand. Unfortunately the publishers didn't find the manuscripts compelling, and one by one they were returned.

Moore subsequently applied to the Binghamton City Welfare Department for a casework position, and was appointed on September 27, 1954. Social work had been suggested by his discharge counselor, and Moore found that he related comfortably to his clients—sometimes too comfortably. His supervisor, Clarence Sackey, counseled him about lending them money. By Moore's first anniversary he'd given them nearly two thousand dollars out of his own pocket. This overidentification disturbed Moore's father, who reminded him that "it's not necessary to tell everyone you meet that you've been in an insane asylum."[20]

Moore joined the local chapters of the War Resisters League, Turn Toward Peace, and the World Federalists, an organization which maintained that, after Hiroshima, mankind's choice was either to create a world government with the power to force nations to cooperate or face atomic annihilation. He also marched in New York City with A. J. Muste's Fellowship for Reconciliation to protest nuclear armament testing.

Moore's pacifism placed him on the fringes of American society in 1954. To many, disarmament was considered an unpatriotic, even treasonous, cause. In 1956, the House Un-American Activities Committee (HUAC) charged that peace activists disseminated "Communist propaganda aimed at discrediting the United States and promoting a dangerous relaxation in the ideological and military strength of our country."

Moore's association with the peace movement further strained his relationship with his father. His sister, Louise, and brother-in-law, Dick, were his closest confidants. When Louise told him that Dick had accepted a promotion and that they would be relocating to California, Moore was devastated. Louise had provided the only consistent encouragement he'd had since Gus Youngstrom died.

After his sister moved, Moore rented a room in a neighbor's home and drifted into a predictable routine of working, reading, writing, attending pacifist meetings, and visiting the Binghamton State patients he'd left behind. He visited so often that his counselor ordered him to stay home and concentrate on his own life.

Disciplining himself to spend more time in the library, Moore discovered a copy of Clifford Beers's 1907 autobiography, *A Mind That Found Itself*, which completely captured his imagination.[21]

Clifford Beers, founder of the National Association for Mental Health, had been institutionalized for what was most likely manic-depressive illness. After Beers's release, he gained the support of the governor of Connecticut in investigating the state hospital system. Patients were warehoused in filthy wards, restrained, and even caged, since many staff in 1907 still believed that the mentally ill were possessed by demons.

"No one knows what causes mental illness," Beers wrote, "or why some recover and some don't, but lifelong stigma must be removed from those who do." Beers believed that people recovered when they had a purpose—a reason for "marshaling their powers," just as he had marshaled his to reform the hospital system.

Moore was so captivated by *A Mind That Found Itself* that he put aside his novels and began writing about his experience at Binghamton State, crafting a manuscript from his many journals. When this manuscript suffered the same fate as his novels, Moore decided to self-publish. This book was a testament to his sanity, and he was determined to get it circulated.

Edward Uhlan, of Exposition Press in New York City, contracted with

Moore for thirty-five hundred dollars, which he borrowed from Louise, to publish *A Mind in Chains: The Autobiography of a Schizophrenic* in December 1955. Moore promoted his book on WENE, a radio station in Endicott, New York, at library lectures, and by presentations to community groups. Uhlan remembered that during the promotion tour, Moore never seemed sensitive about answering questions about his time in the hospital, and he often referred to himself as a twentieth-century Don Quixote. He sold all three thousand copies.

Activist

Nothing will ever be attempted if all possible
objections must be first overcome.
—Dr. Samuel Johnson

By 1956 Bill Moore had become convinced that what discharged mental patients really needed was a self-help network like Alcoholics Anonymous, which had been created twenty years before. He opened up his apartment on Carey Street to support groups of ex-mental patients who tried to assist each other through the difficult transition from institutional to independent living. He offered a program based on AA's self-help principles, calling it "a fellowship of people who share experiences, strength and hope with each other in a mutual search for friendship, understanding, and mental stability."

While Moore continued to work at the welfare department, Mental Health Anonymous became his passion. His volunteers advocated for outpatient clinics at Binghamton State, for more doctors, and for more effective patient government. Despite the fact that Alcoholics Anonymous volunteers were permitted to hold inpatient meetings, Binghamton State's director, Arthur Rodgers, refused to grant the MHA volunteers the same privilege.

"So long as MHA restricts itself to its present brand of therapy through sociability, I'm all for it," Dr. Rodgers said, but he denied MHA's repeated requests to hold meetings with inpatients.

"That could be very harmful," Rodgers insisted. "A hospitalized person needs professional treatment or he wouldn't be in a hospital."[1]

But Dr. Oswald Boltz, a Binghamton psychiatrist who'd treated Moore, disagreed. "It's certainly worth trying," he argued, and he petitioned his colleague Dr. James Ivory, a member of the board of directors of the Broome County Mental Health Association, to recommend that MHA be granted a trial run with inpatients.

"From my standpoint," Boltz said, "it is the germ of a first class idea."[2]

Still, Rodgers refused. He considered MHA's founder a mental case himself. That was *exactly* the point, Moore argued. That was *exactly* why MHA was needed. Ex-mental patients were *always* crazy until proven otherwise. Despite the professional encouragement that MHA received and the fact that MHA volunteers had prevented three suicides through their hotline work, Rodgers would not take a chance on them.

Mary

Moore was still stinging from Dr. Rodgers's disdain when he met Mary Hamilton Weyant, the neighbor of a blind Harpur College graduate student named Bart, whom Moore read to three times a week. Bart told Moore that he thought Moore should meet the nice lady who lived next door.

Mary Weyant was immediately impressed by Moore, a social worker who'd been to college, written a book, and knew a lot about politics. She was touched by his generosity in spending his free time reading to Bart, who was also a veteran.

Moore became fond of Mary and her three children, eleven-year-old Lyn, ten-year-old Shirley, and nine-year-old Danny. When he told her about where he'd spent a year and a half of his life, instead of withdrawing, Mary shared her own troubles. She was separated from her husband, who was an angry abusive man, and she feared for her children's safety. One Sunday Moore accepted her invitation to come to church with the family.

The Park Terrace Heights Gospel Chapel's old hymns, fiery preaching, and after-service fellowship reminded him of the Russell Baptist Church. Moore had always admired the teachings of Jesus, but he found Christian theology puzzling. If God was pure love and Satan was pure evil, then there must be *two* gods, he reasoned, and if Jesus *was* God whom was he talking to when he cried out on the cross, "My God, my God, why have You forsaken me?"

While Moore envied the comfort that Mary's faith brought her, he could not accept Christianity. After attending services for a few weeks he finally confessed his atheism, carefully explaining that he didn't despise religion and was willing to attend church with her, but that he'd never be a believer.[3]

Bill Moore possessed a gentle, cheerful personality, and he was kind to Mary Weyant's children. She chose not to make an issue of what she believed was his religious confusion. Faith, after all, was a gift.

Moore had assumed he'd never marry because there was so much he wanted to accomplish, but he had not counted on falling in love with Mary Weyant, and she wanted to get married. Mary was the first person who'd ever needed Moore, and he felt protective of Lyn, Shirley, and Danny.

Mary told her friends that "Bill taught me how to want to live again, and I owed my life to him."[4] She wanted to marry him, but was terrified of provoking her husband's wrath by asking for a divorce.

Mary helped Moore locate jobs for MHA members, and she assisted with support group meetings, eventually becoming a full partner in Mental Health Anonymous. But even with her help Moore was growing dissatisfied with MHA. He knew that he'd never be able to further its agenda while Dr. Rodgers was director of Binghamton State. Moore decided to travel to Chicago, to investigate a new self-help program, Recovery, Inc., and learn how its membership coped with the medical establishment.

Mary was also growing restless. She was unhappy about the long hours Moore spent with MHA, the World Federalists, and the War Resisters League. She wanted more time with him for herself and the children. He was aware that she struggled sometimes, trying to decide whether he was a reformer or some nut who thought he was Don Quixote. He was both, he tried to tell her. When he told her about his Chicago trip she asked to go with him. He said he might be away for weeks, even a month, but she was insistent. Finally he suggested that they send the kids to stay temporarily with her parents in Hillcrest, remain in Chicago until they had learned everything they could about Recovery, Inc., then move to Florida and establish another MHA. In Florida Mary could get a quick divorce; they could be married, and send for Lyn, Shirley, and Danny.

At first Mary was thrilled, but she quickly got cold feet. Could Bill Moore really settle down? she wondered. And what about her church? Their plans flew in the face of Scripture. Wasn't living with a man who wasn't your husband a sin? Yet, she wanted to be with this guy who believed that everything was possible and who made her laugh, and she wanted to get away from Binghamton.

On May 11, 1956, Mary sent Lyn, Shirley, and Danny to stay with their grandparents, and Moore resigned both his caseworker position and the directorship of MHA. They drove to Chicago, where they joined Recovery, Inc., for four months; then they moved on to Jacksonville, Florida, where they rented two apartments for propriety's sake, and Mary filed for divorce. When her decree was granted, she and Moore drove to Camden County, Georgia, where they were married in Kingsland on November 1, 1956.

Moore took a day job at the Jacksonville Maxwell House Coffee plant, but once again focused all his energies on working with ex-mental patients in the evenings. He opened their apartment for SEARCH, an acronym for service, education, action, recreation, character and health. (They weren't able to use "MHA" since the Jacksonville Mental Health Association was already using it.)

Moore held public forums on the subject "Self-Help in Mental Health" with panelists that included physicians, psychologists, and psychiatric social workers. The *Jacksonville Times Union* praised his efforts.

"The underlying thought in this group [SEARCH] is the idea that people gain strength in overcoming a weakness by leaning on each other," an editorial noted. "More importantly, organizations like these are building their programs on spiritual motivation. . . . Present indications point to the fact that the group therapy movement in the United States may become one of the most noteworthy developments of our time."[5]

Mary was a full partner in the SEARCH organization, which grew quickly. Moore was ecstatic when the District of Columbia Public Health Service requested information about it. Mary was proud of their achievement, but she disagreed with Moore about its spiritual basis. She considered it a Christian mission, while Moore defined it as "strictly a social and service group."[6]

Mary also missed her children and didn't believe they'd be happy in the

Jacksonville heat. She grew homesick for Binghamton, and put her foot down when Moore applied to the National Institutes of Mental Health for a sixty-thousand-dollar grant to survey mental health self-help groups across the nation. His research would require extensive travel, and Mary was not interested in spending time alone in Jacksonville. Nine months after they had left Binghamton, the Moores were on their way home.

Binghamton Redux

Back in upstate New York, Bill and Mary Moore rented a small house at 3 Franklin Street near the Chenango River. Lyn, Shirley, and Danny returned to live with them. In their attempts to mend the family rifts their elopement had caused, only Mary was successful. Her mother became very fond of Bill, but Robert Moore cut off all communication with his son and daughter-in-law.

In order to meet the financial obligations of a house and a ready-made family, Moore was forced to accept the first job he was offered, that of a janitor on the night shift at Binghamton's Vail-Ballou Press Book Bindery. Mary found work with Transformers, Inc., an electronics plant in nearby Endicott.

Although still a newlywed, Moore didn't seem to mind working nights. The graveyard shift gave him time to resume his activities with the World Federalists, the War Resisters League, and MHA. During the day he opened his home to ex-patients, drafted magazine and journal articles, and canvassed the city asking small businessmen and factory foremen to hire MHA members. With Mary's help, he published a bimonthly newsletter including articles by physicians and psychiatrists and essays offering practical advice about starting self-help groups.

As Moore concentrated on reviving MHA, his supervisor at the book bindery began to criticize him for working too slowly and talking too much. Because Moore had committed himself to an endless series of meetings, Mary had to deal with plumbers, electricians, the landlord, and teachers—in addition to holding down a full-time job and copublishing MHA's newsletter. She encouraged Moore to take a more active role in the family, and when he didn't immediately respond, she began to criticize. Moore refused to argue, but he didn't alter his routine.

Binghamton was a city which functioned in some ways like a small town, and when Mary Moore vented her frustrations to one of her husband's coworkers at the bindery, her story traveled. In desperation, she even asked Robert Moore to speak with his son. Robert was not fond of Mary. He considered her elopement while still a married woman to be scandalous behavior, but she confirmed his suspicions about his son's irresponsibility, and he agreed to appeal to Bill to take his family obligations more seriously.[7]

If Mary believed that building a constituency could pressure Moore into changing his behavior, she was wrong. Pressure only increased Moore's stubbornness. The very qualities that had attracted him to her—his refusal to get upset, his gentleness and humor, his childlike enthusiasms—began to irritate her as she found the weight of their family life resting squarely on her shoulders, just as it had in her first marriage.

Perhaps as a result of her alliance with his father, Moore grew progressively oblivious to Mary's unhappiness. Focusing almost exclusively on his activism, he spent hours writing for the pacifist journals *New World Review*, the *Independent*, and the World Federalists' *Liberation*, while continuing to edit and publish the MHA newsletter.

Mary ultimately took her frustrations to her pastor, Rev. Bob Drewry. In addition to concerns about her husband's behavior, she became increasingly anxious about his atheism. She asked Drewry to speak with him. Moore agreed with the minister that he wasn't being fair to his wife and the kids. He knew he spent too much time at meetings, and in the library—but he was trying to establish himself as a writer and he believed he was entitled to his own religious beliefs.

Late in 1957, Moore resigned his job at the bindery and took a federal civil service test. He worked in the frozen food department at a Grand Union supermarket for a year and a half, until he was appointed a career substitute carrier at the Binghamton post office on March 16, 1959.

The following month *Parade* magazine, a national Sunday newspaper supplement with a circulation of fifteen million, accepted his article "An Ex-Patient's Heartening Plea: How You Can Help Keep Thousands Like Me Out of Mental Hospitals." It ran on Sunday, April 26, 1959, to kick off National Mental Health Week.

"Perhaps the most destructive factor with which the ex-mental patient has to deal is the idea that he is somehow different and as such undesirable and unapproachable," Moore wrote. "We are not different. Not really. Not deep down inside."

The article carried pictures of Moore and Mary working on the MHA newsletter, of the meetings in their home, and of Moore canvassing for job opportunities. It portrayed him and Mary as partners, and celebrated Moore as a role model. Excessively upbeat, it perhaps overstated the case, and its success increased Moore's appetite for publicity.

He spent the next three years sorting other people's letters for the post office during the day and banging out his own on an old manual Remington typewriter in his basement at night. His letters to editors, congressmen, and town council members addressed issues as diverse as recognition of Communist countries and opposition to the marking of intersections with four-way stop signs.

Moore's correspondence with the editor of the *Binghamton Evening Press* reveals him to be a social liberal, supporting federal programs to prevent poverty, disease, and illiteracy, but he was also a strong advocate of individual rights. He supported labor during the 1959 nationwide steel strike and advocated extending public housing to college students, but opposed the use of public funds to construct a nativity scene on the Broome County Courthouse lawn.

In the spring of 1960, Moore picketed the courthouse after he, Mary, Shirley, Lyn, and Danny all came down with infectious hepatitis. The town's sewer system, which had been poorly maintained, was seeping into their well. Moore wrote to the *Binghamton Press* that "the important thing to bear in mind is that if people will not keep their gripes to themselves, but air them openly in a friendly manner to those in a position to do something about them, what a wonderful thing a free society is! And because so comparatively few take an active interest in such things as community improvement, the efforts of those who do something count for that much more."

In May 1962, Moore stood beside an Atlas missile display in the Water Street Armory parking lot wearing a sign that read "Reverse the Drift To War." Defining it as a vigil rather than a demonstration, he declared that "it is altogether fitting that I stand here before this giant missile in a memorial to the dead of World War III. For after such a war, there may be no one left to pay tribute." He also began to travel to New York City to participate in disarmament demonstrations and peace vigils.

Moore tried to interest his family in his activism, but when the *Binghamton Press* put his picture in the paper, his stepdaughters felt humiliated. Moore tried to make them understand how important it was to protest injustice. He explained that if he didn't attract attention, he couldn't attract support.

Fourteen-year-old Danny, however, was proud of his stepfather for taking on Principal Wiley at the Maine-Endwell Junior High School. Moore supported the students who maintained that their constitutional rights had been violated when they were forced to sit through a long assembly about patriotism. He collected their essays and published them in a pamphlet entitled "The Student Response."

When he was threatened with arrest for distributing the pamphlet, Moore replied, "If arrest is the price one must pay in order to circulate students' opinions free from censorship, then it is a [sacrifice] I am prepared to make."[8]

Moore deeply loved his stepchildren, although he often seemed baffled by his role as a parent. While they called him Poppa, he acted more like an older brother. Danny loved to roughhouse with him, and Lyn recalled that he made sure she had piano lessons, even when money was very tight.

But Mary was exasperated. "What you want is right," she told her crusading husband, "but I don't like the way you go about it." Moore often responded by quoting Clarence Darrow, who said that if 80 percent of the people ever agreed with him he would be convinced that he was wrong.[9]

Moore plunged into the 1957 water fluoridation controversy by supporting the addition of fluoride to the town's water supply despite the fact that some Binghamton council members were calling the simple health precaution "creeping socialism."

The dispute was driven by fear of "mind control," a terror which had been introduced by the Korean War. Communists were accused of plotting to drug America's reservoirs. Robert Shelton, Imperial Wizard of the Ku Klux Klan, fueled the general hysteria by charging that fluoridating public water was a subversive tactic to make southerners comply with school desegregation. "What's a better way to take over this country than to give an overdose of fluoridation?" he asked.[10] But Moore argued against withholding the demonstrated benefits of fluoride. Tooth decay was a major public health hazard. Binghamton voted not to fluoridate, but history ultimately affirmed Moore's position.

By the summer of 1962, Moore was clearly a controversial figure. His stand on religious freedom brought him outright notoriety when he supported atheist Madalyn Murray's suit against the federal government to remove "In God We Trust" from U.S. currency because it violated the First Amendment. Few issues could have upset Mary more. Angry and desperate, she wrote her own letter to the editor of the *Sun Bulletin* on August 27, 1962.

"I would like it publicly known that I am not at all in agreement with my husband, Mr. William L. Moore," she wrote, "in his political or religious stand which has recently roused the public ire. I have received numerous phone calls protesting the statements he has made and I am sympathetic with their sentiments. I do not wish to be identified with his philosophy.

"My three children and I are born-again Christians and would be very happy if prayer and Bible reading were observed in the public schools. We believe that this nation was founded on Christian principles and we deplore the atheistic trend that is making such headway today. Our Constitution was framed to guarantee us freedom of religion, not freedom from religion. . . ." She signed it Mrs. William L. Moore.

Ironically, just as his hometown reputation and home life were eroding, Moore was receiving encouragement from the wider activist world. In June 1962 *New World Review* published his review of Erich Fromm's *May Man Prevail*. Fromm argued that the world's troubles could not be reduced to a series of communist plots. Moore noted that "it is refreshing to read this inquiry into the facts and fictions of foreign policy by Fromm, a psychoanalyst of world-wide reputation. It is interesting also to be told by him that sometimes statistically normal people can be guilty of pathological thinking."

In August *NWR* published "My Friend in Viet Nam," Moore's essay about his friendship with Dang at Southampton College in England. Moore had lost contact with Dang, whose father was a Vietnamese businessman, and he did not know if his old friend lived in the North or the South, but knew he would suffer either way if the United States expanded the war with his country.

"We cannot win this fight in Viet Nam," Moore wrote, "at best one day we will withdraw as did the French, licking our wounds." He pointed to the "ideological blindness on the part of Americans who refuse to see the realities of the situation but think that they are on some moral crusade to defeat the Devil, which now they give the name Communism."

In October *New World* released Moore's review of *Dear Mr. President: An Open Letter on Foreign Policy*, written by Harrop and Ruth Freeman.

By the autumn of 1962, Bill Moore was straddling two worlds, increasingly ridiculed in one and increasingly respected in the other. They were set on an inevitable collision course.

Crusader

Where shall I hear words such as in elder ages drew men to leave all and follow—father and mother, house and land, wife and child?
—RALPH WALDO EMERSON

Hot. Eating ice cream and drinking lots of liquids, almost no solid foods. Chattanooga and Birmingham newspapers quoted fairly Bobby Kennedy's prediction of an end to segregation in about ten years. . . .[1]

Moore put his pen down, set aside his journal, and rubbed his throbbing legs. Highway 11 was all hills, and his calf muscles were painfully stretched. He'd counted on being in better shape, having walked from Baltimore to Annapolis a month before and from Baltimore to D.C. just two weeks after that. Well, he was thirty-five, after all. Not a kid anymore.

At 4:30 he'd passed an "Alabama Welcomes You" sign and adjusted his watch to central time. It was 5:30 P.M. back in Binghamton, New York. The kids would be home from school. Moore hadn't seen them or Mary since January. Although he missed everybody, he couldn't honestly say he was sorry that he'd moved. Despite some early misgivings, he felt every bit as alive as he had the last time he'd lived in Baltimore—that time when he'd believed Gus was still alive and pulling strings for him. Only this time he wasn't deluded.

Moore had joined Baltimore's Fellowship of Reconciliation, the Congress of Racial Equality (CORE), and the American Civil Liberties Union as soon as he'd gotten settled. He'd become friendly with the ACLU president, Dr. Irving Murray, a white Unitarian minister who was also active in the NAACP and Planned Parenthood. Moore began attending Murray's First Independent Church, where in 1819 the legendary William Ellery Channing had asked his parishioners "to look back on the history of the church and say whether the renunciation of reason is not dangerous." That kind of preaching appealed to Moore.

He also contacted atheist Madalyn Murray (no relation to Irving Murray) at her headquarters on North Calvert Street and volunteered his services. Murray was suing Baltimore for exempting churches from paying taxes. Churches, she argued, hosted flea markets and bingo games and were used for the administration of secular social service programs without contributing to tax revenues. Moore also supported Murray's lawsuit against prayer in the public schools, a position he was probably unaware that Martin Luther King, Jr., also endorsed. When the Supreme Court later upheld Murray, Dr. King commented: "In a pluralistic society such as ours, who is to determine what prayer shall be spoken, and by whom? Legally, constitutionally, or otherwise, the state certainly has no such right. I am strongly opposed to the efforts that have been made to nullify the decision. They have been motivated, I think, by little more than a wish to harass the Supreme Court. When I saw brother Wallace [Governor George Wallace] going up to Washington to testify against the decision at the congressional hearings, it only strengthened my conviction that the decision was right."[2]

In February 1963, Moore joined a group of black Morgan State College students in a stand-in at the box office of the segregated Northwood movie theater. The following month *CORElator*, CORE's national newsletter, published his account.

> *Exactly four hundred thirteen persons were arrested in six days in the campaign to desegregate the Northwood theater, and I was one of them. The theater is located in a white, middle-class neighborhood with a Negro college, Morgan, only a few blocks away. For eight years, students at this college had demonstrated periodically against this conveniently located movie which refused to admit them.*
>
> *On February 15, twenty-six students attempted to enter the lobby and were stopped by the manager. The state trespass act was read and they were arrested. Next day, continuous picketing began and mass arrests occurred*

nightly. Bail was set at one hundred dollars and some students would get out of jail only to be re-arrested.

A couple of days later, I happened to pass by, entered the lobby and saw twenty-five students standing peacefully near the ticket booth. The manager suddenly appeared and started to read the trespass act. Not a student moved. I was no less willing than they were to sacrifice for human rights. So, I decided to stand with them. . . .

Picketing spread from the theater to the police station and city hall. Neighborhood residents and college professors joined the picket line at the theater. White students from Johns Hopkins University and Goucher College joined Negro students of Morgan College in picketing. For two more nights, the arrests continued. Then, on February 21, the owner decided to desegregate the theater and the pickets gleefully tore up their placards. Those still in jail were released without bail.[3]

Later, Moore joined CORE picket lines at Gwyne Oak Amusement Park to protest Jim Crow practices in Westminster, home of the National Football League's Maryland training camp. They convinced the Baltimore Colts to choose another site for the 1964 season unless segregation was discontinued in Westminster. It was.

If mental illness had robbed Moore of his chances for professional success it had not dampened his ambition. The civil rights movement provided an outlet for his pent-up energies, and he would always be grateful to Jim Peck for getting him involved.

Peck, a former labor organizer and elder statesman in American peace and justice circles, was the author of a monthly column, "As Jim Crow Flies," in the *Independent*, a journal published by anticensorship activist Lyle Stuart. Moore had followed Peck's column since his release from the hospital. A radical pacifist, Peck applied the principles of conscientious objection to the fight for racial justice. In 1958, he was arrested for sailing into an H-bomb testing area on the peace ship *Golden Rule*, and in 1961 he'd nearly been killed on a Freedom Ride in Anniston, Alabama. It took fifty-seven stitches to sew Peck's head together after a white mob finished beating him.

Peck's message was similar to Martin Luther King, Jr.'s, but without the Christian foundation, and that made it compelling to Moore. Like Moore, Peck was an atheist. Back in Binghamton Moore had served on a War Resisters League planning committee to honor Peck, who was also editor of their journal, the *WRL News*. When Peck returned from the

Freedom Rides, the WRL asked him to deliver the keynote address at their 1961 annual meeting.

Moore was so excited about the activist's visit that he insisted on personally picking him up at the airport. Peck was pleased to find Moore so conversant with *As Jim Crow Flies* and with his articles in A. J. Muste's journal, the *Liberator*. They spoke at length about the peace movement, labor organizing, and civil disobedience.[4]

Peck explained that when he'd been incarcerated in Danbury Prison for refusing to serve in World War II he had become aware of hundreds of other conscientious objectors. They were happy to find each other in prison since few had realized how many CO's there were in America. Most had lost the respect of their friends and families for sticking to their pacifist beliefs since opposition to war was considered either cowardice or mental derangement.[5]

Peck had been encouraged by President Kennedy's pledge to enforce the regulations of the Interstate Commerce Commission to protect interstate travelers, but was sorry that it had taken the brutality of the Freedom Rides to get the president to uphold the guarantees of the Constitution.

He argued that the fight for human rights was a single struggle and that America's political and economic systems needed to be challenged by a united activist front. Nonviolent protest, economic reform, and racial justice were inseparable.

Demonstrating opposition to war was important, Peck said, but realistically, one person, even one country, could make little impact on world peace. Civil rights activism, however, could bring about real reform. He pointed to what Mahatma Gandhi had done for India.

"Why are you wasting your time here in Binghamton?" Peck asked Moore. It was a pivotal moment. That question focused Moore on the civil rights movement as a cause for which he might be uniquely qualified. Most of CORE's white Freedom Riders were northerners who disdained the white South. But Moore understood it. He'd grown up in Mississippi and had at one time shared his family's belief in segregation. With relatives in Alabama, Tennessee, Georgia, Florida, Arkansas, and Texas, he might become a bridge builder. What indeed *was* he doing in Binghamton? Hadn't the state hospital already taken two precious years of his life?

Peck understood Moore's frustration. Because of his own record he'd never been able to fulfill his dream of becoming a journalist. Although no major news organization would hire him, Peck found work editing the national newsletters of CORE (the *CORElator*) and the War Resisters League. His two years in federal prison also rendered him ineligible to teach. Even acquiring a New York State driver's license had been difficult. Peck had been forced to produce three letters of recommendation by persons of good character.[6]

CORE's strategy of "creating crises" like the Freedom Rides and the sit-ins appealed to Moore. Neither he nor Peck ever shied away from reporters or cameras. The temperaments of the two men, however, were very different. While Moore's manner was calm, and he was always able to laugh at himself, Peck was more intense. Journalist Murray Kempton once commented that Jim Peck would walk a hundred miles just to get beaten up. Peck enjoyed public speaking, while Moore, who often stammered, preferred writing. Moore was a gentle crusader whose goal was to convince rather than convert.

Still, Moore admired Peck's radical pacifism and insistence on ignoring laws that conflicted with his idea of justice. Jim Peck was thirty-six years old, and, while he'd devoted his entire adult life to social activism, he'd been able to raise two sons and keep his marriage together. Moore admired that. What he didn't know was that Peck's nonstop crusading had already taken a toll on his wife, Paula, who was suffering from chronic alcoholism, a disease that would kill her in 1972.

After Peck's Binghamton visit he and Moore kept in touch. Moore made the nearly-five-hour bus trip into New York City frequently to participate in disarmament demonstrations and peace vigils with him, and joined the New York City chapter of CORE. In May 1962 they attended a mass demonstration against nuclear arms testing in Times Square, and Peck introduced Moore to Dorothy Day, pacifist founder of the Catholic Worker Movement, which provided desperately needed social and health services to impoverished families on New York City's Lower East Side.[7]

The Route 40 Freedom Ride

Late in the fall of 1961, Jim Peck issued a *CORElater* call for volunteers to staff a Freedom Ride along U.S. Route 40 in Maryland. Before Interstate 95 was completed, U.S. 40 was the main connection between New York City and Washington, D.C. Black diplomats from new African nations traveling between the capital and the United Nations were often refused service at the restaurants and hotels along Highway 40. *Life* magazine dubbed it "the Highway of Shame" since nearly one-quarter of UN members represented black countries.

Wallace Nelson, a black CORE member and a veteran of the 1947 Journey of Reconciliation (one of the earliest Freedom Rides), and his wife, Juanita, organized sit-ins in northeast Maryland to protest the injustices suffered by the African diplomats. The Nelsons spent fourteen days in jail and attracted wide attention when they went on a hunger strike. Peck, who had ridden on the Journey of Reconciliation with Nelson, proposed that CORE support their protest.

The Maryland State Assembly had recently defeated an equal accommodations bill which would have required Maryland's hotels and restaurants to stop discriminating. CORE activists threatened to subject Maryland's Eastern Shore to "the largest Freedom Ride in history."

On December 16, 1961, eight hundred volunteers answered Jim Peck's call. Baltimore CORE dispatched integrated teams to test service in Highway 40's restaurants and motels. Two national chains, Howard Johnson and Holiday Inn, were targeted because they held interstate franchises and were directly subject to federal Interstate Commerce Commission regulations.

Over Mary's strong objections, Moore pledged a week of his vacation time to the Route 40 Freedom Ride. Once he understood that Maryland's Eastern Shore was as segregated as any county in the Mississippi Delta, Moore couldn't resist. Working with the volunteer teams he learned that some Howard Johnson restaurants provided only take-out service for blacks, some offered special seating areas but not use of bathrooms, and others simply refused service.

The Eastern Shore braced for CORE's campaign as the press recalled images of the Freedom Rides complete with burning busses and angry mobs. The advance publicity greatly assisted their cause. As volunteers began arriving from all over the nation and the pressure increased, the managers of Route 40's Howard Johnson restaurants and Holiday Inns agreed to negotiate, and segregation in their tourist facilities was broken.[8]

The CORE activists were drunk with exhilaration. Their campaign expanded further south and became a freedom highways campaign in the Carolinas, Georgia, and Florida. Moore returned to Binghamton determined to move to Baltimore. Mary, however, wasn't about to leave New York State again.

"The integration movement is too dangerous," she insisted. "We'd be targets down there!" But Moore applied to the post office for a transfer anyway, hoping that when it came through he'd be able to change Mary's mind.

Throughout 1962, Moore followed the civil rights movement closely, touching base with Peck often. In July, Martin Luther King, Jr., was arrested in Albany, Georgia. In September, Governor Ross Barnett denied James Meredith admission to the University of Mississippi, and Oxford became an armed camp.

On Columbus Day in 1962, Moore, Peck, and four other activists set out on a "peace sail" to protest the sentencing of pacifist William Worthy, Jr., a black reporter for the *Baltimore Afro-American*, who had reentered the United States from Cuba without a valid passport. Travel to Cuba had been banned in January 1961, and Worthy had previously run afoul of the State Department by traveling to Red China in 1956. After that trip he'd been refused a passport renewal.

Worthy, Peck, Wallace Nelson, and black activist Bayard Rustin had all been members of the 1947 Journey of Reconciliation. Worthy had subsequently been named by the Internal Security Subcommittee (along with the poet Langston Hughes and Jim Peck), as a subversive for cooperating with the Fair Play for Cuba movement to "exploit America's racial troubles." Mississippi senator James O. Eastland pointed to articles that Worthy had written in the *Baltimore Afro-American* urging Negroes to vacation in Cuba where they would receive "first class treatment as first class citizens."

Worthy faced a five-year prison sentence for the passport violation charge. Ten years earlier Moore might have criticized his defiance, but now he felt compelled to resist the growing spirit of repression in America. In a democracy the government was responsible for insuring the rights of individuals, since it derived its power from the consent of the governed. Moore still believed that his hospitalization had been a rights violation, and he demonstrated alongside Peck to protect Worthy's freedom of speech. Moore was not sympathetic to either the Communist Party or Fair Play for Cuba. Most Americans, however, did not make distinctions among nuclear disarmament, civil rights, and communism.

The activists boarded a motorboat in Atlantic Highlands, New Jersey, and went out beyond the three-mile territorial limits of the United States. Worthy met them as they entered New York Harbor, and all walked to the U.S. Immigration and Naturalization Service office on West Broadway, where they reported themselves and surrendered. The INS would not arrest them, but their demonstration was covered by the *New York Times*. An editorial in the *New York Post* observed that Worthy had become the first U.S. citizen to be arrested for the "crime of coming home." On appeal, his sentence was reduced to three months' probation.

A Long, Lonely Highway

Moore had taken part in the Worthy demonstration without first discussing it with Mary. His interracial activism terrified her. With the exception of the school prayer issue, she'd supported most of his causes and had worked hard for Mental Health Anonymous, but she drew the line at CORE.

From 1923 to 1927 Binghamton, New York, had served as state headquarters for the resurgent Ku Klux Klan. Several of Mary's uncles and cousins had attended the Klan's 1924 New York State convention held in the downtown municipal auditorium.[9] They were outraged by Moore's activism. Mary found herself in the middle, defending both sides. She did, however, have the sympathy of her father-in-law on this particular issue. Robert Moore told her on several occasions that he was disgusted with his son's "nigger-loving" activities.[10]

Mary brought her fears and frustrations to her pastor, Bob Drewry, and asked him once again to try to reason with Bill. Drewry agreed to, but he was not optimistic. It was hard for Drewry to imagine that a civil rights activist could be a nonbeliever. In January 1963, Moore's last visit home, he'd explained to Drewry that nonviolence and civil disobedience were *tactics* which had nothing to do with religious belief. CORE's goal was to force the American government to keep the promises of its Constitution.

Drewry called that secularism, arrogance, salvation by works, none of which could hope to succeed. He and Moore often debated late into the night.

Secularists lack humility, Drewry told Moore, who heartily agreed. It was impossible to insult him or to provoke his anger. Finally, Drewry said that Mary was terrified that he'd be arrested in the South and asked Moore to consider her feelings. Again, Moore acknowledged that he was right, and offered no argument.

How could he argue? It was no secret that interracial activism was dangerous. CORE's mission was in direct opposition to white American values. The organization was committed to working for full integration in a society that was bound by law and custom to separation of the races.

In 1963 CORE was an integrated organization. Black members were considered revolutionaries, and whites either communists or malcontents. This was a year before Freedom Summer, six months before the March on Washington, and two years before Selma—before whites going south to organize became respectable.

Many white Americans did not consider blacks fully entitled to participate in society or government. Moore felt a particular affinity with the excluded, because, as a man who had suffered a mental illness, he was often not viewed as fully capable or fully entitled either. How could he explain that? How could he hope to make Bob Drewry understand his motivation when he insisted on attributing everything to God?

Moore wasn't happy that Mary had shared their problems with the minister, but he didn't confront her. What was the point when he didn't plan to change? He would try to accommodate his wife's feelings, but he would not curtail his activism.

In the fall of 1962 when Governor Ross Barnett had attempted to keep James Meredith from attending classes at Ole Miss, Moore had tried again to convince Mary to move south. She told him, "You can't force this, no matter how right you think it is. . . . What do you expect to do by yourself when the entire U.S. Army can't stop the anti-integrationists?"

Once she handed him a clipping from the *New York Times*. "Look here," she said, "it says that 'Americans outside the South make sharp distinctions between legal appeals and political activism in the civil rights struggle. While a majority support legal challenges to the system, direct activism is felt to be too disruptive by a majority of white Americans.'[11] Didn't I tell you?"

"Yes, Mary," he said. "You told me."

A Security Risk

The sun baked Highway 11, and heat vibrated from the blacktop. Moore wiped his brow with the back of his hand and his hand on the seat of his pants. At Sulphur Springs, Alabama, he sat down and loosened his shoes. One sock was sticking to the raw flesh of his heel. Painfully, he pulled it away and held his handkerchief on the spot until the bleeding stopped.

He hadn't been able to change Mary's mind about leaving Binghamton, and when the post office transferred him to Baltimore on November 17, 1962, he'd moved alone. Mary left their home on Franklin Street and moved into a trailer next door to Rev. Drewry and his family in Park Terrace Heights. Crusading solo seemed to be Moore's fate.

When he'd first arrived in Baltimore—six months before his walk—he'd joined the Maryland Council for Democratic Rights and volunteered to work with its Committee to Abolish HUAC. It was part of a national movement begun in 1960 by people like Bill Worthy and Jim Peck who'd lost jobs and reputations when they refused to cooperate with HUAC and its counterpart committee in the Senate, the Subcommittee on Internal Security. Like many activists, Moore resented HUAC's lumping together all organizations that advocated disarmament and promoted civil rights and labeling them "communist fronts."

MCDR had been established on August 26, 1961, in response to a Supreme Court decision requiring organizations advocating the overthrow of the American government to register with the Justice Department. When the Communist Party refused, its officers were indicted. Although still a vocal anticommunist, Moore believed that the Court's decision contradicted the Bill of Rights, which guaranteed freedom of speech and freedom of assembly.

MCDR activists charged that HUAC encouraged hysteria about communism. The McCarran Act (originating with HUAC) had created a Subversive Act Control Board in 1950. If petitioned by the attorney general, that board could order any organization to register with the Justice Department and surrender its membership and financial records.

MCDR's goal was to secure a ten-thousand-signature petition to abolish HUAC and to deliver it to Maryland congressman Samuel Fridel, who was a member of the House committee that controlled HUAC's funding.

At first Moore was content to pass out MCDR flyers, but later, when he offered his apartment as a meeting place, he became involved with the executive board. MCDR's meetings were open to the public, and when Attorney General Kennedy announced that the Justice Department would investigate forty-one anti-HUAC groups, Moore invited Kennedy to come to Baltimore to attend a meeting at his apartment.

Moore hadn't cleared the invitation with the board, but he believed that, since it was his apartment and MCDR had nothing to hide, it would be all right. It wasn't. Moore argued that there was no reason to fear the attorney general. He promised to withhold names if he was personally deposed, but MCDR's executive board voted to expel him in December 1962. Some accused him of working undercover for the government.[12]

What Moore did not know was that his brief association with MCDR and his letter to the attorney general had placed his name on an FBI list of suspected subversives. During a subsequent investigation of his background an informant reported that he'd attended an MCDR benefit banquet at New York City's Astor Hotel on October 17, 1962, with Jim Peck and other known members of the Communist Party. No direct links, however, were ever found between Moore and the Communist Party.

Surviving copies of FBI interviews with Moore's family show how his relationship with them had deteriorated. Robert Moore told the investigators that his son's activities were embarrassing to him, but he assumed that Bill had never recovered from the emotional upset that had put him in the hospital. Robert believed that all his son's troubles had begun in high school when he was influenced by a teacher who taught him "to read minds and take the opposite side of every issue. That man mixed him up generally," Robert said. "[Now] he puts his interest in this peace movement ahead of his wife and stepchildren, and yet he is very fond of them and continues to send money home. It is indicative of the fact that he is unstable."[13]

Bill and Mary had lived less than five miles from Moore's parents, yet neighbors who'd lived next door to Robert and Clara for ten years told FBI investigators that they never knew the Moores had a son.

Mary admitted that she knew Bill was connected with some kind of "committee of concern" in Baltimore, but she didn't know much about it. "He gets carried away," she explained, "trying to do things for people who he should have no interest in, and he is so sincere he does so even if it requires him to leave his family." She said that Moore could brood all day over things which normal people would simply dismiss from their minds.

When asked about their marriage, Mary replied that she didn't know whether her husband would return to her. She complained that whenever she asked him not to do something he would seem to go out of his way to do it. They had trouble talking, she said, and she believed it was better to let him go his way and hope that he'd be able to get whatever concerns he had out of his system.

A Freedom Walk

Moore considered himself an optimist and in many ways a lucky man, yet he was troubled by the pain he knew he'd caused Mary. While he hoped she wasn't sorry she'd married him, he suspected that that was exactly how she felt. Moore was much happier with their separation arrangement than she was.

But Mary had come to demand the same things that Robert had demanded—that Moore stay home, be content, be ordinary. He loved his family—Mary, Lyn, Shirley, Danny, his father, maybe even Clara—but he couldn't turn his back on the wider world. It would be like being locked up all over again.

Early in March 1963, just seven weeks before he set out for Chattanooga, Moore had walked from Baltimore to Annapolis as a follow-up to the Route 40 Freedom Ride. He wanted to personally deliver a letter to Maryland's governor, Millard Tawes, urging him to reintroduce the failed equal accommodations bill.

On March 22, just a month before his Mississippi or Bust trek, Moore walked to Washington, D.C., from Baltimore, this time hoping for an opportunity to discuss segregation with President Kennedy.

The letter he carried for the president said simply, "I am a mailman, and this is the farthest I have ever walked to deliver a letter. . . . It is not so much that I need the exercise as that I must do what I can toward achieving human brotherhood. Walking and letter delivering are my so-called 'professional skills' as legislation and administration are yours, and we must do the best we can with the abilities we have. . . . Two of my great-grandfathers from Mississippi fought for the South in the Civil War. I was raised for seven years in that state: relatives of mine live there and in Alabama, Tennessee, Georgia, Florida, Arkansas and Texas. The South is like my second home. I used to think as they now think. But I have had the advantage of living most of my life in states with greater racial tolerance. I am employed in your totally integrated Post Office Department. . . .

"I can see the harm to whites as well as to colored people where racial prejudice and denial of civil rights is the custom."[14]

"Walks" were traditional protest vehicles in peace and justice circles. The idea of a walk was to spread the message to local communities on the way to the goal. It was an exercise in discipline and endurance, and it held special significance for Moore, a mailman.

In October 1961 the "San Francisco to Moscow Walk for Peace," sponsored by the Committee for Non-Violent Action (CNVA), had sent out a call for volunteer "walkers, runners, and stand-and-waiters" who were willing to "go the distance for peace."[15] When sixteen Peace Walkers reached Washington, D.C., in December, Arthur Schlesinger, Jr., representing President Kennedy, met them outside the White House as they began the second leg of their anti–nuclear arms protest to the Kremlin. (The president had been cautioned not to be photographed shaking the hands of activists on their way to the Soviet Union.)

In August 1963, four months after Moore's walk, a group of antiwar activists walking from Quebec, Canada, to Guantánamo, Cuba, detoured to the nation's capital to join the March on Washington.

Still, when Moore described his plans for a one-man walk through the South to Walter Carter, executive director of Baltimore's CORE, Carter was not enthusiastic. Even fearless Jim Peck said that the idea of a white man traveling alone through Mississippi and Alabama to protest segregation was crazy. Yes, peace walks were traditional, but Peck reminded Moore that the Southern Peace Walkers (whom CORE had supported) had been arrested in Johnson City, Tennessee, less than a year before. It had been an interracial walk, and Tennessee whites, who had no quarrel with their "Defend Freedom With Non-Violence" signs, were enraged at the sight of whites and blacks marching together. Whites were repeatedly asked, "Why are you walking with them niggers?"

"Get a group to walk with you," Peck advised.

Moore assured Peck that he was used to traveling alone, and that camping by the side of the road didn't bother him. Besides, he knew Mississippi. But Peck felt so strongly that he refused to intervene with either Walter Carter or with CORE's National Action Council on Moore's behalf. Even Peck didn't understand that the idea was to meet with Governor Ross

Barnett *alone*. Barnett might turn a group away, but a white southern mailman just might be able to deliver a message in terms the governor would understand. Moore never told Peck that after CORE refused to support him he'd asked the Baltimore NAACP for sponsorship and had been refused by them as well. Only the Baltimore ACLU endorsed his walk.

Moore's walk is best understood in the context of the radical pacifist movement which he'd discovered while still a patient at Binghamton State Hospital. Moore never expected to single-handedly redeem the South, nor did he ever view himself as a savior. His walk was an act of conscience, planned in the same spirit as that of former navy captain Albert Bigelow, who had undertaken his 1958 peace sail into an H-bomb testing area near the Marshall Islands on his ship, the *Golden Rule*. (Jim Peck had been a member of his crew, and three years later Albert Bigelow accompanied Peck on CORE's Freedom Ride.)

"I am going," Bigelow wrote, "because however mistaken, unrighteous, and unrepentant governments may seem, I still believe all men are really good at heart, and that my act will speak to them."

Martin Oppenheimer, describing the *Golden Rule* sail in the summer 1958 issue of *Dissent* magazine, asked, "If, as they admit, their effort may bring no real change, why do it at all? . . . They did it because they could do no other, because no one else did it for them, because politics failed to do it, because the hour was late and because they had to. Effectiveness had little to do with it. This was the individual act undertaken against a state and a condition which seemed omnipotent; above all this was propaganda of the deed, one's physical body thrown into a void where no other bridge seemed to exist."[16]

In April, two weeks before Moore left for Chattanooga, he wrote to Mary that his walk "could be something big, [something] for which my whole life has been a sort of preparation."[17] When Mary wrote back asking him not to go, he was firm."I don't intend to back out now. No one really has any idea what will happen—doing it, walking down there, is the only way to find out. It would not be surprising if I were beaten and arrested more than once . . . so I'm planning as best I can for any eventuality."

Mary told him that she was frightened by the news of the demonstrations in Birmingham, and that his father was also very upset. "Are you sure you're ready for this?" she asked.

Moore told her he was as ready as he'd ever be, and that she shouldn't worry.

"You don't have a care in the world, do you?" she asked, tension crackling in her voice. When he didn't respond, Mary took the opportunity to make him promise to be off the road every night before dark.

Moore hoped Mary understood that when he sent her his post office life insurance policy it wasn't because he really expected anything to happen to him. He was just trying to be practical, responsible, as she wanted him to be.

Native

Two times two equals four even if a paranoiac makes the statement.
—Viktor E. Frankl, M.D.

By the end of Moore's second day on Highway 11 he had put Georgia behind him, but his back hurt, his muscles ached, and for the first time he wondered if he'd really make it all the way to Mississippi.

In Hammondville, Alabama, he'd offered copies of his letters to a few, mostly elderly, people he'd encountered. Nobody was interested. Nothing had been written about his walk in the *Gadsden Times* or the *Birmingham Post-Herald* either. Martin Luther King's demonstrations were the big news. The minister was out of jail now and talking about his "next phase." Moore would be in Birmingham by Sunday, his thirty-sixth birthday, and he'd see for himself what the next phase was all about.

After an hour's walk without passing a soul, Moore came upon an old black man struggling to change a tire on a broken-down farm truck.[1] He was short and broad with dark skin and white hair. A little girl and an elderly woman were with him. They were the first black people Moore had seen since Chattanooga. The man sang as he worked, "If you trust and never doubt, he will surely bring you out. Take your burden to the Lord and leave it down."

Moore remembered that song from when he wasn't much older than the little girl. "Morning," he smiled.

"Mornin', mister." The old man grinned. The woman nodded nervously.

"That's a powerful voice you've got."

"A gift from the Lord, ain't that right, Mallie?"

The little girl smiled shyly. "This here is Mallie Fae, my granbaby, and Sezelle, my missus."

"Good to meet you. I'm Bill Moore."

"Azie Riggins."

"You a Freedom Rider, Mister Moore?" Mallie asked.

"A freedom *walker*, maybe," Moore laughed. "I'm on my way to Mississippi to talk with the governor."

"'Bout what?"

"I want to convince him that segregation is wrong."

"That what it say on your signs?" she asked.

"That's right."

"Mighty brave, mister," her grandfather said.

"So they tell me. Can I give you a hand?"

"That would be appreciated." As they pulled together on the wheel, the lug nut released and Moore was able to change the tire.

"I'd offer you a lift, mister, but I'm headed Chattanooga way," the man said.

"Couldn't take it anyway," Moore replied. "I've pledged to walk."

Riggins rubbed his chin with the back of his hand. "You want to be careful, mister," he said. "People can get ugly if they don't like what you're sellin'."

"Pray hard and hope. That's what we do," his wife told Moore. Her round, earnest face dripped with perspiration, and she patted it gently with a blue-and-white handkerchief.

"Yes," Riggins agreed. "If you're a hard-praying man, Jesus hears. He can make it different."

Moore nodded.

"Maybe you just ain't met the Lord yet," the black man said gently. "Bible say was the demons first recognized him. Takes the rest of us a mite longer."

Moore smiled. "I'll keep watching."

"Amen to that." Azie Riggins turned to his family. "Ready, ladies?" Mallie Fae grinned as she and her grandmother climbed into the truck.

. . . *Jesus makes it different.* Moore had tried to believe that when he was a boy. He'd prayed to Jesus every night like his grandmother taught him. Billy Moore believed with all his heart that Jesus would take care of everything.

When he moved to New York and worked in his father's A & P he used to pray for one of the customers who was blind. Moore was convinced that his faith was strong enough to make the blind man see, but he prayed and prayed, and nothing happened.²

His father had no patience with the blind man and made him stand around longer and longer before he'd wait on him. After a while the man stopped coming to the store. Where was Jesus?

Suddenly the gravel on the shoulder of the road crunched loudly, and Moore turned to see a police car pulling up. An officer got out, left the door wide open, and walked toward him with one hand resting on his buckle, the other on his gun. A name plate above his badge read *Knowles*.

"I hear you been passing out invitations," Deputy Knowles said slowly. "Where's the party at?"

"Jackson," Moore said. "How did you hear?"

"It's all over the radio. We been told to keep an eye out for you, mister. You must be awfully tired."

"Not too bad." *The radio!* So there *was* publicity after all! Moore took out a mimeographed copy of his letter and handed it over.

"This what you been givin' out?"

Moore nodded, and the deputy pushed his hat back, lifted his sunglasses, and began to read:

> *Dear Governor Barnett:*
>
> *I have always had a warm place in my heart for Mississippi, the land of my childhood and my ancestors. I dislike the reputation this state has acquired as being the most backward and most bigoted in the land. Those who truly love Mississippi must work to change this image.*
>
> *Frankly, I do not know which is worse—to be raised to believe that one should be happy to live in poverty and die twice as fast as the white man and to be told to reject the ideas of those who tell you democracy means the right to vote whatever the color of one's skin; or is it worse to be raised as members of a sort of 'master race' which fights a losing battle to preserve injustice with barbaric laws and police state methods.*

The British were wise in that they dissolved their empire before they were forced to do so. Consequently, the governments of countries such as India and Nigeria are stable and friendly and democratic. The French, on the other hand, held onto their empire as long as they could. Thus the bitter strife in Laos, Vietnam, Algeria.

The end of Mississippi colonialism is fast approaching. The only question is whether you will help it to end in a friendship like the British, or try to hold onto what is already lost, creating bitterness and hatred, as did the French. For our sake, as well as the Negro's, I hope you will decide to try the British way.

The white man cannot be truly free himself until all men have their rights. Each is dependent upon the other. Do not go down in infamy as one who fought democracy for all which you have not the power to prevent.

Be gracious. Give more than is immediately demanded of you. Make certain that when the Negro gets his rights and his vote that he does not in the process learn to treat the white man with the contempt and disdain that, unfortunately, some of us now treat him.

Sincerely,
William L. Moore[3]

"You believe this, do you?" Deputy Knowles asked.

"I do."

"You know it ain't real popular thinkin'. . . ."

"Yes, sir," Moore said. "I'm from the South."

"Got identification?"

Moore showed his post office ID.

"Baltimore ain't rightly the South."

"I grew up in Mississippi. I live in Baltimore now."

Knowles scratched his head. He'd seen men like this one before, men who never seemed to know how much trouble they were in. "Look, Mr. Moore, it's mighty hot," he said. "I'd be pleased to take you to the bus station."

"Thanks, but I made a pledge to walk all the way to Jackson."

"You gotta cross Alabama to get to Mississippi. Know what I'm saying?"

"Yes."

"This highway gets lonelier in the direction you're headed. You sure you know what you're doing?"[4]

"I'm an American, walking in my own country. If I'm not safe here, where am I safe?"

"Suit yourself." The officer made a gesture that looked a little like a salute as he climbed back into his patrol car.

"Wait," Moore called. "How far am I from Ft. Payne?"

"Ten miles."

"Thanks."

As the sun began to set, the highway did seem lonelier. Nothing stirred. Two-lane blacktop stretched as far as Moore could see. Flat fields ran to tree lines where huge firs stood like soldiers at attention defending the mountains behind them. It all seemed designed to make humans feel small and insignificant. Once in a while a crow cawed or a cricket chirped, nothing else. Moore tried to focus on the beauty of the countryside, but silence, heat, red dust, and the pain of his blisters kept distracting him. His back muscles were straining, and he breathed more heavily each time he crested a hill.

At six-thirty he entered Gault Avenue in Ft. Payne, which was a real town with a hardware store, pharmacy, five-and-dime, and restaurants. He stopped at Byron's Café and ordered the blue plate special, so hungry he didn't care what it was. At a nearby table three men were arguing about some preacher named Lloyd Hill, who'd been jailed for snake handling. One of them didn't believe it was right to lock up a man for the way he witnessed. Moore wished he had the energy to get himself into that conversation, but it was an effort to lift his fork.

He decided to spend a few unbudgeted dollars on a motel room for the night, even though he didn't have much money. After he had paid his rent and the mortgage on Mary's trailer there hadn't been a lot left over, but visions of a hot tub and a soft bed called to him. He found Black's Motel sometime after nine o'clock. C. C. Gilbreath, the owner, stared at his signs and asked if he was a salesman.

"No," Moore said.

"Mebbe you'd better get yourself a license tag for that thing," Gilbreath chuckled, pointing to the cart and handing Moore his room key.[5]

"I'll make sure to do that," Moore smiled. Inside the small, hot room he dropped onto the bed and lay staring at the ceiling. His body pulsated, his mind raced, and he wondered if he'd be able to make another forty miles before the sun set tomorrow. He tried to write in his journal, but words wouldn't come, so he turned off the light and eased onto the lumpy mattress.

Agitator

Change and decay in all around I see;
O Thou who changest not, abide with me.
—Henry F. Lyte and W. H. Monk

On Tuesday, April 23, Moore rose at sunup, settled his motel bill, and limped toward Highway 11 on stiff legs and swollen feet. Another endless stretch of road bordered by railroad tracks and mountains rolled out before him. He stopped twice before entering the crossroads of Collbran, Alabama, at the turnoff to Little River Canyon. It was 10:30 A.M. Collbran was nothing more than a grocery store–service station, a church, and a cemetery.

The grocery was a simple white plank building with two wooden posts supporting a pitched tin roof which jutted out to form a shelter. Tires, hay bales, and a rusted RC Cola sign that had been used for target practice leaned against the sides of the concrete steps leading to the front door. Three men were standing outside by the gas pumps, which offered Gulftane high-test for thirty-three cents a gallon.

"Morning," Moore nodded.

"Would you look at this, Floyd," one of them said to a tall wiry man with graying brown hair and a mouth as narrow as a mail slot. Looking Moore and his signs up and down, the second man asked, "Ain't from around here, are you, buddy?"

"Outside Meridian, actually, but I'm just passing through."[1]

"Why's that?" Floyd asked.

Moore explained that he was a mailman on a walk of reconciliation. "See, almost ten years ago the Supreme Court. . . ."

"Them buzzards," the first one snorted.

". . . but the Constitution guarantees. . . ."

"Didn't nobody ever tell you that the Constitution was written by white men, *for* white men?" Floyd asked.

Moore opened his mouth, but the third man cut him short. "I heard about you on the radio last night." This man was older than the others, and he wore heavy brown coveralls and a khaki shirt buttoned up to his Adam's apple. "They said you was walking clear to Mississippi."

"That's right. On the radio?" Moore asked.

"WGAD. But they said you was from Baltimore."

"That's where I live now."

"You really gonna talk to Ross Barnett?"

"Yes." Moore was grinning. Lots of people must have heard.

"And what's it you'll be tellin' him about *our* rights . . . ?"

"Leave him be, Floyd," the old one laughed. "Some folks ain't happy 'lessen they're lookin' under the cow's tail."

But Floyd paid no attention. "You tellin' me you *want* your kids goin' to school with a bunch of runny-nosed niggers?"

The smile dropped off Moore's face.

"You ever seen a nigger quarterback, mister?" the first one asked, taking off his straw hat and wiping his brow.

"You ain't part of that nigger preacher's crew in Birmingham, are you?" Floyd asked.

"Martin Luther King?" The questions were coming too fast. Moore was getting confused.

"Yeah. *Martin Lucifer Coon.*" They all laughed.

"Strange cargo for a Meridian man to be hauling," Straw Hat said, staring at the Jesus poster attached to Moore's cart.

"Just a question of mind over matter, Jack," Floyd said, his lips so thin they seemed to disappear.

"What's that supposed to mean?" Jack growled.

"Means *I* don't mind, and *he* don't matter."

Moore felt his face burning. Jack was still glaring at the poster. "You oughta get rid of that thing," he said.

Moore began to explain, but Jack shook his head. "It ain't right." He spit on the ground and walked into the store. Floyd and the old man followed him.

Moore limped on, passing the cemetery, the parsonage, and the Gravel

Hill Baptist Church. He had to expect this. He was saying exactly what most folks didn't want to hear.

The road between Collbran and Portersville was lined with stands of pines, broken only by an occasional filling station, stone house, or tiny graveyard. Split-rail fences enclosed chickens, goats, horses, cows, and hay barns (some advertising Rock City). Both sides of the road were bordered by the powerful mountains. It was beautiful country, not at all like the poor section above Ft. Payne.

By the time Moore stopped under a shade tree it was nearly noon. He pulled off his shoes and rubbed his swollen toes. Better to leave the shoes off, he decided. The soles were almost gone, and he'd need the shoes if he met up with newsmen in Birmingham.

He took out his journal and drafted another telegram to the Associated Press. Carefully he skimmed his letter to the president for the right phrase. "I am not making this walk to demonstrate either federal rights or states [*sic*] rights, but individual rights. I am doing it for the South, hopefully to illustrate that the most basic of freedoms of peaceful protest is not altogether extinguished down there." All those words would be expensive, but if the national news picked them up it would be worth the investment.

Somewhere near Portersville a little black dog had begun to follow him. The pup stayed back at first, but as Moore wrote, it inched closer, with its tail wedged between its legs. It was hungry and needed a good dose of Happy Jack's mange medicine.

Moore took a sandwich out of his cart, pulled out the bologna and fed the dog. It ate quickly, greedily. "It's okay, boy," Moore said soothingly. "It's okay." The dog whimpered. It was still hungry. All he had left was a chocolate MoonPie, and the dog devoured that, too.

"*I* was at the White House last week. What do you think about that?" Moore asked as the dog licked the MoonPie wrapper. Recalling the expression on the White House guard's face when he handed him the letter addressed to President Kennedy, Moore shook his head. "Figured I was a crackpot. Just like those guys back at the store." He pulled out the letter. "See what *you* think, ole boy," and he began to read:

Dear Mr. President:
    After I attempt to leave this letter for you at the White House, I will start for my native Mississippi. I will take the bus to Chattanooga, then walk

*from there wearing signs on my front and back opposed to segregation. I will
also bear an open letter for Governor Ross Barnett, which I will attempt to
deliver personally.*

    *If you, Mr. President, wish to write to Governor Barnett, I would be
delighted to have the opportunity to deliver your letter, also.*

    *I expect that the Southern hospitality which I have cherished so much in
the past will manifest itself in less desirable forms this time. I may well feel
like I am living the Perils of Pauline, with no hero around to come to my
rescue.*

    *I will be engaged in interstate travel, and, theoretically, under the protec-
tion of the 14th Amendment to the Constitution, guaranteeing—on paper—
equal rights and privileges to all citizens. I am not making this walk to
demonstrate either federal rights or states [sic] rights, but individual rights.
I am doing it, among other things, I feel, for the South, and hopefully, to
illustrate that the most basic of freedoms of peaceful protest is not altogether
extinguished down there. I do not believe that such a walk has ever been
undertaken before. I want to show that it can be done.*

Sincerely,

William L. Moore.[2]

    The letter slipped from his hand as he grabbed at a painful cramp in
his calf. He'd been walking up and down hills for almost three days and
had spoken to no one since he left the store that morning. Nobody.

    Sitting in the beating sun on the deserted highway, with a day's growth
of beard and surrounded by his signs, Moore resembled one of the Old
Testament prophets—perhaps the lonely Jeremiah, who'd wandered Jerusalem's streets with a yoke around his neck, or the mystic Isaiah, who'd
walked naked for three years, or even the determined Ezekiel, who'd eaten
an entire scroll, all to demonstrate the evils of self-righteousness.

    Be patient, wait! That's what Moore had been told all his life. *You don't
understand, but you will when you grow up,* his parents had said. *You'll understand it better by and by,* the preachers told him. That's what the blacks
were being told, and that's exactly what they were tired of hearing.

    It was the same treatment that mental patients got—privileges granted,
privileges revoked, and they were always told to be grateful. Why should
patients be grateful? Real convicts at least knew the length of their sen-
tences.

    Moore knew how impatient he sometimes made people, especially
Mary, when he talked about social justice. All his life he'd been told that

reality was more complicated than he understood it to be. But how difficult was it to see that it was wrong for black men who'd fought in World War II, in Korea, and now in Vietnam to come home and find that they couldn't even vote for the government that had sent them off possibly to die?

Moore rummaged through the cart and pulled out his journal. "Walking again," he wrote. "Couple of passing cars have yelled nigger loving so-and-so. Saw a sign that said 'Alabama Welcomes You.' Changed tire. Adopted by hungry, thirsty, road foolish dog."³ The pup sniffed him, and Moore closed the book.

He had to do something about the dog before it got attached to him. He continued south. Every step was painful. It was humiliating for a mailman, an ex-marine, to be in such miserable physical shape. He limped through Collinsville with the dog trailing him, and stopped at Cat Harris's service station, where he bought a sandwich, a container of milk, and a few cans of dog food. Mr. Harris gave the pup a bowl of water. Some kids were playing nearby, and Moore asked if they knew where he could find a home for the dog. Two brothers agreed to take him. Harris gave them a length of clothesline to tie around the dog's neck, and Moore gave them the dog food. It was harder to give the pup up than Moore had expected, and that made him angry at himself. He hurried on as fast as his pained legs would carry him, not looking back.

Mixer

Beware of the man whose God is in heaven.
—GEORGE BERNARD SHAW

"I'm telling you, the man's askin' for it. He's carryin' signs about eating with niggers like it was some kinda his business." The DeKalb County farmer could barely contain his anger.

"What did I tell you?" his neighbor asked. "It'll take another ten years to make the damn Yankees get it through their thick heads that we ain't gonna mix."

"When the schools close it's the niggers who'll suffer. Don't consider that, do they?"

Up and down DeKalb County, speculation was growing about the big white stranger with his strange signs—so much so that state and local authorities were growing concerned.[1] Alabama didn't need any more publicity than Birmingham was already providing. After reading Deputy Knowles's report, DeKalb County sheriff Harold Richards called Captain Ben Allen at the department of public safety and asked him to pick Moore up for mental observation. That was the only excuse the sheriff could think of for detaining a man he was sure would get himself killed. Allen promised to have Inspector Roy McDowell take care of it.

Moore, unaware of their interest, was worrying about being ignored. Nobody had said another word about his being on the radio, and there was still nothing in the newspapers.

In Collinsville he saw homes that were prettier than any since Chattanooga. Some were made of stone and others of cinder blocks; a number had wide wooden porches. There were motels, a drive-in movie, and a few gospel chapels. The sign in front of one warned that "if you give Satan an inch he'll want to become a ruler."

Walking was easier without shoes, and Moore was so absorbed in his thoughts that he didn't notice when an old black Buick pulled up in front of him. It stopped abruptly, throwing up a blinding cloud of yellow dust. Two men got out, and Moore recognized Floyd from the grocery. The man with him was older, but not the same old man he'd met that morning. He wasn't Straw Hat either.

"Hey there, hey fella!" Floyd called.

Moore pulled his cart to the shoulder.

"Want you to meet a friend of mine," Floyd said. "This here is Gaddis Killian. He's a mailman. Didn't you say you was a mailman, too?"

"That's right."

Gaddis had a broad, rugged face and a haunted look. He took Moore in, then averted his gaze.

"I told Gad here that you was marching clear to Mississippi. He didn't believe me, did you, Gad?"

"Never said that," Gad snapped, then turned to Moore. "My cousin said you got a picture that defames the Lord Jesus Christ."[2]

Gaddis was so riled that he was shaking. *The poster?!* Moore turned the cart around to face them. "*This?*"

Gaddis glared at the rebel-looking, thick-bearded Jesus, then bent down to read the type: *Wanted—agitator, carpenter by trade, revolutionary, consorter with criminals and prostitutes.*

"What *is* this?" he asked, ripping the poster off the cart. His face was so pale it seemed he'd surely pass out.

"It says that Jesus was a revolutionary, which he was," Moore said, taking his poster back.

"Where did you get a thing like that?" But Gaddis didn't wait for an answer. "Jesus healed the whores," he said, "and them *criminals* were his disciples! Far as I know he never said nothing about a revolution!"

"He kicked over the money changer's table in the temple," Moore offered. "That was pretty revolutionary. . . ."

"Are *you* a Christian, mister?" Floyd asked.

"No." Moore knelt to refasten his poster. When he looked up, Floyd and Gaddis were nodding at each other.

"Why you tying that damn thing back on your wagon?" Floyd asked.

"Never mind that," Gaddis snapped. "If you ain't a Christian, what *are* you, one of them Catholics?"

"No."

"You believe in God?"

Moore took a deep breath. "Depends. I don't believe in the God who condemned everybody because Adam ate an apple."

Gaddis began scratching first one shoulder, then the other, as Floyd looked up and down the highway.

"If you prayed for faith you'd believe," Gaddis said, his voice still shaky. What was the matter with him? "What *do* you believe in, mister?"

"People, I guess." Moore mumbled, keeping one eye on Floyd, who was craning his neck to look down the highway. Things were starting to unravel again, just like back at the store.

"The hell you say." The corners of Floyd's thin lips twisted in an ugly smile. "You believe in black, white, and yeller, all mixing and intermarrying together. Ain't that right?"

"I believe in integration, yes."

"Well, *we* don't. We take our orders from the Lord, not the Supreme Court!" Gaddis sputtered.

"The Supreme Court only interprets the law. . . ."

"Not *our* law. Those nine old communists sit up there in Washington spitting on my granddaddy's grave. I got no respect for any one of them," Gaddis said.

Floyd folded his arms across his chest. His shirt was brown plaid and short-sleeved like Moore's, but Floyd's was starched stiff.

"Any man who believes in integration is dead from the neck up," he said. "The nigger ain't just a dark-skinned white man, he's an animal, just like the Bible says."

"That's enough, Floyd," Gad said, wiping his neck with the back of his hand. "I didn't come here to talk about niggers." He turned to Moore. "You sound just like a communist with all that talk about revolution."

Moore jerked his head around. "No, I'm making my walk for peace, not to start any revolution."

"Then let me straighten you out," Gad growled. "You got your nigger crusadin' and your religion all mixed up. You agitators can't find the middle aisle of a church, but you think you know where the truth is. Well, I'll tell *you* what. Jesus died for our *sins*. We believe that. He's a *personal* savior. *All men*, even niggers, can claim salvation no matter *what* they done."

Floyd nodded. "You make Jesus sound like some kind of a beatnik."

Moore ignored Floyd and looked at Gaddis. "Does that mean Hitler could have been saved?" he asked.

"You don't have no notion what I'm talking about, do you?" Gaddis coughed hard and spat on the ground.

"You believe that Jesus Christ rose from the dead?" Floyd asked suddenly.

"No."

"You calling Jesus a liar?"

"I'm not calling anybody a liar," Moore said. "I'm answering your question."

"And I'll answer *your* damn question," Gaddis sputtered. "If Hitler gave himself to Jesus before he done them things, then yes, I suppose he *could* have been saved."

"I don't believe it. . . ." It was out of Moore's mouth before he could catch it.

"Course you don't!" Floyd said in a low, grinding tone. "You don't believe in nothing! Didn't I tell you, Gad? I ain't ever in my life seen a man carrying a picture of Jesus Christ and proud to say he don't believe in God! Know what I'm thinking . . . ?" He moved closer to Moore, who braced himself.

But Gaddis put a hand on Floyd's shoulder. "Listen," he said, wiping away the sweat that was running into his eyes, "Jesus said the poor could enter the kingdom just like everybody else. When him and Paul lived, the Romans owned slaves. Paul told them to knuckle under, and Jesus never said one word about them. They knew what was important. Don't matter where your next meal is coming from or how much freedom you got if your soul is lost."

Gaddis's skin was yellowish-grey and moist. "Ain't you got nothing to say for yourself?" he asked.

"Never mind, Gad," Floyd said, "we know what he is."

Still, Moore said nothing.

"C'mon, Gad. I got to get back to the store. I got no more time for him. He won't make it past Birmingham." Floyd turned and walked toward the car.

Moore sighed with relief, resting his weight against the cart handle.

"You best look to your soul," Gad warned.

"Come *on*, Gad," Floyd called. "You're wasting your breath."

After the Buick spun around, Moore took off his signs and stretched out flat on the grass. He was drained, shaken. For the first time he felt blood-chilling fear. He didn't want to die. He wasn't ready for everything to end. He'd known enough mental patients to understand that Gaddis was in trouble—sweating and twitching like that, calling people who didn't agree with him communists . . . and who could tell what Floyd might be capable of?

Attention at Last

Moore left Collinsville at about six o'clock and found newsman Charlie Hicks of radio station WGAD waiting for him on the highway.[3]

"How are you?" Hicks asked.

Moore pointed to his bare feet. "Except for blisters, not too bad. Got to expect some when you walk a hundred miles."

People had been calling the station all day asking about the white stranger walking on 11 South wearing integration signs, Hicks told him. "They want to know if you're part of Martin Luther King's campaign in Birmingham."

"I'm not part of any movement," Moore said, explaining that he was simply a mailman walking to Governor Ross Barnett's home to deliver a message. "My letter to him is a plea to accept the inevitability of integration and to be gracious about it."

But the newsman hadn't told Moore everything. One thousand callers would never have lured Charlie Hicks out of a cool studio on such a hot night, but at seven o'clock a man's voice, deep and raspy, had whispered that "a news story of some consequence" was heading down Highway 11 seven miles north of Reece City.[4]

Hicks asked Moore if he was afraid of getting hurt. Despite the encounter with Floyd and Gaddis, Moore said simply, "I'm walking this highway as an American citizen under the protection of the 14th Amendment. Besides, I grew up in Mississippi, and I don't believe the people of the South are that way."[5]

"What exactly are you going to say to the governor?" Hicks asked.

"That it's about time we got rid of the black eye we've got when it comes to race relations. I believe the governor's wrong when he says that *all* Mississippians want segregation."

Flashing headlights caught Hicks's eye. A car pulled up behind them and a tall man got out.

Hicks knew him. He was a reporter from the *Chattanooga Daily Times*. They shook hands and Hicks introduced Moore. "Just the man I'm looking for," the Tennessee newsman boomed. "Mr. Moore, there's speculation that you've come down here to cause some trouble. You got anything to say about that?"

Moore was glad that the *Times* was finally interested, but he was still shaken from his encounter with the men from Collbran. "I don't think so," he said. "I'm certainly not planning to harm anybody, and like I told Charlie, I don't think that people would mistreat me."[6]

"Do you think the Negroes will thank you for this?" the reporter asked.

"I'm not asking for their thanks," he said. "Segregation is against federal law."

"I should be getting back to the studio," Hicks said, clearly disappointed in the "news story of some consequence." "I'm due on the air in ten minutes. Can I give you a lift, Mr. Moore?"

Moore declined.

"Be careful," Hicks warned, "and good luck to you."

The Tennessee reporter nodded. "I need to find a phone, too, but I'll be catching up with you again, Mr. Moore."

"Thanks." Moore waved as the men pulled away. Too bad he hadn't remembered to bring a transistor radio so he could hear Hicks's broadcast—he might even make the Mutual Broadcasting News. Things were happening fast.

Moore stopped at Robinson's Hilltop Grocery and bought a can of corn and a small pecan pie for thirty cents. It was seven-thirty. If he made Reece City before ten he'd be in good shape.

Suddenly another car appeared, and someone called out his name. Moore tensed. Who was this? The man approached him slowly, holding up a badge. "Roy McDowell," he said, "I'm an investigator for the state of Alabama, and I'd like to ask you a few questions." He gestured for Moore to get into the car.

For thirty minutes McDowell questioned Moore about his background, his purpose, and his plans.

"I'd like to drive you to the Mississippi border, Mr. Moore," he said, finally.[7]

"That's very kind," Moore replied. "But I told one of your deputies this afternoon that I made a pledge to walk to Mississippi and I mean to keep it."

"There's a lot of trouble with the racial situation down here just now," McDowell said.

"Am I breaking the law?"

"No, sir, but if you could take off those signs I think it would go better for you. You're getting a lot of notice. I just want to keep you from getting hurt."

"I appreciate that, officer, I do," Moore said. "But I'm trying to prove something. If I turn back or take off my signs I'd be giving up."

"I hope you know what you're doing, Mr. Moore. If I could take you in I would, but it's a free country, I guess."

"Just trying to keep it that way." Moore smiled.

McDowell succeeded in making Moore promise to stay at the D & J

Truck Stop Cabins for the night. They were only three miles down the highway, and Moore insisted on walking.

McDowell let him out and made a U-turn. He'd report back to Captain Allen that there wasn't much they could do. He couldn't arrest a man who hadn't committed a crime. Moore crossed the road and continued walking on the left side of the pavement. He rested only once—just a short break to catch his breath and make notes in his journal. He wanted to get it all down so he could write about it someday.

"Third day on the road," he scribbled, "walking again. Traffic cop waved greeting. Chatted with a few men who heard about my walk on TV. They didn't think I'd finish it alive. Sheriff's car stopped to ask how long I'd been walking. Took a leaflet, wondered if I'd make it to Mississippi. A couple of men drove up and questioned my religious and political beliefs. And one was sure I'd be killed for them, such as my Jesus poster on my buggy. Feet sore all over. Shoes too painful, walking without them."[8]

He wasn't afraid anymore. Lots of people were looking out for him now—reporters, state police, even the department of public safety, and he was finally getting publicity.

Ten miles north of Attalla he passed through the little farm community of Keener, Alabama, and spotted a sign for "roadside tables." It was a small picnic area less than one hundred yards off the road. Although it looked like a comfortable place to stop he'd promised Inspector McDowell that he'd spend the night at the truck stop. A car was idling nearby with its headlights off. As Moore passed, a door opened and slammed; then he heard footsteps behind him. McDowell again? He turned.

Not McDowell. There was a loud crack. Moore felt burning, searing pain behind his eyes, and everything went dark.

Larry Keener, the night switchboard operator at the *Gadsden Times*, had received an anonymous call at 7:30 P.M. requesting that a reporter be sent to an area seven miles north of Reece City on U.S. 11; the police should also come, the caller said. Thom Wilkerson and Bill Basenberg were dispatched, but they didn't rush and they didn't call the police. Cranks were contacting the paper nearly every day now. The troubles in Birmingham were making everybody crazy.[9]

When they arrived in Keener, Wilkerson and Basenberg found the police already there, calming a distraught motorist, Willis Elrod, who was talking so fast that they could barely understand him. Elrod had pulled over to use the roadside park's rest room on his way home from work and had tripped over the body of a tall, barefoot white man lying face up on the road with a set of bloodstained signs next to him. He ran across the highway to the Sizemore farm and called the police.

"It looks like he asked for trouble and he got it," Carl Alverson, manager of a local gas station who had walked up the road to see what all the commotion was about, told them.[10]

Victim

All over Alabama the lamps are out.
—JAMES AGEE

"White Mixer Slain on 'Bama Highway," the banner headline of the April 24 *Jackson (Mississippi) Daily News* screamed. The murder victim was identified as "a white integrationist from Maryland who had been a mental patient. . . ."

"Robbery was not a motive," Etowah County coroner Noble Yocum reported from Alabama. "Mr. Moore had fifty-one dollars cash in his pocket and his watch was still on his wrist. . . . From the angle of the bullet, it appears it was fired at close range."

One slug had struck Moore in the left temple, the other had ripped into his neck. Yocum estimated the time of death was between 8:00 and 8:30 P.M.

Etowah's sheriff, Dewey Colvard, theorized that the killers parked near a roadside table ten miles north of Attalla, and waited for Moore. "They were in such a hurry to get away," he said, "that they didn't even touch him after he fell. They must have been scared or they would have dragged him off the highway into the ditch."[1]

Yocum speculated that the murder was a "civil rights case," and that the racial demonstrations in Birmingham were probably involved. "I personally don't think this is a local matter," he said.[2]

Deputy George Knowles of the DeKalb County sheriff's office said he'd warned Moore that things could get rough for him farther south on Highway 11, and while Moore appeared to understand, he was determined to keep going.

"In these cases," Knowles offered, "you'd naturally look for something mental, so I looked at him very carefully. He had a nice expression, very open. And he didn't bother anybody; he didn't seem to have spoken to anyone unless they spoke to him first. We got every man we have working on it."[3]

Newsman Charlie Hicks was badly shaken. "He was a nice, friendly, intelligent guy," he said. "I just talked to him. . . . I told him something might happen, but he was determined to go on alone."[4]

Moore's aunt Helen and uncle Charlie Cagle, who'd begged him not to stop at their home, drove from Birmingham to identify the body. Moore's signs, leaflets, money order receipts, wallet, watch, and journal were secured in the sheriff's office, along with the copies of his letter to President Kennedy and his plea to Governor Barnett.

All Moore's possessions except the "Jesus sign" were accounted for. Deputy Tony Reynolds noted that it called Christ an alien, a Jew, and a man known to associate with criminals. He and Sheriff Colvard felt that getting rid of it was the least they could do to calm the very distraught Helen Cagle. Her husband, Charlie, would later comment, "The thing that upset those people most was that sign about Jesus Christ. They were nice Christian people."[5]

Four hours after Moore's body was found, Mary Moore received a collect call from Coroner Yokum's office informing her that her husband had been in an accident. The caller instructed Mary to dial back after she'd found someone to stay with her. She ran barefoot next door and got Rev. Bob Drewry.

"I knew the minute that phone rang at midnight that Bill was dead," she said.[6] Early the next morning she called his father, Robert Moore, who said in response, "Mary, we've got to keep this thing quiet."[7]

As Moore's body was being prepared by the Etowah County mortician for shipment to Binghamton, New York, the national media began struggling to make sense of the puzzling story of a southerner who favored integration, an atheist who died carrying a picture of Jesus, and an activist

associated with both CORE and the NAACP who died alone on an unauthorized march.

Lee White, President Kennedy's press aide, scrambled to locate
Moore's letters, neither of which had reached the Oval Office. White suggested that Kennedy refer to the postman's murder during a routine press
conference and embarrass Governor Wallace, who had recently prevented
the integration of his alma mater, the University of Alabama.

Kennedy, angry at Wallace's remarks about Washington being an im-
perialist invader, put Moore's name on the front page of every national
newspaper when he said that "we had an outrageous crime, from all accounts in the State of Alabama, in the shooting of the postman who was
attempting in a very traditional way to dramatize the plight of some of our
citizens being harassed on the road. We have offered the services of the
FBI in the solution of the crime.

"We do not have direct jurisdiction," the president continued, "but we
are working with every legislative legal tool at our command to insure
protection for the rights of our citizens, and we shall continue to do so."[8]

George Wallace grudgingly agreed to a request from William W. Rayburn, circuit solicitor (state district attorney), to offer a one-thousand-
dollar reward for information leading to the arrest of Moore's killers. Rayburn assured the governor that it would take some of the heat off the state.
"This crime is a terrible thing," Rayburn told reporters. "It hurts our
Southland in the eyes of the rest of the nation."

On April 25, 1963, an editorial in the *New York Post* observed that "he
[Moore] spent his life tugging at the world's coat sleeve. When at last it
began to listen, William Moore was gone." Bill Moore couldn't have said
it better himself.

The Suspect

I have never known a racist who was an atheist.
—REV. HENLEE H. BARNETT, 1961

"Disagreements over the principles of integration and religion are the only issues involved in this murder," William Beck, Floyd Simpson's attorney, insisted after his client was arrested on April 25, 1963, and held as a material witness in the matter of the murder of William L. Moore.

"The guilty man fits the two categories of integration and religion, and my client fits neither. I've known him for thirty years and he's not fanatically religious."[1]

While the national press appeared uninterested in Moore's atheism, it was a fact that many in the white South were anxious to broadcast. If black Christians and white Christians could agree on any one thing it was that nonbelief was a sin.

Many white Alabamians feared that the murder of a northern integrationist would provide an open invitation for agitators to come south to stir up the black population. Focusing on Moore's atheism was a way of tarnishing his message. Informing blacks and whites that Moore was both a blasphemer and a mental case seemed prudent.

William Moore's last journal entry had steered investigators directly to Floyd Simpson and Gaddis Killian. Sheriff Dewey Colvard was "pretty sure" that Simpson was the person Moore referred to in the diary.

Simpson's ancestors had settled in DeKalb County, Alabama, before the War between the States, and the grocery he'd leased from Gad Killian just seven months earlier was a popular gathering place for Collbran locals.

A sergeant first class in the Alabama National Guard and a veteran of both the Korean War and World War II, Simpson was forty years old. He and his wife, Lucille, and their six children—Paul, eighteen (who'd recently gotten married), Carolyn, sixteen, Mary, fourteen, Marsha, twelve, and Todd, seventeen months—all lived behind the rented grocery store. Simpson had worked for many years as a fixer for Southland Mills before going into business for himself.

Gaddis Killian, a forty-four-year-old mailman and father of four, lived in the big house next to the grocery. He suffered from a variety of nervous disorders which periodically landed him in the hospital. Killian had been out delivering mail when the sheriff came for him, and he'd voluntarily surrendered the following morning.

Killian's wife reported that Gaddis, a devout Baptist, was interested in a sign on Moore's cart which called for the capture of Jesus Christ. She and Lucille Simpson said their husbands had left the store early in the afternoon to drive down Highway 11 to catch up with Moore, but they had returned by four o'clock and had not gone out again.[2]

Killian explained that on April 23 he'd stopped at Simpson's grocery at 11:30 A.M. on a break from his mail route. Killian's cousins, Jack and George, told him that, an hour before, they'd talked with a race mixer on his way to Jackson, Mississippi, who was carrying an obscene picture of Jesus Christ. Killian wanted to see the picture for himself. When he left work at 3:00 P.M. he and Simpson had driven down the highway looking for the man. Killian admitted that they'd spoken with Moore, but he denied any knowledge of the shooting.[3]

Killian's neighbors reported that he was deeply concerned about moral and spiritual laxity in America. "Gad's gotten to be a terrible radical lately," one said. "You can't talk to him anymore. He just keeps on saying we been sold out to the Communists and the Catholics."[4]

Sheriff Colvard was holding Simpson on an open charge, but he couldn't lock Killian up because he was claustrophobic. "He's a sick man," Colvard told reporters, "and that's why I allowed him to go home and go to bed."

Although Simpson assured the sheriff that he and Killian merely "felt sorry for that fellow Moore," and in a friendly spirit had warned him that he'd never get past Birmingham, he refused to take a lie detector test.

"We couldn't believe that a fellow thought like that," Simpson said. "He believed in integration and intermarriage and said that he didn't believe in God."[5]

Colvard asked what Simpson had done after four o'clock on the day of the murder and if he'd loaned his car to anyone. "I'm sorry, Sheriff," the grocer said, "but I can not, and will not, answer any more questions."

Rev. Benny Parker, pastor of the Gravel Hill Baptist Church, located next to Simpson's store, visited with Lucille Simpson and they prayed together.[6]

On April 28, which would have been Moore's thirty-sixth birthday, Sheriff Colvard received an FBI ballistics report matching the slugs found in Moore's body with bullets fired from Simpson's rifle. Floyd Simpson was formally charged with first-degree murder.

Colvard's arrest warrant was based on the FBI ballistics report and on the fact that several eyewitnesses had placed Simpson's car near the scene of the shooting, that Simpson admitted speaking with Moore at least twice on the day he was murdered, and that Simpson refused to tell investigators what he'd done after four o'clock on April 24.

Three witnesses reported seeing Simpson's black Buick in Keener at approximately seven o'clock, and they testified that he was with a second man who was not Gaddis Killian. One described the car as a 1950 or 1951 black Buick with #28 on the license tag, the designation for DeKalb County.[7]

William Don Wessonate, who worked at the Attalla Gulf station, reported driving north on Highway 11 at 8 P.M. on April 24 and passing a black Buick pulled off to the side of the road at a rest stop near the Sizemore farm. The taillights, he said, were blinking, and a man was walking toward the car from the left side of the road. Wessonate had missed Moore's murder by seconds.

All the witnesses described the second man in the Buick as heavyset. Killian, whose build was slight, was released, and six officers were dispatched to DeKalb County to investigate. Sheriff Colvard assured the FBI that when the second man was found he'd be arrested and held on an open charge.

When Captain Ben Allen of the department of public safety drove one of the witnesses up to Simpson's store to positively identify the Buick, the witness informed Allen that Jasper Fike, who was standing in front of the grocery, looked a lot like the man he'd seen with Simpson. Allen brought Fike to Gadsden, and placed him in a lineup; two other witnesses picked him out. Fike submitted to a lie detector test, and passed. Sheriff Colvard released him.[8]

Despite the convincing physical evidence and the testimony of eyewitnesses, Circuit Solicitor William Rayburn did not request a special grand jury session. He told Assistant Attorney General Burke Marshall that, in his opinion, even with a signed confession he couldn't get a conviction in Alabama. Many of those interviewed stated that, while they didn't believe in murder, they were against marches like the one Moore was on, and were incensed that others were being planned. Rayburn agreed to a five-thousand-dollar bond until the grand jury's scheduled September session.

The *Birmingham News* noted with relief that Simpson's arrest climaxed a case "which has gained nation-wide attention and brought numerous out-of-state newsmen to Gadsden." Ft. Payne locals hoped to keep confidential what many outside journalists suspected. Floyd Simpson was a member of Klavern #13 of the United Klans of America (UKA). His was a familiar presence at weekly Ft. Payne meetings, where open Bibles were displayed on "sacred alters" [sic]; at cross burnings; and at "naturalization" rites, where new Klansmen left the "alien world" and entered the benevolent brotherhood singing "The Old Rugged Cross."[9]

Chartered in 1961, the United Klans of America was a federation of Klaverns stretching from Alabama to Louisiana, through southern Mississippi, and including Tennessee, Florida, and parts of Georgia. Under the motto *Non Silba Sed Anthar* (Not for Self, but for Others), its membership had grown to almost twenty-five thousand by the time of Moore's murder.

As a young man Floyd Simpson had placed his left hand on a Bible opened to the twelfth chapter of Romans, which exhorted Christians to show "godly conduct and godly character." He'd raised his right hand and pledged to, at any time and without hesitating, go to the assistance or rescue of another Klansman. "At his call I will answer," he'd promised, "and I will be truly Klannish toward Klansmen in all things honorable.

"I swear that I will most zealously and valiantly shield and preserve by any and all justifiable means and methods, the sacred constitutional rights and privileges of free public school, free speech, free press, separation of church and state, liberty, white supremacy, just laws, and the pursuit of happiness against any encroachment of any nature by any person or persons, political party or parties, religious sect or people, native, naturalized, or foreign of any race, color, creed, lineage, or tongue whatsoever.

"All to which I have sworn by this oath I will seal with my blood, be Thou my witness, Almighty God. Amen!"[10]

Asa Carter, head of the Gadsden Klan (who would become Governor George Wallace's chief speech writer), and a number of Simpson's associates from Ft. Payne had helped Birmingham's Eastview Klavern #13 viciously beat the Freedom Riders (including Jim Peck) in Anniston and Birmingham in 1961. Just weeks after Moore's murder they would dynamite Martin Luther King's room at the A. G. Gaston Motel in Birmingham and the home of his brother, Rev. A. D. King, and five months later they would bomb the Sixteenth Street Baptist Church where four young black girls would lose their lives.

Governor George Wallace would press Al Lingo, director of the Alabama Department of Public Safety, to take action before the FBI completed its investigation, and Lingo would arrest Charles "Arnie" Cagle, the son of a Baptist minister and a cousin by marriage of the postman William Moore.[11] Robert Chambliss and John Wesley ("Nigger") Hall were also held on charges of "illegal transportation and possession of dynamite." (Cagle had earlier been arrested for transporting dynamite to the University of Alabama campus after Governor Wallace had stood in the doorway to block the integration of his alma mater.)

Cagle, Chambliss, and Hall, represented by UKA Grand Klonsel Matt Murphy, Jr., were convicted of a misdemeanor, fined a hundred dollars each, and sentenced to 180 days in jail. Lingo charged them with lesser crimes in order to take control of the evidence and prevent the FBI from building a murder case. Chambliss would not be indicted for the Sixteenth Street Baptist Church murders until 1977.[12] Cagle was never indicted.

Rev. Willis Griffen, chaplain (Kludd) of Simpson's Klavern, was an ordained Baptist minister who wrote a weekly newspaper column championing white supremacy, the subject of most of his sermons. He made a tract of his land available for rifle and pistol practice on Saturday afternoons.[13] Griffen said of Floyd Simpson, "He's a religious man. Of course his business keeps him away from church sometimes, but his family goes regularly. And there's a Baptist church right next door to his property."

Ft. Payne Klansmen speculated that some tramp had killed Moore and that the state police, anxious to take the heat off themselves, had served Simpson up because Moore had mentioned him in his journal.

On April 29, 1963, Simpson was released on a five-thousand-dollar bond pending the September grand jury session. Five days later, Jack Hopper, a staff reporter for the *Birmingham News*, arranged an exclusive interview with him.

"I am emphatically denying any part in the slaying of William Moore," the grocer told Hopper. "I had no reason to slay him, and my interest in him was merely as a curious individual. I wanted to talk to a man who apparently had no belief or faith in God, as I had never talked to a man of this character."

Simpson admitted that he and some friends had discussed religion, integration, and intermarriage with Moore outside his store on the morning of the murder, but noted that Moore seemed to enjoy talking about his beliefs. There had been no quarrel, Simpson insisted, even when he and Gaddis Killian caught up with the man eighteen miles further on Highway 11.

But during that second conversation Moore became evasive, Simpson said. "He wouldn't give exact answers to our questions concerning God and about the segregation issues."

Simpson described a picture that Moore had taped to his shopping cart. "To the best of my recollection," he told Hopper, "it said 'Jesus Christ, son of a carpenter.' I don't remember the rest of the writing, but the thing appeared to be low-rating Christ."

Simpson said that during both conversations, neither of which he estimated was longer than fifteen minutes, he got the idea that Moore was being paid for his attempted march through the South. "I don't see how anybody could believe in such things as intermarriage between the white and Negro races unless he was being paid for it. . . . I told him they are having trouble in Birmingham, and I advised him to turn back as he would never get through Birmingham."

Finally, Simpson told Hopper that he had no interest in either segregation or integration. "I have never taken any part in any racial difficulties, nor indicated any interest in these type of problems. We just don't have them around here."

White Americans React

No excellent soul is exempt from a mixture of madness.
—ARISTOTLE

Back home in Binghamton, New York, flowers, cards, and expressions of sympathy filled Mary Moore's trailer home on Parkway Street. She took little comfort in them, however. Mary resented all the reporters' questions and insinuations about Bill's activism, and she was amazed when Governor Nelson Rockefeller declared that "the slaying of William Moore, a man expressing his beliefs in the worth and dignity of every human being, is a tragedy."[1]

Yes, it *was* a tragedy, but it was also a humiliation for her and the children. She tried to be gracious to the endless parade of strangers who came to her door, called, and sent telegrams, but she didn't really know what they expected of her.[2]

"Everybody wants to know how a wife feels when her husband is out to change the world," she told reporters. "Well, I did ask him not to go. But he would not be stopped. He was too determined. You must know Bill to understand he hates to see anyone oppressed. He was a freedom fighter from way back. He thought he could change the world and make it better."[3]

New York state representative Howard Robison wired, "I came to know William Moore through the correspondence we had—usually over the one matter, civil rights. . . . [He] was quite evidently a man of courage and conviction."

Most surprising was a letter from Clarence Sackey, Binghamton's former city welfare commissioner and Moore's ex-boss. "This is typical of the kind of thing he became involved in," Sackey wrote. "He was very much a standard bearer in terms of what he thought was justice, very much on the offensive for underprivileged people."[4]

Mary could hardly forget that Sackey had warned Bill about getting too close to his clients and ordered him to stop giving them money. (Moore had distributed nearly three thousand dollars during the two years that he worked for the welfare department at a time when his annual salary was thirty-four hundred dollars.) When Moore resigned, Sackey had classified him as ineligible for rehire.

CBS-TV news reported that Moore was a World War II veteran who'd seen action on Guam. Bill would have had a good laugh about that, Mary thought. He'd often joked about all the "action" he'd seen from the motor pool. The media seemed determined to create a white hero of the resistance like Mississippi's 1962 black hero James Meredith. Like Meredith, Moore was a veteran and an independent activist engaged in a constitutionally protected activity when he was attacked.

The *Chicago Sun-Times* blamed Moore's murder on "all who have condoned violence,"[5] and the *Denver Post* asserted that "Moore's blood is on the Governor's [Wallace's] hands—and on the hands of all those who encourage the people of the South to defy the laws that guarantee basic American rights to the Negroes."[6]

Few national correspondents were interested in either Moore's atheism or his "Jesus poster." They assumed that his disagreement with Simpson and Killian had been over segregation. Race was the issue which made Moore's story newsworthy. Journalists logically connected his walk with the Birmingham demonstrations less than one hundred miles from where he'd been killed.

Moore's memorial service was held on Thursday, April 25, at the William R. Chase Funeral Home around the corner from city hall, where he had conducted so many of his one-man crusades.

Mary Moore announced that her husband's funeral would be open to anyone who wanted to attend. She said that all the national publicity would have pleased Bill. "It's just what he would have loved. He said in his last letter [to me] that this might be the biggest thing in his life. I'm sorry he can't be here to enjoy it."

Rev. Robert Drewry, a slender middle-aged man with a long face, dark hair, and darkframed glasses, told the 150 mourners (half of whom were black) that, while Moore was an avowed atheist and they saw "eye to eye on almost nothing," he considered him a friend. Drewry described his friend as "a man with singleness of purpose from which he never swerved."

Governor Nelson Rockefeller sent his associate George Hinman to represent him, and Congressman John V. Lindsay (who would later be elected mayor of New York City) sat among the mourners.

Drewry read extensively from Moore's autobiography, *The Mind in Chains*.

"I always dreamed of Utopia," Moore had written, "and I was not content merely to dream[7]. . . . [S]atisfactory as my present life may be there is something inside me which whispers that I cannot remain content for long. . . . I think of all the troubles over all the earth and I wonder if I'll ever really be able to do my share to help save the world. . . . I cannot rid myself of the notion that all the important events of my life were more or less planned, that they were meant to be."[8]

Drewry asked God to grant that some good might come from Moore's cruel death.

Jim Peck delivered the eulogy. "It is heartening to see this big crowd," he told the mourners, "but it's not enough. We must redouble our efforts for peace and brotherhood . . . for all the things Bill Moore fought for."[9]

One hundred students joined the forty-car funeral procession when it reached Harpur College, Moore's alma mater, and followed it to Vestal Hills Memorial Park.

At the grave site a marine rifle squad fired three volleys, and a bugler sounded taps. Marine reservists folded the American flag which draped Moore's casket, and handed it to Mary. "I hope and pray to God it wasn't for nothing," she said, "maybe this will help to wake people up to how horrible segregation is."

Mary's mother, Ruth Hamilton, told Jerry Handte of the *Binghamton Evening Press* that her son-in-law was "one kind man. He was wonderful to the children, even though they were not his," she said.

Handte wrote that "Bill Moore's life was full of paradox. Although he was a vigorous crusader, he was a gentle one. He adopted such causes as civil rights, world peace, and bettering the lot of mental patients without the bitter invective and seeming hatred of opposition often characteristic of reformers.

"His letters to newspapers were marked by humor, a quality usually conspicuous by its absence in the declamations of idealists.

"Most crusaders are didactically sure of their ground: Mr. Moore usually admitted the possibility that he was not the sole possessor of wisdom, inviting men of good will to examine the issues in question together.

"People with balanced outlooks and peaceful temperaments are often shy of public expressions of their views. Mr. Moore sought and welcomed publicity in behalf of whatever causes he embraced."[10]

The day after Moore's funeral, Mary and his three stepchildren were placed under police protection because they had received a series of mysterious hang-up calls and a barrage of hate mail. Mary was also notified that she'd be laid off from her job at the Transformers plant at the end of the week. It was routine, her supervisor explained, a cutback resulting from the cancellation of a navy subcontract.

Another St. Stephen

Outside the South, Bill Moore was initially cast by the media as a twentieth century abolitionist. Some journalists and politicians described him in what today would be considered excessively religious language (especially since the victim was a self-identified atheist). The April 25 *Chicago Daily News*, for example, crowned him a "latter day St. Stephen."

"Perhaps the most revered martyr of all time was that figure of primitive Christian days, the deacon Stephen," its editorial of April 29 observed. "He was stoned to death for blasphemy because of his faith in the gentle teachings of Jesus. His unflinching courage has inspired many a follower and remorse for such cruelties of men has doubtless preceded many a reformation.

"William Moore the Baltimore postman has earned a place in the company of Stephen . . . the simple appeal for humanity in his letter should melt a small corner in the heart of even a Mississippi legislator."

The April 25 *Milwaukee Journal* hailed Moore as "a pilgrim," while the April 25 *Binghamton Evening Press* declared him "a true martyr."

Councilman Vincent Capozzi, whose seventh ward included Binghamton, remarked, "I believe that it has been sufficiently proved that racial segregation is a sin against justice. And I also believe that racial segregation is a sin against charity, and that one can go to hell as easily for committing a sin against charity as he can for sinning against justice, perhaps more easily."[11]

Even Murray Kempton, writing for the very liberal *New Republic*, observed that "Moore's condition seems to have been paranoid not in the delusion of being persecuted, but in the conviction of being specially blessed, which was the paranoia of evangelical times and with which George Fox, for one, may have built a church."[12] (Fox founded the religious order of Quakers.)

The atheist's walk began to evolve into a kind of passion narrative with Moore in the role of itinerant mailman, crucified by those who misunderstood and feared his message. His murder was expropriated by clergymen, activists, journalists, and politicians as a platform on which to articulate their own convictions and fears.

But this adulation was fleeting. When an increasing number of sympathetic activists, black and white, began to announce their intentions to finish Moore's walk to Mississippi, the national focus began to shift away from what had been seen as his sacrificial death to issues concerning his sanity. As a lone crusader Moore cut a noble figure, but as more and more whites rallied to his cause, angry voices countered that he'd willed his own death in an insane attempt to achieve martyrdom.

Evidence that a growing number of committed white idealists like Moore were willing (though not eager) to die to end segregation was unsettling to a majority of white Americans. Two years earlier, after the brutal 1961 attack on the Freedom Riders in Birmingham, a Gallup Poll reported that 63 percent of white Americans who were aware of the event disapproved.[13]

The *Wall Street Journal* noted that "the so-called Freedom Riders went looking for trouble, in one of the most likely parts of the South, and they found it."[14]

White activists were often accused of inciting blacks to overthrow capitalism and usher in a communist revolution. Anne Braden, a southern white activist, recalled that "whites in the movement were always on the fringes, always the outcasts and never respectable."[15]

By 1963, most working-class whites had achieved a standard of living that they could not have dreamed of before World War II. Opening up the postwar prosperity to blacks who would compete for their jobs, lower their property values, and overcrowd their schools seemed foolish. Many did not understand how other whites could march with blacks and advocate black advancement.

Many white Americans suspected that "the Negro cause" attracted white eccentrics, escapists, and neurotics—conscience-stricken fanatics like the abolitionist John Brown, who was clearly unbalanced. Activists who pointed to the discrepancies between the promises of the United States Constitution and the realities of American life were considered disloyal.

Even liberals questioned the effectiveness of white activists demonstrating in the South, fearing that their presence would precipitate violence. Many white liberals sincerely wanted change, but change without pain.

Moore had understood that those who called attention to society's shortcomings paid a price. Change never came without challenge, but in the early 1960s, it is fair to say, most white activists did not believe they would have to pay with their lives. Destruction of reputations and lack of professional advancement were sacrifices they did expect.

It was, therefore, not surprising when speculation began to grow that the murdered postman had provoked his own death. What better way to achieve martyrdom than by walking through the Deep South protesting segregation?

Those who knew how determined Moore had been during the last six months of his life might have ended such conjecture. Moore was certainly eccentric, most likely naive, and in some ways irresponsible, but he was not suicidal. No one, however, stepped forward.

Jim Peck was not anxious to reopen the issue of CORE's refusal (with his approval) to sponsor Moore's walk, and Mary Moore could not defend her husband's move to Baltimore without drawing attention to their troubled marriage. She was desperate to maintain Moore's image as a visionary, and she feared that discovery of his local Binghamton activism would fuel the doubts about his sanity and put a damper on CBS's plans for its documentary "Death of a Mailman." Mary had no income and no prospects. She hoped that the documentary might attract needed support for her family.

As the tide of sympathy for Moore turned, Harpur College president Glenn Bartle declared him "a sincere individual," but noted that "his methods supporting those issues in which he strongly believed may be questioned. . . ."

Moore had walked for thirty-four hours and covered ninety-five miles. An April 26 editorial in the *New York Times* called this "a pitifully naive pilgrimage." John F. Kellogg of Binghamton took issue, and his letter to the *Times* was printed on the op-ed page on May 5.

"The method [Moore] chose to further his ideals was simple and direct," Kellogg wrote. "The letter he was carrying to Ross Barnett was a gentle, articulate, well-reasoned document neither pitiful nor naive. . . . He never indicated that he believed the war against bigotry could be won overnight. *That* would have been pitifully naive.

"It has been a fairly easy matter to rationalize in terms of the bigness and complexity of modern life our inactivity and our silence in the face of evil, stupidity and injustice. What can a single individual do in the face of forces so large we have asked ourselves. And then we have turned our backs on the problems that have momentarily disturbed us.

"Through his moral intensity and by means of his good-natured lonely individual effort William Moore has shown us the falseness of our comfortable rationalizations."

Admitting that Moore had a local reputation as "somewhat of a nut," Kellogg went on to say that "his eccentricity was to believe in good and work for it no matter how unpopular the cause nor how ludicrous he might seem in the course of his work.

"The history of the progress of man's heart is largely the history of nuts such as Moore, people who were unwilling to leave the world in as sorry a state as they found it."

The *Binghamton Evening Press* of April 25 noted that "it was an odd thing [Moore] was doing when two bullets ended his life . . . he was marching straight through the deep South with signs stressing the equality of the races."

Nine professors and nineteen Harpur College students also responded angrily. "It may be said that [Moore] was not 'realistic,' they wrote, "that he was somewhat lacking in 'common sense.' This is only to say that the sense he had was not common in today's America, a sense that asserted both that injustice must end, and that the impossible must be accomplished. In the philosopher Albert Camus' terms, William Moore was both a rebel and an absurd man."[16]

Fifteen Minutes of Fame

Bill Moore's violent death turned Mary Moore into something of a local celebrity. She continued to receive hundreds of telegrams and telephone calls expressing both sympathy for her loss and support for Moore's cause.

A white woman in Gadsden, Alabama, sent her two dozen American

Beauty roses with a gift card that said, "It's a lonesome road. He wrote his own sign. He did not hide behind another's."[17]

"This is the type of thing Bill would have loved," Mary told the *Binghamton Sun-Bulletin*. "He would be glad to know that people are really thinking."

She said that since her family was under twenty-four-hour sheriff's protection and she no longer had a job, she was considering making a trip to Alabama to confront Floyd Simpson, her husband's alleged murderer. The *Sun-Bulletin* offered to sponsor her trip and to assign a reporter to accompany her.

"I want to ask him why he did it," she said. "I want to know where all that hate comes from."

Five days after Moore's funeral, Mary and Binghamton's mayor, John J. Burns, appeared on WINR-TV's Channel 40 *Hometown* to discuss the murder. During the live interview with host Tom Cawley, Mary emphasized what a good father Moore had been, and said firmly that, despite the rumors, he was not an atheist.

"At times he said he was," she allowed, "but I would definitely say he was not an atheist. Bill was a very complex man."

When Cawley asked about their life together, Mary laughed. "When I first met Bill, I thought, what's with this fellow?" she said. "He was different, and often irritated people. . . . But I was quite a weak individual in those days, and he caused me to think, to be brave. He taught me to be independent."

Mary insisted that she had encouraged Moore's move to Baltimore and that they'd planned it for nearly a year. She denied that their marriage was troubled. "It was something he had to do," she said. "He was a very complicated man. People didn't know quite what to make of him."[18]

Mary told Cawley that she'd asked that her husband's bloodied signs be given to a group of students who were completing his walk, but the Alabama police had refused to release them. She'd also requested his journal. "Bill always kept good records," she said. "I hope nothing's lost."

When Cawley questioned her about Floyd Simpson's release on bond she said, "It just doesn't seem possible. It's ridiculous. Down there they cling together. They've been cooperative, but not as thorough as they might have been. They don't condone what happened, and yet they let this man go. What is the world coming to?"[19]

When Cawley asked about the possibility that Moore had intended to become a civil rights martyr, Mary shook her head firmly. "No," she said. "Bill was very much afraid of death. I don't know how he walked down that road. . . . I was really worried because I knew about the [Birmingham] Alabama riots. I'm positive that he knew in his heart that death could be waiting, but he wasn't looking for it. It took an awful lot of courage for him to do what he did."

(On this point Mary seems to have understood her husband very well. The May 1963 issue of *Civil Liberties*, the newsletter of the American Civil Liberties Union, carried a board resolution expressing deep regret for the death of its member William Moore. "Mr. Moore," the resolution said, "was in touch with the ACLU before beginning his Walk about his legal rights and possible need for legal aid. [Moore] asserted that he did not want to be a test case, nor, it was clear, did he intend to become a martyr. Yet he died for his belief in civil liberties.")

Mary concluded that some people thought her husband was an oddball, but he was always looking out for the underdog. "You would have to know him to understand him," she said.

Mayor Burns nodded. "This taught us a lesson," he agreed. "Bill Moore was scorned here. I think now we're all sorry he was. Maybe the next time someone wants to picket the courthouse, we will tolerate brave people."[20] Mary smiled at him.

Meanwhile, back in Birmingham, Helen Cagle refused to speak with reporters about her nephew, Bill Moore. From behind her locked screen door she shouted, "Too much has been said already! We don't want to read any more about him! If you men will grant my request and his family's you'll print nothing more about him. He wasn't responsible. . . ."[21]

Black Americans React

*The American ideal is, after all, that everyone should
be as much alike as possible.*

—James Baldwin

Many black activists embraced Moore's symbolic walk and understood it
in ways that escaped even sympathetic white liberals. Journalist John O.
Killens wrote in the *New York Times*, "To the average white man, a courthouse . . . is a place where justice is dispensed. To me, a black man, it is a
place where justice is dispensed-with. . . . You give us a moody Abraham
Lincoln [as a hero-symbol], but many of us prefer John Brown whom most
of you hold in contempt and regard as a fanatic; meaning, of course, that
the firm dedication of any white man to the freedom of the black man is
prima facie evidence of perversion and insanity."[1]

Phyllis Garland, reporting for the black *Pittsburgh Courier*, referred to
Moore as "a sacrifice on the altar of hatred," and noted that "it was a
striking thing that a white man was willing to risk his life to carry the
message of integration to the governor of Mississippi.

"It would have been significant if a Negro was murdered, but here was
a white man who did not have to risk his life. In another time he could
measure up to Joan of Arc or even Christ."[2]

Rev. Marlin Ballard of Baltimore's Fellowship of Reconciliation attended Moore's funeral and told reporters that "we feel [Moore] emulated
what Christ did 2,000 years ago. It may do more for the cause of integration than much past effort has done."[3]

Mary Moore never visited her husband when he lived in Baltimore, but
early in May she agreed to accompany Jim Peck to the Baltimore CORE's
memorial service for him at the First Unitarian Church.

Rev. Irving R. Murray, a stocky, dark-haired white man with piercing
eyes, told the 450 mourners (who were mostly black) that Moore "burned
with a fierce conviction that brotherhood and democracy must prevail."

Murray counseled that Moore ought not to be considered a maverick since the methods he used were the same ones used by the Hebrew prophets.

"If [Moore] was a screwball," Murray said, "then the prophets Amos and Isaiah were screwballs too. . . ."[4]

Mary met some of the people who'd become important in Moore's life, most of whom were black. Ralph Matthews, a correspondent for the *Philadelphia Afro-American*, had met Moore during the Northwood Theater stand-in. Matthews recalled him as a quiet but friendly guy who rode around town on a blue motor scooter. Often he'd be the only white person working at the CORE chapter on North Avenue. He was low-key and didn't talk a lot, others told her.

Moore had become involved with CORE during the period when the organization was evolving from a pacifist group of predominantly white intellectuals into a militant black movement. Baltimore CORE's members, unlike those in many large cities, were overwhelmingly black.[5]

"[Bill's] calm puzzled me," Matthews remembered, "until I came to understand that his inner peace came as a result of his having discovered what being a white American really meant. Bill would never have put it in these words, but I think he felt that [white] America had sinned against Black America and it needed to publicly confess and atone."[6]

One week before Moore left for Chattanooga, Matthews and a few friends had gathered in his apartment to wish him well. Some were students he'd met during the Northwood stand-in, and others were friends from the earlier Route 40 Freedom Ride.

One young black woman sadly recalled that she'd joked with Moore about where he wanted his body sent. She tried to talk him out of his walk, and when he wouldn't reconsider, she asked him to at least take somebody with him.

Moore said that was a good idea, "only I can't find anyone who wants to come. Why don't *you* walk with me?"

"You're white and they'd get you," she'd laughed. "I'm colored and they'd get me twice as fast . . . and if they saw us walking together, *well. . . .*"

Moore had shared his plans with only one post office coworker, Herbert Gardner, whose daughter Anne had also been arrested at the Northwood Theater. Gardner, a black man, recalled that "Bill was from the

South and he seemed to feel that he was going home and that the Southern white people and his own family would listen to him."[7]

He told Gardner that the time was coming when the nonwhite races would be in power because the world is 75 percent nonwhite. Moore said he hoped the colored races would be kinder to his people than they had been to them.

Ralph Matthews recalled that his last words of advice to his friend were: "Bill, you'd better carry a gun.

"We all told him he'd be killed. But who of us honestly expected, even knowing of the racial madness there, that what we prophesied would come true? I think what we were really saying was 'Please make it, man,' because if he had, it would have [signaled] a genuine wind of change."[8]

The Civil Rights Establishment Reacts

The lone man belongs to the wolf.
—ARABIC PROVERB

"Who the hell *was* this guy?" the members of CORE's National Action Council asked each other. "What did he think he was doing, and how is this crazy business going to reflect on the movement?"

Although countless blacks, named and unnamed, had been killed in the struggle to claim their constitutional rights, and many whites and blacks had been beaten and injured, Moore's was the first murder of a white nonviolent social justice activist.

While Walter Carter, executive director of the Baltimore CORE, had wired Mary Moore that "[t]his [tragedy] has struck us deeply, Bill was very close to us even though he had been with us only a short while," he had refused to sponsor Moore's walk. Now Carter was terrified that the press would learn that some CORE members had considered Moore a "kook."[1]

Doris Derby, who was in the twelve-member SNCC delegation to

Moore's funeral, assured Mary that "[w]e're determined to continue [Bill's] work." When SNCC formally expressed an interest in completing Moore's walk, however, CORE's National Action Council decided to reclaim him.

CORE's public relations director, Lloyd Taylor, requested that Attorney General Robert Kennedy order a federal investigation of the assassination. "It is a sad reflection upon American democracy," he said, "when a citizen cannot walk the streets in non-violent protest without being physically harmed. We as good Americans cannot rest until justice is brought in this case and all America is free from racial hatred."[2]

Now that Moore was dead, his reputation could be managed, and CORE could support him to a degree that had been impossible while he lived.

On Wednesday, April 24, 1963, James Forman, executive secretary of the Student Nonviolent Coordinating Committee, left a message for Mary Moore, requesting that she contact him if she thought that her husband would have wanted SNCC to finish his walk.

Mary telegrammed back: "Appreciate your feelings. Covet your prayers. My blessings as you plan to finish Bill's hike. If I can procure blood splattered signs in time, would appreciate your carrying them to the finish."[3]

Concurrently, James Farmer, CORE's executive director, called an emergency meeting of the National Action Council. After an all-night session, despite a state injunction prohibiting CORE from demonstrating in Alabama, the council voted to join SNCC's effort to finish Moore's walk.

On April 27, Forman and Farmer issued a statement declaring that their organizations, which had collaborated successfully on Freedom Rides, sit-ins, and voter registration campaigns, would be walking together to Jackson, Mississippi. Only disciplined activists would be selected for what was considered a dangerous mission.

"This is the thing we [also] want to do," Rev. Ralph Abernathy, deputy to Dr. Martin Luther King, Jr., told the *New York Times* on April 29, referring to the walk. "It's just a question of timing."[4] Dr. King was scheduled to appear in Memphis, Tennessee, on Wednesday, May 1, but Abernathy said that he was considering cancelling that appointment to join the walk.

The National Association for the Advancement of Colored People

(NAACP) declined to participate, but its Chattanooga chapter offered a canteen truck to the marchers.

Carry It On

On the evening of April 30, 1963, ten volunteer Freedom Walkers from SNCC and CORE gathered for a press conference at the black Fairview Presbyterian Church on East Ninth Street in Chattanooga, Tennessee. CORE's Richard Haley read a prepared statement."We want to hold America's attention for a while yet on the hope and belief of William Moore," he said. "We must reiterate this man's single yet profound purpose—to express the idea of human brotherhood by a peaceful walk through the American countryside. . . . This will not, of itself, open a lunch counter, integrate a school, or add a single Negro voter to the list of the nation's registered voters. But it affords a magnificent occasion for the people of the towns and cities through which we pass to participate in this Moore Memorial Trek. They can do so simply by giving their quiet consent to our passage."[5]

Every one of the volunteer walkers was deeply committed to nonviolent resistance and to the principles of "soul force," or "satyagraha," a system of personal ethics. They believed in openly violating unjust laws and refusing to cooperate with oppression, while at the same time conducting themselves in a spirit of love for the oppressor.

All believed that racial hatred was symptomatic of spiritual illness and that white privilege, not individual white people, was the enemy. They opposed violence because it destroyed individuals but left oppressive systems intact. Like the Freedom Riders, the Freedom Walkers accepted the possibility that revolutionary suicide might be required of them.

Robert Gore, a young CORE activist and the only black man to have completed the Committee for Nonviolent Action's (CNVA) Southern Peace Walk from Chattanooga, Tennessee, to Washington, D.C., in 1962, assured reporters that "[t]he way America responds to our march will indicate how America feels about what happened to William Moore."[6]

Part II

The Freedom Walk

*There is nothing that so strikes men with fear
as saying that they are all the sons of God.*
—G.K. Chesterson

Passing the Torch

*[I]t was in my heart like a fire burning, bound up in my bones, and
I grew weak with holding back. . . .*
—JEREMIAH 20:9

*"Pass me not oh gentle Savior, hear my humble cry, While on others Thou are
calling do not pass me by. . . ."*
Fifteen hundred black citizens of Birmingham, Alabama, lifted their
voices at the St. James Missionary Baptist Church on Tuesday evening,
April 23, 1963, to welcome Rev. Martin Luther King, Jr., just returned
from eight days in jail for defying an injunction against parading without
a license. The midweek service was to honor the city's youth: college students, high school students, and other teens who'd been participating in
nonviolent workshops, picketing against Jim Crow, and demonstrating in
front of the downtown stores.

Rev. Fred Lee Shuttlesworth threw his head back, spread his arms wide,
and shouted, *"Keep on walking, keep on sitting-in, keep on picketing, and use
the whites-only water fountains at city hall tomorrow morning!"*

The crowd cheered wildly, shaking the foundations of the brick church
and rattling its wooden windows. Three white students from nearby
Birmingham-Southern College shouted with them.[1] Barbara-Jo McBride
and Sam Shirah had been marching with the Miles College Anti-Injustice
Committee, and Marti Turnipseed had completed a sit-in shift at Wool-
worth's.

Rev. Shuttlesworth called the trio to the altar. The two young women dressed in skirts and blouses looked like typical college coeds, but Sam Shirah, with his close-cropped hair, wrinkled flannel shirt, and muddied jeans, looked more like the rednecks who'd cursed at the demonstrators.

Dr. King congratulated them for "having the courage to do what you learned in Sunday School," and when Rev. Shuttlesworth wrapped his long arms around the young women many in the congregation jumped up and hooted.

The following morning Sheriff Bull Connor demanded that Dean Ralph Jolly expel all three. A Sunday school teacher himself, Connor was outraged by reports of an interracial embrace at the St. James altar. Dean Jolly assured the sheriff that Martha Turnipseed, who had been warned about her radical activities, would be asked to leave Birmingham-Southern and that Barbara-Jo McBride would be suspended but that there was nothing he could do about Sam Shirah. Shirah had already been expelled for "encouraging white students to join the Negro marches."[2]

"We're tired of waiting!" Rev. Shuttlesworth roared from the pulpit that night. "We've been waiting for three hundred and forty years for our rights. We want action. We want it now."[3]

As the minister waved his arms above his head a young man slipped a small piece of paper in front of him. Shuttlesworth picked up his reading glasses, scanned the note, and looked out into the congregation. In a voice filled with tension he told them that a white mailman, William Moore, protesting segregation by making a one-man peace walk from Chattanooga, Tennessee, to Jackson, Mississippi, had been shot dead on a highway near Gadsden, Alabama.

As the congregation gasped and murmured, Shuttlesworth called for silent prayer. Then he asked James Dombrowski, his white colleague from the Southern Conference Education Fund, to say something.

Dombrowski laid aside his prepared speech. "Mr. Moore's brutal slaying is a dramatic symbol of the hate and violence bred by segregation and white supremacy," he said. "It is the logical, inevitable, and natural result of the policies of Governor George Wallace and those who uphold segregation. The killer of Moore undoubtedly felt that he was a patriot ridding the country of a dangerous radical who sought to subvert the Southern Way of Life."[4]

Sam Shirah bolted up so quickly that he tripped over his own feet. Abandoning Marti and Barbara-Jo, he fled past rows and rows of packed pews and out into the street to find his motorcycle. He had to reach his friend Bob Zellner, who was in Norfolk, Virginia. Shirah was scheduled to meet Zellner at Virginia State College on Friday, when he would be introduced as Zellner's successor as white southern campus coordinator for the Student Nonviolent Coordinating Committee. Most of the SNCC staff were already there. Shirah figured that if he rode all night he could probably reach Norfolk in time to volunteer for whatever demonstration SNCC was planning to protest the mailman's murder.

Campus Traveler

Samuel Curtis Shirah, Jr., was born to Rev. Samuel Curtis Shirah, Sr., and Fredna Oneita Hodges Shirah on April 27, 1943, in Troy, Alabama.[5] He and his brother, Richard, born in 1944, and sister, Sue, born in 1946, were raised in the Methodist parsonages of the Alabama–West Florida Conference.

Sam, Sr., was ordained in 1944 and after serving a series of assistant pastorships was appointed to the Methodist church in Seale, Alabama, in 1949. He was given responsibility for a five-congregation circuit covering Phenix City and Ft. Mitchell, Alabama. Phenix, known as "sin city," was the capital of a lucrative gambling and prostitution industry which served the soldiers of Ft. Benning in Columbus, Georgia.

On Sundays, Sammy, Richard, and Sue often heard their father preach five times. Their mother, a diminutive woman with an iron will, played the piano. In the summer of 1951 at a revival meeting in Goat Rock, Alabama, seven-year-old Sammy responded to his father's altar call and gave his life to Jesus.

"Big Sam" Shirah was an intelligent, soft-spoken, ambitious man. While tending his five-congregation flock he managed to complete a graduate degree in theology by commuting 115 miles to Emory University's Candler Seminary in Atlanta. Only five feet, five inches tall, Shirah had a warm smile, bright red hair, and dancing eyes. During his travels he'd write long letters home addressed to "My Sweetheart and Other Hearts." A liberal Christian, Shirah believed that God had called him to minister to the militant segregationists of Alabama and west Florida.

In 1956 Big Sam was appointed to the Frazer Memorial Methodist Church in Montgomery where he joined the Montgomery Improvement

Association and met regularly with Rev. Martin Luther King, Jr., pastor of the nearby Dexter Avenue Baptist Church. During the year-long bus boycott, Shirah and his family were continually threatened by white Citizens' Council activists, some of whom were members of his own congregation.

Only weeks after the Council of Methodist Bishops passed a resolution supporting the Supreme Court's 1954 *Brown* v. *Board of Education* decision, a group of dissenting Methodist laymen organized the Methodist Laymen's Union in Birmingham in order "to prevent either sudden or gradual integration of Negroes and Whites" in the southern churches.[6] Birmingham's sheriff, Bull Connor, a trustee of the Highlands Methodist Church, had been an enthusiastic participant.

To dissociate themselves from the laymen's union, Shirah, his friend Rev. James Zellner, and a group of liberal clergy from the Alabama–West Florida Conference organized the Andrew Sledd Study Club. Jim Zellner referred to their collaborations with black clergy as "making big medicine."

Their namesake, Professor Andrew Sledd, was a Methodist minister and professor of Latin who'd been forced to resign from Emory in 1902 after he published "The Negro: Another View" in the *Atlantic Monthly*. He'd held the white South accountable for the practice of lynching because "nobody roused themselves to prevent it."

The study club preachers vowed that they would never permit themselves to be driven from the South (as Sledd had been) because of their opposition to segregation.

They angered their parishioners by publicly supporting activists like Methodist bishop G. Bromley Oxnam. Oxnam's 1960 Volunteer Civil Rights Commission recorded testimonies of southern blacks who'd been denied the right to vote, and he delivered the tapes to Congress in an effort to build support for a comprehensive civil rights bill.

In 1959 Big Sam was sent to the First Methodist Church in Clayton, Alabama, located directly across the street from Judge George Corley Wallace's home. Sue Shirah attended second grade with Bobbi Jo Wallace, the judge's daughter, and Big Sam and Oneita considered the future governors George and Lurleen good neighbors and good friends. When Lurleen locked George out after a heated argument, he slept on the Shirahs' couch.

The Wallaces were members of Big Sam's congregation, and George served as Sammy's seventh-grade Sunday school teacher.

That year Big Sam and some of his Alabama–West Florida Conference colleagues joined the militantly antisegregation Southern Conference Education Fund (SCEF), whose mission was to eliminate Jim Crow through the joint efforts of southern blacks and whites. SCEF activists believed that not every white southerner was a segregationist and not every segregationist was one for life. Rev. Jim Zellner had in fact once been a Klan organizer.

Led by James Dombrowski (a white man), the black Birmingham preacher Rev. Fred Shuttlesworth, and the white journalists Anne and Carl Braden, they called themselves "Southern radicals" to distinguish themselves from white liberals (North and South) who urged caution in dismantling segregation.[7]

A year after the Montgomery bus boycott the Bradens were recruited to staff SCEF's education and communications unit. Anne edited the newsletter, *Southern Patriot*. In 1960 she met Jane Stembridge, a white native North Carolinian who had left her studies at New York's Union Theological Seminary to work full-time with SNCC. Stembridge and Braden jointly proposed that SNCC and SCEF work together to involve white students in the southern freedom movement. White southern student activists could expand SCEF's work. The board ultimately granted SNCC five thousand dollars to hire a white student willing to take a year off to promote white campus activism. Jim Zellner's son, Bob, was appointed SNCC's first white student coordinator in 1961.

Zellner set up the program, but when he graduated from Montgomery's Huntingdon College in 1963 he resigned to become SNCC's first white field secretary. He recommended that his friend Sam Shirah, a sophomore at Birmingham-Southern who was active in the Methodist Youth Fellowship, replace him.

Day One

Even in the shadow of death, two and two do not make six.
—Leo Tolstoy

Four days after his twentieth birthday, Sam Shirah stood in front of the Greyhound bus station in Chattanooga, Tennessee, with hand-lettered reproductions of William Moore's bloodied signs hanging around his neck.

It was 8 A.M., May 1, 1963, and the six-foot, 160-pound Shirah was surrounded by five black and four white volunteers from SNCC and CORE. They'd gathered on the spot where Bill Moore had begun his walk nine days before. All were determined to deliver the mailman's message, *Mississippi or Bust*, just as the signs said. Most were dressed in "city clothes": white shirts, jackets, and ties. Shirah, however, wore a checkered flannel shirt, jeans, work boots, a green felt fedora, and sunglasses.

He watched as Richard Haley, CORE's black national program director, and Bob Zellner tried to deal with the nearly one hundred people who'd come to check them out. The crowd was about evenly divided between the angry and the curious. Some clearly did not like the idea that Haley was a coleader; others seemed fascinated by the well-spoken black man.

"We hope to impress the people we meet not with our uniqueness, but with our humility...," Haley shouted through a bullhorn. "We are fighting the frustrations we have felt before when good men were killed in the struggle, and no one remembered why...."[1]

Haley could barely be heard above the carnival din of two white preachers who were taking turns informing the crowd that William Moore had been an atheist. Lifting up an atheist was blasphemy, one shouted. The other declared that all demonstrating was vanity, and displeasing to God.

Suddenly a black woman stepped forward and identified herself as Rev. Lovert Barkley from the Fourth Avenue Church of God. Clutching a Bible in her right hand, she shouted, "I ain't got no education, but I got religion, thank God for that!"[2] She offered to pray for the walkers' safety. "As long as you got Jesus it don't matter," she assured them.

"Yes, yes," other voices affirmed. Haley nodded.

Rev. Barkley closed her eyes and rolled her head back. "We are going to go under the mark of the beast, friends. I wish I could go with you. Let's pray that God takes us safely through it, friends. Ask Him to be with you on the road."

"Help them, Jesus!" an old black woman cried.

"*No!*" thundered an elderly white lady in a powder blue spring coat. "No! They're not a-carryin' the Bible; they're not a-carryin' God. . . . They *don't* have Jesus with them!"

Then she burst into song. "Oh Glory Hallelujah! *Hallelujah!*" she crooned. "Don't you say this old woman's crazy! You know they made fun of Jesus? They did. You *better* ask him to be with you on the road. . . ."[3]

Shirah shuddered. The tension between the black woman and the white woman was palpable. He was grateful to be among veteran activists. Every one of the volunteer walkers had been beaten up, arrested, or thrown in jail at least once. Every one, except him. But he was determined to prove himself, and to make Bob Zellner glad that he'd included him.

At the Norfolk conference it had been difficult to convince Zellner that he was ready to march with them. But he was certain that he was exactly where God wanted him. College could wait.

His mother understood. After he was expelled from Birmingham-Southern she'd written to Dean Jolly, "Our hearts are breaking for our son for we are better able to comprehend the cost of the cross he has chosen for his life than he is at the tender age of twenty years. Even though our hearts are heavy, we give thanks to God that he has faith and courage enough to try to make his performance in life match his Christian profession. May God help us who taught him these Christian principles to search our own consciences and do the same."[4]

Oneita Shirah was proud of her son's determination to march with the Freedom Walkers. She always encouraged him to follow his heart. Big Sam, however, had trouble understanding how dropping out of college demonstrated the strength of one's commitment.

Ranging in age from twenty to forty-six, the ten volunteers hailed from New York, Ohio, Illinois, North Carolina, Alabama, and Mississippi. Five came from big cities, three were rural southern blacks, and two were rural southern whites; two of the ten were Jewish. Some had been working on voter registration, others had been Freedom Riders, and the rest had organized sit-ins, boycotts, and farm cooperatives all over the South. Two had completed the Southern Peace Walk from Chattanooga to Washington, D.C., just a year earlier.

Only men had been accepted for the assignment, because it was feared that white women and black men walking together would enrage southern segregationists and provoke violence. Jim Peck had volunteered, but a bout of bleeding ulcers forced him to back out. None of the walkers had known William Moore, but they assumed that his assassination was a warning to other whites who might be tempted to help out in Birmingham. They understood that he was a human rights activist and that his solo campaign was being called irresponsible and suicidal. Few were aware that he was an atheist, and when the press reported that he'd spent time in a mental institution they were not shocked. Nearly all of them had been called unstable, reckless, or naive because of their dedication to pacifism, nonviolence, and racial justice. Moore had become a symbol, and they were anxious to demonstrate that his idealism had not been wasted.[5]

They would follow his path across the valley between Lookout and Sand Mountains, down the edge of Georgia through Rising Fawn (in the State of Dade), and into Alabama through Sulphur Springs, Ft. Payne, Attalla, Birmingham, Bessemer, and Tuscaloosa. The *Chattanooga Times* reported that this route would bring them "through the rugged hill country of northwestern Georgia and northeastern Alabama . . . an area marked by pockets of KKK activity and the antipathy toward Negroes felt by many mountain whites."[6]

Finally, at 8:30 A.M., with all public prayers, speeches, and announcements completed, the Freedom Walkers began marching up Market Street, across Eleventh to Broad Street, and south on Highway 11 to Lookout Mountain. It was oppressively hot. Chattanooga was experiencing a humid spring. The men carried backpacks and canteens, and perspiration dripped from every neck.

Lawrence Curry followed in a big white NAACP "freedom canteen" filled with sandwiches, coffee, soft drinks, and bandages. The local NAACP field secretary, Vernon Jordan, waved them on and wished them luck.[7]

Three dozen newsmen trailed the canteen, zigzagging back and forth to interview the activists and people in the crowd and to call out to staff photographers to capture a particular shot. Locals, hecklers, and curious teens kept up with them for a few miles along the dusty blacktop.

A reporter for the *Chattanooga Times* walking beside Zev Aelony, a white CORE field secretary, pointed to a hill overlooking the city and asked, "See up there?" Aelony nodded.

"That's where the elites live. They bankroll the white trash, 'cause they like keeping them around to threaten folks like you."[8]

As they passed through the railroad district near the spot where Moore had been accosted by the black man who tore his sign, a well-dressed white man in a black Jaguar pulled up beside them.

"Boys, those look like pretty good niggers," he shouted. "Can't see why they wanna walk with you damn Jews."[9]

But not everyone was hostile. Several people, black and white, put out their hands for the walkers to shake, and an elderly black lady with tears streaming down her cheeks said, "I wish my husband were here to see this."

Two unmarked police cars shepherded them to the foot of Lookout Mountain, where dogwood trees blossomed on both sides of the highway. By this time most of the stragglers had fallen away, and everything was eerily quiet. In the distance, towering white oaks seemed to stand at rigid attention. The silence was broken only by the grinding hum of cicadas.

In 1829 federal troops had marched the Cherokee Indians out of the Georgia hills to Oklahoma along the "Trail of Tears" at the spot where the Chattanooga police turned the walkers over to a single Tennessee highway patrolman assigned to escort them to the Georgia state line.

By ten o'clock the sun was burning brightly, but a soft cool wind promised relief as they walked single file across the Tennessee River at Moccasin Bend. *Chattanooga News-Free Press* photographer Jim Mooney carefully framed the gray stone Moccasin Bend Psychiatric Hospital behind them before he snapped his shutter. The photo appeared on page one the following day.

Out in the countryside, people watched from their porches in grim silence. Shirah, still leading, sang out in a rich baritone voice:

Ain't gonna let nobody turn me 'round, turn me 'round, turn me 'round,
Ain't gonna let nobody turn me 'round

Keep on a-walkin', keep on a-talkin',
Marching out to Freedom Land. . . .

The Appalachians, worn by centuries of wind and water, are gentle soft mountains covered with lush forests, but the walkers had little opportunity to appreciate their beauty. Everyone was on alert for ambush.

Five miles outside Chattanooga, just beyond the Tiftonia railroad overpass, they stopped for lunch. As Lawrence Curry passed out roast beef sandwiches, apples, potato chips, and soft drinks, a group of young white men gathered. They were especially intrigued by Sam Shirah, who looked just like them. His drawl was thicker than their own, and they could not believe that an Alabama boy, one who'd been a student in George Wallace's Sunday school class (as he never tired of telling them), would march with black men and Jews in support of integration. To segregationists Shirah was worse than the blacks, worse than any outside-agitating Jew—he was a homegrown race traitor.

"Well, you *may* burst, by god," one of them told him, pointing to his bloodied *Mississippi or Bust* sign, "that other'n did." When Shirah put out a hand for him to shake, the man recoiled in horror.[10]

But another local, an older burly white man in a blue denim jacket and leather cap, said that he'd actually spoken with Moore. "I wouldn't say that guy was fitten to be killed," he reflected. "I'd say he was doing what he thought was right. I shook hands with the man and he seemed alright to me."[11]

As they packed up after lunch, a farmer shouted from across the road, "There'll be a committee waiting for you boys at Trenton."

With a comprehensive civil rights bill pending in Congress, interracial activism was national news. Martin Luther King's demonstrations in Birmingham dominated the fifteen-minute television newscasts, and the progress of the Freedom Walkers, as they were being called in the North (Mix-Hikers in the South), was carefully detailed in the national press.

The *New York Times* warned that "the freedom walk might grow into a massive anti-segregation protest similar to the freedom rides with all of the implications of potential violence and Federal-state controversy this would entail. . . ."[12]

Mississippi's Greenville *Delta Democrat Times* described the walkers as "a band of hard core integrationists," while the *Birmingham News* called their walk a "gross exploitation of a tragedy by groups from outside Alabama."

But if the activists thought that the attention they were attracting would pressure the FBI into protecting them, they were mistaken. "We have no federal police force," J. Edgar Hoover insisted, and Attorney General Robert Kennedy, to whom President John Kennedy had delegated responsibility for civil rights matters, concurred.

James Forman, SNCC's executive secretary, had telegraphed Alabama governor George Wallace three times before the march began, informing him that volunteers from SNCC and CORE would be continuing Bill Moore's walk. He asked, "Will the State of Alabama provide protection?"[13]

Wallace had wired back, "Your proposed actions, calculated to cause unrest, disorder, and a breach of the peace in the state of Alabama, will not be condoned or tolerated. Laws of the State of Alabama will be strictly enforced."

When Forman assured the governor that the activists would be walking, with or without protection, a war of the wires ensued. Wallace continued, "Supplementing my previous telegram of April 25, Alabamians deeply regret the killing of William Moore and every possible effort is being made to apprehend the persons responsible. Your proposed activities will serve no useful purpose but on the contrary would hinder and impede efforts to investigate the crime and apprehend the perpetrators.

"Your apparent desire to bally-hoo this tragic incident for political and selfish reasons would be an affront to the dignity of the people of Alabama and to the family of the deceased. I strongly urge you to abandon your project. If you persist, the laws of Alabama will be strictly enforced."

Forman fired back: "Regarding your two telegrams received, we share with citizens of the state of Alabama regrets for the murder of William Moore. We share with his widow the desire to see his walk completed so that he will not have died in vain. Alabamians can show genuine sorrow if you guarantee us our constitutional rights to walk the roads of Alabama without fear of arrest or assault.

"We think this is the best way you can show to the nation your concern for this tragic murder in your state. Further, we maintain that you, as governor, can set the tone for the rest of the citizens of Alabama, a tone of peace and respect for individual rights to travel in the United States."

Forman's third telegram was addressed to President John Kennedy. "Will the Federal Government provide protection for our walkers?"

He never received a reply.

The caravan of ten walkers and forty newsmen continued to travel single file along what appeared to be deserted country roads, yet each time they stopped, a crowd gathered. They were not aware that the *Chattanooga Free Press* had printed their itinerary, listing their names and detailing their activist histories in the morning edition.

When they arrived at the Georgia border at 2 P.M., the Tennessee state trooper who'd been escorting them turned around and headed home. No Georgia official arrived to relieve him. The road ahead was eerily deserted. Was there safety in this indifference, they wondered, or was it the calm before a storm?

They hadn't decided where to spend the night. One possibility was to return to Chattanooga each evening, but many, including Shirah, felt that it would look like they were running scared every time the sun went down, so they chose to camp out along the road.

SNCC and CORE routinely appointed observers to serve as links with the outside world during potentially violent demonstrations. Four black SNCC field secretaries, Landy McNair, Avon Rollins, Eric Rainey, and Willie Ricks, served this function for the Freedom Walk. In addition, two white women, SNCC communications worker Dottie Miller (who was Bob Zellner's fiancée) and Casey Hayden (former wife of SDS leader Tom Hayden), helped deliver food and supplies on the first day out.

Scouting ahead for campsites the observers found a welcome at the Mt. Calvary Baptist Church in Hooker, Georgia, the only black community in the State of Dade. The church was close to the spot in Wildwood where Bill Moore had camped in the abandoned school bus.

The walkers reached Mt. Calvary at 2:30 P.M. and found a group of black teens waiting outside to deliver the keys. Young boys playing in a churchyard would not call attention to themselves in the way that a committee of adults might. Neither the minister nor any member of his congregation showed up to welcome them. It was dangerous enough to have offered the shelter of their church.

The teens accepted the walkers' invitation to supper, shared a game of softball, and sang songs with them. Shirah, accompanying himself on guitar, crooned "Pistol Packin' Pappa" and "Glory, Glory How Peculiar," while Bob Gore played freedom songs on the piano. Chico Neblett, one of the original SNCC Freedom Singers, and Richard Haley, a former music professor at Florida A & M, contributed their rich baritone voices while Zellner harmonized. Like Shirah's, Zellner's voice had been honed in Methodist church choirs.

The only visitor the walkers had that night was Dade County sheriff Allison Blevins, who said he'd driven out just to check on them. They credited Blevins's visit with preventing violence.

As darkness set in, they rolled out their sleeping bags between the church pews. After the journalists returned to Chattanooga for the night, cars began to fill the gravel parking lot. Motorcycles roared, headlights blazed into the sanctuary, and someone set off firecrackers. An angry voice shouted, "Don't worry, we won't get you tonight! We'll do it in broad daylight!"[14] The men shivered through an unseasonably cold night and took turns keeping awake for guard duty.

Eyewitness

As night fell on their first day out, Bill Hansen, SNCC's white Arkansas field secretary and a former Freedom Rider, wrote in his diary:

> *8:30 P.M. Cars have been gathering in front of the church for almost an hour now. There seem to be in the neighborhood of thirty-five whites, most of them young. They are about fifty yards from the church. Eric Weinberger is out there talking to them. . . . The walkers are a little wary of the situation but we are all rather calm at this point. Zellner and Chico are asleep. Eric just came in. He said they don't seem to be visibly hostile, but that could change.*
>
> *8:45 P.M. Bob Gore is playing the piano . . . the rest of us are just sitting around talking. It's getting rather chilly and we only have one bucket of coal but we've started a fire anyway.*
>
> *10:00 P.M. We turned out all the lights and prepared to go to sleep. About a half hour later cars with headlights on pulled into the yard. They stayed for quite a while, but I went to sleep and don't know what time they left.*[15]

Day Two

I have been a stranger in a strange land.
—Exodus 2:22

Even the most seasoned of the walkers would have had trouble envisioning the odd assortment of characters who were waiting for them on the road on Thursday, May 2. The men welcomed the bustle of returning newsmen and cooked an outdoor breakfast. Over oatmeal and coffee, a *New York Post* reporter handed Richard Haley a copy of James Wechsler's column which had run on April 30.

At the church in Chattanooga the night before the march began, Wechsler had asked Haley what he thought about the revelation that Bill Moore had spent almost two years in a mental hospital.

"It [gives] the white public a comfortable feeling that he was a crackpot," Haley said, "and that what he was trying to do had no purpose and can be forgotten."

Two days later Wechsler wrote, "For a long time I have been disturbed by the tendency of complacent citizens to view the freedom riders and other rebels against the segregationist system as slightly deranged. The corollary is that those who attend all white churches on Sunday are truly sound of mind and body, and that there is nothing schizophrenic about the gap between Christian prayer and racist performance."[1]

For a second time in as many days a vaguely restless and decidedly angry religious sentiment washed over the Freedom Walkers.

The men left the hamlet of Hooker, Georgia, at 8 A.M. Winston Lockett, who'd worked to desegregate Holiday Inns and Howard Johnson restaurants on Maryland's Eastern Shore the year before (unaware that Bill Moore was also among the Route 40 Freedom Riders), took the lead wearing Moore's signs.

The walkers rotated responsibility both for wearing the signs and for bringing up the rear. The end man was always in the most vulnerable position. Bob Zellner took cleanup that morning, and led the singing of "We Shall Overcome" as they stepped off:

Moore died not in vain,
Moore died not in vain,
Deep in my heart I do believe
That Bill Moore did not die in vain.

One of Sheriff Blevins's deputies arrived with the state of Georgia insignia on his radio car covered over by a hand-lettered sign that read "State of Dade." Despite the official escort, firecrackers were thrown at the walkers, and a Cadillac with Georgia plates tried to run them down. No one was arrested, however. The deputy gave the excuse of not wanting to encourage the newsmen.

Outside Trenton, Georgia, a young man sitting on the rusted fender of an abandoned car in a field of wild onions shouted, "You won't make it. Georgia may take it, but Alabama won't ever stand for it."[2]

At 9 A.M. when they arrived in Trenton, an angry group of about seventy-five white men began to close in on them. Sheriff Blevins suddenly appeared, dispersed the mob, and personally escorted the walkers to the county line.

When they stopped for lunch near Wildwood, curious locals gathered once again, and a late-model Corvair driven by a white man accompanied by two black ministers and two small black children pulled up. The short stocky white man wore a dark-blue suit, powder-blue tie, and horn-rimmed glasses. When he jumped out of the car, cameras began clicking wildly. The reporters had recognized thirty-eight-year-old Billie Sol Estes, the richest man in west Texas. He'd once traveled in the circle of Vice President Lyndon Johnson, Speaker of the House Sam Rayburn, and Texas senator Ralph Yarborough, but he'd recently been convicted of extorting $24 million in a federal loan scam.

A Church of Christ lay preacher whose grandfather hailed from Ft. Payne, Alabama, Estes was celebrated as an outlaw-hero by many southerners, black and white. He'd cultivated his Robin Hood image by spreading his wealth among the poor folks of Clyde, Texas, where he'd grown up.

Estes told the walkers that he was conducting a personal goodwill tour of the integrated Holiness churches in Chattanooga while he awaited sentencing. At the West Nineteenth Street Church where he'd been preaching about love, he'd met Rev. Andrew Carrey and Rev. Floyd Rose, whom he introduced to them.[3]

It was one more irony of the times that Estes could express his support for the Freedom Walk, preach to integrated congregations, and still enjoy white favor. The white South appreciated him as a good businessman, a champion of states' rights, and a good-hearted missionary who reached out to blacks in an acceptable, paternalistic way. His religion, like theirs, was based on salvation, redemption, charity, and maintaining the status quo.

It was rumored that Estes donated large sums of money to black schools and churches, and the reporters began firing questions at him. Holding up both hands, he'd only say that he intended to preach at the East Third Street Church of Christ that night and that he and his new friends had just stopped to wish the walkers well.

Bob Zellner recalled it as a "surreal experience."

"Please don't involve us in your controversy," Haley had implored him.[4]

Estes agreed to leave. He shook each man's hand and promised to pray for them. Then he climbed back into his car and hoisted one of the children onto his lap. When his passengers were settled, he spun the Corvair around and headed back toward Chattanooga.

After lunch, as Winston Lockett slipped back into Moore's signs, a white teen asked, "You really goin' through Alabama?"

Lockett nodded.

"But them people have different plans."

"Well, our plans are to follow William Moore's trail."

"Maybe you'll end up like him," the teen smirked.

"We need to keep his spirit alive," Lockett said.

"Well, what did he *want*?" The boy was getting impatient.

"A country where people can walk to Mississippi in peace," Lockett told him.[5]

"Look," Zellner explained, "we're trying to show if your idea is better than ours you don't have to beat us up. You can try to convince us instead."

"Aw, come on," another man growled. "Moore was just trying to prove he was right and we're wrong."

"We're fighting fear, buddy," Shirah assured him. "Fear of mixing with anyone we please. It's not a race problem, it's a human problem."[6]

"If we don't take up what Moore started," Zellner continued, "everyone will forget about him and what he was trying to do."

"That'd be a good thing," an old man mumbled, and the teens laughed.

Detour

At four in the afternoon the walkers stopped at a crossroads near Rising Fawn, Georgia, to wait for Lawrence Curry to restock the freedom canteen so they could head down the mountain to Rome, Georgia. The black deacons of Rome's Thankful Baptist Church had invited them to participate in a mass meeting honoring the city's youth who'd been sitting in at Rome's downtown lunch counters. Sixty-two teens had been arrested. Rome was fifty miles off course, but the walkers believed that it was important to support the young activists.

As they waited for Curry to return, the crowd grew restless. Bill Hansen pulled out his diary.

"4 P.M.," he wrote. "We have finally stopped for the day. Everyone is completely shot. My legs ache everywhere—up and down, up and down these mountains. We are 6.8 miles from the Alabama line. Newsmen who have driven to the border tell us a couple of hundred people await our arrival along with Al Lingo [Alabama's commissioner of public safety] and the Alabama State Police."[7]

Shirah strummed his guitar, and Zellner, stretched out beside him, practiced a Jimmie Rodgers yodel. At about 5:30 P.M. a burly young man stepped forward and knocked Zellner's hat off, then stood on it.

"My name's Goat," the teen said, daring Zellner to challenge him. When Zellner didn't flinch, Goat snatched his sunglasses and tossed them across the road. Zellner and Shirah stood up slowly.[8]

"Oh, lookie here, I stepped on your hat, sorry, buddy, didn't mean to do that," the young man taunted.

As Zellner reached over to pick the hat up, one of Goat's friends yelled, "Hey, Goat, he swung at you!"

Goat jumped into an exaggerated fighting stance. After he got his laugh he lowered his fists and smirked at Zellner. Tension rose to a palpable level as the crowd moved in for a better look.

The three scouts ran for their cars and quickly herded the walkers inside.

The road between Rising Fawn and Rome runs through the Chattahoochie National Forest over treacherous mountains. Ten miles along Highway 136 the walkers realized that they were being pursued by three cars full of Goat's friends. The teens pulled out in front of them, boxed them in, and played "fender tag" on the winding roads for fourteen miles. There were no guard rails and the valley directly below was a thousand-foot drop.

"We were scared to death," Winston Lockett remembered. When they reached the Thankful Baptist Church and told their story, members of the congregation insisted that they stay in Rome for the night. "We did," Richard Haley said. "Wild horses couldn't have gotten us out of there."[9]

Some of the church elders counseled them to end the walk. But the men explained that they'd made a commitment back in Chattanooga to fulfill Moore's pledge to meet with Governor Ross Barnett. They'd promised to do whatever it took to prevent Moore from being silenced. If attacked, they would not resort to violence; if arrested, they would not accept bail. ("Jail/no bail" conserved badly needed funds.)

But had they thought about what might happen if they were locked in a county jail surrounded by angry people, the elders asked? It raised the ugly possibility of lynching. Were they being provocative, even suicidal, as Bill Moore was accused of being?

If they allowed terrorists to stop them, they explained, it would make matters worse for black people than if they had never volunteered to walk. The enemy would gain strength and the fight would be harder to win. Bill Moore had understood that; it was a condition of participation that they'd all accepted.[10]

Two years later, reflecting on the activism of 1963, theologian Howard Thurman, a black man, wrote, "A strange and wonderful courage often comes into a man's life when he shares a commitment to something that is more important than whether he himself lives or dies. It is the discovery of the dynamic character of life itself. This may not be a conscious act as far as the rationale for it is concerned. It *is* a discovery of the conditions under which fresh resources of energy are available. When a person is able to place at the disposal of a single end, goal, or purpose the resources of his life, his strength is magnified a hundredfold or even a thousandfold. He relaxes his hold upon his own physical existence because he is caught up in the kind of enlarged consciousness or expanded awareness that is triggered by the commitment that his life becomes important only in terms that fulfill the inscrutable demands of the commitment. Such an experience is spiritual; yea, it is religious. In such a moment a man has the feeling that he is totally encompassed, totally alive, and more completely himself than he has ever been before. Under such a circumstance, even death is a little thing. This is the reason why there is a kind of fervor—not hysteria but a kind of fervor—that so often illuminates the countenances of those who are peacefully demonstrating in the face of the threat of violence. I recognize that there may be mass hysteria into which people are caught up and the ability to stick by one's witness under duress may be created out of hostility and overriding anger. But there is another and vaster possibility which has made itself manifest here and there during these fateful days: a deep spiritual awareness that one's life is in vital touch with the Source of Being that holds and makes secure against all that destroys and lays waste."[11]

Freedom's Main Line

The Freedom Walkers became keenly aware that as they approached the Georgia/Alabama border the crowds waiting for them were growing larger and angrier.

Near Sulphur Springs, Georgia, a dozen whites holding baseball bats stepped in front of them. After a quick huddle the walkers decided to demonstrate nonviolent engagement. Chico Neblett began singing, "This May Be the Last Time," and the others joined him as they walked toward the blockade fully expecting the bats to start swinging. But the Georgia state policemen, who initially appeared to ignore the menacing locals, moved swiftly to disburse them. No arrests were made, but clearly someone in authority wanted the Freedom Walkers to leave Georgia alive.[12]

Across the border in Alabama, however, the air was so electrified that even Mississippi segregationists were urging Alabamians to calm down. An editorial in the comparatively liberal Greenville (Mississippi) *Delta Democrat Times* noted that "apparently Alabama intends to arrest the so-called 'Freedom Walkers' as soon as they hit the state line. . . . What the Marchers say they are testing is whether anyone has the right to march in peaceful protest on state highways. In Georgia they found they do, and Georgia is the better for it. By being jailed in Alabama they will have actually accomplished at least part of their purpose. Alabama will gain nothing but a little more tarnishing of its reputation."[13]

But a determined core of Alabama segregationists who resented the trouble that outside agitators were stirring up in Birmingham vowed not to let the mixers pass.

More Marches

SNCC and CORE were only two of many movement organizations who were interested in completing Bill Moore's walk. On May 1, Diane Nash, a black SNCC activist who'd been a leader of the 1961 Nashville sit-ins, led eight black volunteers (all members of Birmingham's Alabama Christian Movement for Human Rights) to Keener, Alabama (where Moore had been shot), to finish his pilgrimage to Jackson. They were arrested as they entered Gadsden, Alabama, less than ten miles into their march.

Baltimore CORE, Moore's membership chapter, scheduled a memorial march from Attalla, Alabama (near Keener), to Jackson for June 14 so that college students would be able to participate.

Other local NAACP and CORE chapters and campus Friends of SNCC organizations announced memorial walks. None of these marches were granted federal protection. The attorney general was actually flippant. On April 25, two days after Moore's murder, Robert Kennedy (who had initiated the vogue of the fifty-mile hike as part of the New Frontier's Physical Fitness Initiative) remarked that "perhaps [the demonstrators'] energies might be better used in a different direction than taking a walk."

The activists deeply resented his cynicism. His sworn responsibility was to make interstate roads safe if state governments were unable or unwilling to do so.

Not all civil rights activists supported the Moore memorial marches, however. Some complained that the death of a lone white man was attracting more national attention than the year-long violence black voter registration workers had been suffering in Greenwood, Mississippi.[14]

Greenwood was one of the sites of the Voter Education Project (VEP) launched in 1962 by a coalition of movement organizations. On February 23, 1963, Jimmy Travis, a black SNCC field worker, was seriously wounded in Greenwood. (This was the shooting that Moore had referred to in his letter to *Washington Post* columnist Drew Pearson.) Throughout the spring of 1963 voter registration volunteers were ambushed, the field office was torched, and black citizens marching to city hall to register were attacked by state police waving clubs and leading German shepherds.

Like the Freedom Walkers, VEP project directors repeatedly requested federal protection for the registrants, but it was always denied them.

Finally, when eight black Greenwood citizens were attacked on their way to the courthouse by riot-gun-wielding state police, John Doar of the Justice Department petitioned a federal judge for a temporary restraining order.[15]

This was the first time any federal representative had offered support. It seemed to the activists that Greenwood offered a perfect opportunity to call the question of federal protection. Less than a week later, however, on April 4, Doar's superiors rescinded his petition in exchange for the release of the eight prisoners and a guarantee of safe passage for "legitimate applicants." In the end the Justice Department chose to avoid grappling with the constitutional issue of activist protection that Greenwood posed.

Dr. Martin Luther King, Jr., did not participate in either the Greenwood courthouse marches or the Freedom Walk. Later, historians would speculate that he kept his personal distance because the Voter Education Project and the Freedom Walk were joint efforts and would not permit the spotlight to be focused exclusively on his leadership. Only Birmingham could offer him that opportunity.

Day Three

This is our country too.
—David Dennis, CORE, 1963

On Friday morning, May 3, the Freedom Walkers left the safety of Rome, Georgia's black community, and drove downtown. At the junction of Broad and Second Streets they passed a monument to the Ku Klux Klan's first imperial wizard, Confederate general Nathan Bedford Forrest. Forrest had permitted his troops to massacre surrendering black Union soldiers at Ft. Pillow, and when asked what the war was about is reported to have said, "If I ain't fightin' to keep my niggers, then what the hell am I fighting fer?"[1]

The three-car caravan navigated the twisting mountain roads back to

U.S. 11 and Rising Fawn, Georgia. They arrived at eleven o'clock. It was blisteringly hot, and the largest crowd they'd seen yet had created a monumental traffic jam.

The walkers waited while Marvin Rich, CORE's white national community relations director, finished telegraphing their itinerary to Governor Wallace. Rich asked the governor to enjoin the state police from barring their entry into Alabama. He reminded Wallace that all governors take an oath to uphold the Constitution, which defines the United States as a federal union, not a confederation of sovereign states.

"We're sending our itinerary to give the people of Alabama and America another chance," Rich told reporters.

Wallace did not respond. He was seething over a telegram that Sam Shirah had sent to him care of the *Montgomery Advertiser*.

"Dear Governor Wallace," Shirah had written, "I appeal to you as the son of your pastor at Clayton, Alabama and as a past Sunday School student there when you were superintendent and as a fellow Alabaman to let us pass."²

Wallace was also furious that his friend Grover C. Hall, Jr., editor of the *Montgomery Advertiser*, had printed the damn thing. To make matters worse, it was picked up by the wire services. Where did a snotnose like Shirah get the nerve to address the governor of Alabama like that? Wallace was planning to announce his candidacy for the presidency shortly. That smart aleck didn't realize who he was dealing with. He blamed the preacher for the boy's self-righteousness.

After the gubernatorial inauguration, when Wallace had evoked the Klan rallying cry "here yesterday, here today, here forever!" in his vow "segregation today, segregation tomorrow, segregation forever!," Big Sam Shirah had asked how he could encourage race hatred and still call himself a Christian.

"Come on now, Preacher," he'd explained, "you know me better than that. All this talk is just to get me the clout I need to make things right. It ain't me. Once I'm in office it's over, it's all over. You'll see."³

Big Sam had told his children many times that George Wallace was trapped by his own rhetoric, and Shirah, perhaps naively, thought he might be able to appeal to the better angels of his old Sunday school teacher's nature.

Angry locals continued to follow the walkers through Rising Fawn, pelting them with eggs, bottles, and rocks as the two Georgia highway patrolmen assigned to protect them watched. Bill Hansen, Chico Neblett, and Zev Aelony were all hit. The newsmen were also pelted and cursed.

As they passed a stuffed cloth dummy hanging from a split-rail fence with a sign reading "Freedom Walker" around its neck, Zellner threw his head back and warbled, "Ain't gonna let ole Wallace turn me 'round, turn me 'round. . . ." The others joined him, singing, "Keep on a-talkin', keep on a-walkin', walkin' on to Freedom Land. . . ."

"You won't make it through Fort Payne," someone in the crowd shouted as they passed under a row of Confederate flags strung across the highway outside a souvenir shop. It was there that Shirah noticed a little white boy clutching at his mother's skirts. With his free hand the boy waved to them. When his mother realized what he was doing she slapped him hard, and he began to cry.

A wiry young white man with a stand-up crew cut suddenly stepped from the crowd and punched Winston Lockett, knocking him off his feet. "That dirty nigger ran into me," he laughed.[4] No attempt was made to arrest or even to identify the man. Then Robert Gore dropped to his knees, hit by a rock, stunned. It was like being in a war zone, Zellner recalled, you'd be talking to one of the guys and suddenly he'd fall down right beside you.

Werner Czarnojohn, a twenty-six-year-old West German filmmaker, and his twenty-two-year-old assistant, Wolfgang Wawrayevwicz, who were shooting a documentary about the American South, approached Lockett for an interview, but he could not understand what they were saying. Zev Aelony, utilizing his two years of high school German, was able to figure out most of their questions and answer briefly. His interview ran on German and Scandinavian television the following week.

Highway 11's two lanes narrowed abruptly near the Alabama state line, where a billboard beckoned the traffic to turn around: "See Rock City—Out of This World on Lookout Mountain." Colonel Al Lingo, fresh from riot duty in Birmingham, waited inside Alabama with nineteen steel-helmeted troopers and a crowd of nearly fifteen hundred whites. Three helicopters hovered overhead. Lingo shouted through a bullhorn, "You all are welcome to Alabama as individuals, but not as demonstrators. This is a violation of the law. You will be given one minute to disperse. If you do not, you will be arrested and charged with breach of the peace."[5]

Major Joe Smelley kept careful time with his watch as the seconds passed. A Greyhound bus bound for Birmingham pulled over to let its passengers out to watch the circus.[6]

Lawrence Curry drove the big white freedom canteen across the state line first, and the police waived it through without incident. When observers James Forman and Landy McNair followed in a car, the police pulled them over. A trooper asked if they knew the walkers.

"Yes," McNair responded.

"Don't you be saying yes to me," the officer roared. "You say *yes sir* to me!"

Someone from the crowd shouted that Forman and McNair were seen bringing food and water to the marchers. That was enough for the trooper.

"Okay," he said. "Get out. You're under arrest."[7]

Finally, at 3:30 P.M., Shirah, wearing Bill Moore's bloodied signs, led the Freedom Walkers into Alabama. A voice in the crowd screamed, "Get the goddamn communists," and all hell broke loose.

"Throw them niggers in the river," somebody shrieked. "Kill the white men first."[8]

A white woman with her hair set in pink plastic curlers yelled, "Kill him! Kill him! Kill him!" to nobody in particular.[9]

The troopers tackled Zellner and Eric Weinberger first, electroshocking them with three-foot cattle prods before tossing them into a police car.[10] "That's white men dealing with you, brother!" a young man jeered.

Bottles and rocks flew through the air, many hitting the walkers, as each was arrested the moment he stepped into Alabama. Robert Gore, bringing up the rear, was nearly forgotten. He literally ran into the police wagon to protect himself from the angry mob. The Freedom Walk ended twenty-five miles short of the picnic area where Bill Moore had lost his life. His ten replacements were taken to the DeKalb County jail in Ft. Payne, Alabama.

Colonel Lingo insisted that he'd arrested them for their own protection. "These boys would never have made it through Alabama," he told reporters. "They would have been killed. . . . The FBI is in agreement with us that they couldn't get through this section alive. We're going to have law and order regardless of what it takes."

But the public safety commissioner knew that he was defying federal law. The walkers were *entitled* to safe passage between states under the provisions of the Fourteenth Amendment.

Rev. James Zellner later learned that the DeKalb County officials had been willing to allow the marchers to pass, but that Governor Wallace had pressured them to make the arrests. Circuit Judge W. J. Haralson of Ft. Payne was rumored to have favored releasing the walkers on their own bond, but the governor was determined to prove a point, and perhaps settle a score.[11]

"We had a right to make this walk," James Forman argued. "If we can't get this right, it will be impossible to secure our other rights."[12]

Because the men refused bail they would remain in jail until the next regular session of the circuit court, which would convene on June 1.

Jail/No Bail

At the Ft. Payne jail, Deputy Sheriff J. A. Patterson separated his prisoners by race. He approached Zev Aelony, a Jew with dark kinky hair and a deep tan, and asked, "What are you, boy?"

Aelony said he didn't understand.

"Where do your people come from?" Patterson asked.

Recalling the story of Exodus, Aelony replied, "They came out of Africa."

When Patterson directed Aelony to the colored cell the other white men demanded to go with him.[13]

"You all want to go in together?" the exasperated officer asked. When they said yes, he led them to the black holding pen and called Colonel Lingo, demanding that they be taken out of his jail. Patterson did not want to be responsible for protecting such crazy men from the angry locals.

The walkers celebrated the desegregation of the DeKalb County jail all night long. One of the jail trusties loaned Shirah his guitar and they sang freedom songs. Aelony fashioned a chess set from crusts of the stale breads, dark and white, they'd been served at supper, and challenged Shirah to a game on a makeshift board.

When Big Sam was notified of his son's arrest he contacted Rev. Travis Warlick of the First Methodist Church of Ft. Payne and asked him to check on the walkers. Warlick dispatched his associate pastor, Rev. Buddy Freeman, who brought them some books and a Monopoly set.

"I'm against everything you stand for," Freeman told them, "but I'm a Christian and I want to make sure that you're okay." Rev. Freeman spent the rest of the afternoon calling the men's families to let them know that their sons were safe.[14]

He told the activists that while they were being arrested, fire hoses and police dogs had been turned on the demonstrators in Birmingham. Getting arrested had catapulted the Freedom Walkers onto page one of the *New York Times*, but when Bull Connor quipped that he used hoses on the demonstrators before he released his police dogs in order to "wash them niggers off so the dogs would bite them,"[15] forty reporters ran to Birmingham. Connor had upstaged the Freedom Walkers. Despite SNCC's and CORE's joint pledge to send reinforcements along Moore's route until somebody got to Mississippi, on Sunday, May 5, James Forman announced that SNCC had no plans to continue.[16]

The job of protecting the Freedom Walkers was clearly more than Deputy Sheriff Patterson had bargained for. When a SNCC communications worker told a reporter that a silent vigil at the DeKalb County Courthouse was planned, Patterson advised the newsman that he was "fearful that the freedom hikers would be removed from the Ft. Payne jail by force." He said that Sheriff J. Harold Richards was "out with the state boys and the highway patrolmen," and that he [Patterson] was very nervous.[17] Patterson appealed to Al Lingo once again to remove the prisoners from his charge. This time Lingo transferred them to the Etowah County Courthouse in Gadsden, fifteen miles away. The eight black walkers from Birmingham's Alabama Christian Movement for Human Rights were still being held there. An around-the-clock prayer vigil was maintained outside to ensure that if the prisoners were abruptly released they would find themselves among friends.

The Gadsden jail was hot and overcrowded. Prisoners were assigned to segregated unlocked cells which opened into bull pens allowing expansion of the eighty-prisoner capacity to at least twice the normal (and safe) number.

The guards dragged Eric Weinberger up and down the steps when he refused to walk.

"Why does he do it?" the assistant warden asked Richard Haley. "Why won't he just walk up them steps?"

"Because He who is with us is stronger than those who are with you," Haley replied, quoting from the Book of Kings.[18]

The warden shook his head.

On May 14, fifty Gadsden activists held an all-night pray-in outside the Etowah County Courthouse. An enraged Al Lingo retaliated by transferring the ten Freedom Walkers fifty miles south to Kilby State Prison near Montgomery.

Kilby, with its gray concrete walls encircled by barbed wire, looked like a Hollywood prison set. The ten activists were housed in its abandoned "third section," because Warden Holman believed that the white prisoners would kill the white walkers if he put them in the same cellblock and that the black activists would stir up the black prisoners if he put them together.

The walkers were housed in small concrete cells on Kilby's old death row. Less than one hundred yards from where they slept, the electric chair stood at the end of a narrow hall behind a green metal door. The Scottsboro boys, nine black teens accused of raping two white women in northern Alabama in 1931, had once lived on the "third section."

Twice a day the Freedom Walkers were served cornbread laced with sand, which they fed to the fat river rats who roamed at night, terrifying the city-bred Winston Lockett.

Richard Haley challenged his cellmates to a contest to write a song about Kilby, and he soon had the entire troupe warbling, "Kilby, you thrill me, with your stone bread and lethal collard greens. . . ."[19]

The guards were morbidly curious about who was bankrolling the activists. One was sure that they were Robert Kennedy's mercenaries. Those questions deeply troubled Eric Weinberger. He told the guards that he would fast to prove to them that money couldn't influence him to work against his conscience.

Weinberger was the first to develop running sores from being dragged up and down metal stairs and across the concrete floors. Because of his fast he was not taking in nourishment, and his sores didn't heal. After two weeks Zellner, Gore, and Shirah assured him that he'd made his point and that noncooperation with the guards was sufficient. There was no need, Gore said, to give Warden Holman the pleasure of watching him starve to death. But Weinberger refused to eat for another week. Finally, Zellner and Shirah said that they would join his fast if he would agree to eat every seventh day to stay alive. He refused, and would have died if he hadn't been transferred to the prison hospital on May 23 and fed intravenously. Weinberger had dropped forty-five pounds in twenty-one days.

Shirah wrote to his mother, "This witness of Eric's has been one of the most meaningful experiences of my life. He is in effect saying that I had rather die than cooperate with this evil system. . . . What other step can I take at this point than to identify myself with Eric and the truth by taking his place? What other course can I take than to refuse to cooperate with this system that treats so brutally and inhumanly those who disagree with it?"[20]

After Weinberger was hospitalized, the walkers pledged a three-day fast to atone for the wrong that was done to him. They wrote to Governor Wallace describing Weinberger's treatment and explaining their action.

All understood the potential consequences of their letter. All, except Shirah, had suffered brutality in southern jails before. Kilby was Bill Hansen's twenty-first incarceration. At Dougherty jail in Albany, Georgia, Sheriff Cull Campbell had told the white prisoners that "this is one of those guys who came down here to straighten us out." They beat Hansen senseless, and broke his jaw.[21]

Winston Lockett had spent a month in a Raleigh, North Carolina, jail for attempting to integrate a Howard Johnson restaurant, and Jessie Harris and Richard Haley had passed forty long days at Mississippi's Parchman penitentiary. Weinberger had been incarcerated in Brownsville, Tennessee, and Zellner was a former inmate of the jails of McComb, Mississippi, Albany, Georgia, Baton Rouge, Louisiana, and Montgomery and Talladega in Alabama.

A month on death row gave Shirah time to reflect on his commitment to the freedom movement. He read *The Mind of the South* and was fascinated by W. J. Cash's definition of white southern sentimentality as "the will to deny ugliness." He called it "the best analysis of us Southerners I've ever seen."[22] Cash accused southerners of "prettifying" the institution of slavery by boasting of the Great Southern Heart which loved and cared for the souls of black folks. Of the white men who broke ranks with this ideology, Cash wrote, "[T]housands of voices proclaimed them traitors and nigger loving scoundrels; renegades to Southern womanhood and the Confederate dead and the God of their fathers; champions of the transformation of the White Race into a mongrel breed."

Shirah also read John Howard Griffin's *Black Like Me*, the story of the trials of a white journalist who passed for a black man, and he threatened to write his own book, *White Like Me*.

Shirah was grateful for his parents' support, something most southern movement whites couldn't count on. Oneita Shirah ended each of her letters with "Sammy, be true to the very best you know, and remember that we always love you."

Big Sam tried to be encouraging, but he was clearly disappointed that Sam, Jr., had left college to follow Bob Zellner into the movement.

"Your job is to prepare yourself for important work," he wrote. "Remember, Moses spent forty years preparing himself. You must train your mind and let your emotions mature. We have great hopes for you, Sam."

Big Sam often reminded his son that "the Movement will still be there when you graduate."

But Shirah was impatient. College courses couldn't hold his attention while there was so much that needed to be done, and he was desperate to begin his campus work. SNCC had hired him to coordinate a white southern student program nearly two months before, and he had yet to make a single campus visit.

Shirah wanted to settle his nagging doubts about how effective he could be working with white college students who were often overly eager to make concessions and keep the peace. Most had been taught to shut their minds against the oppression of blacks, and those who couldn't usually headed north. Zellner had tried for two years to cut through what he called the "cotton curtain" of obstacles constructed by college administrators and local law enforcement officers to prevent students from getting involved in the civil rights movement. It wasn't easy work.[23] Shirah was anxious to test his ability to do it.

Alabama Reacts

I don't believe in the kind of discrimination that offends anyone.
—GOVERNOR GEORGE C. WALLACE

Although the Freedom Walkers had pledged "jail/no bail," Zellner and Shirah accepted bond twenty-five days into their thirty-one-day confinement. Their preacher fathers bailed them out so that they could attend the annual Alabama–West Florida Conference of the Methodist Church at Montgomery's Huntingdon College on May 28. Governor George Wallace was scheduled to address the gathering.

"Don't you dare wash," Big Sam told them, "I want George to see *exactly* what you look like."[1] They hadn't been issued prison clothes or given the clothing their families sent. What they were arrested in was what they had worn for nearly four weeks. They were covered in rags, emaciated from fasting, and badly bruised from their refusal to cooperate with the guards.

The preachers and their sons stationed themselves just inside the college auditorium to wait for the governor. With them were both mothers, Shirah's brother, Richard, and his sister, Sue.

As Wallace entered, Oneita Shirah called out in a high-pitched voice, "Hold it there a minute, George. I want to ask you why you put my boy Sammy in jail."

Hundreds of heads turned toward the commotion. George Wallace could not believe his eyes. The scrawny, filthy, tattered young man waving to him was the preacher's son.

"Now, Oneita," Wallace said, smiling uncomfortably, "if I hadna arrested Sammy those rednecks would of killed him!"

"Then why didn't you put *them* in jail?" she demanded.[2]

The question seemed first to disorient Wallace, then to enrage him. He was fed to the teeth with being harassed by the self-righteous Shirahs. Momentarily forgetting that he had an audience, he swore he'd personally destroy Big Sam if the preacher and his family kept it up.

Wallace was so rattled that he left without delivering his address.

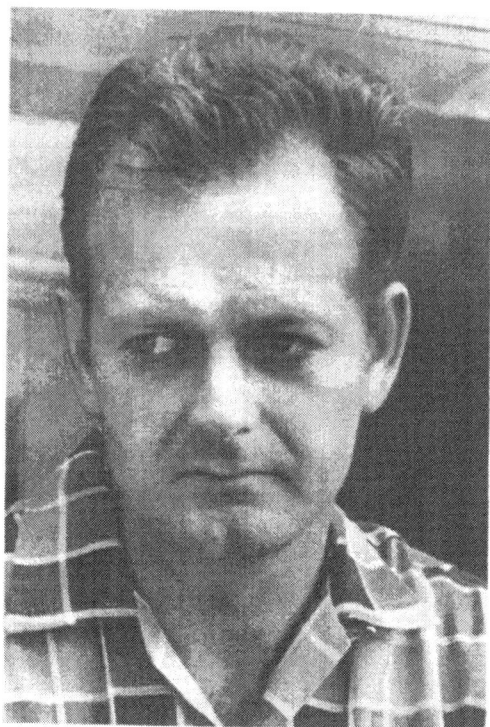

Bill Moore shortly after his release from the Binghamton State Hospital on August 13, 1954. Courtesy of *Binghamton Press and Sun Bulletin*, Binghamton, New York.

Bill Moore demonstrating in front of the Broome County Courthouse in Binghamton, January 1962. Courtesy of *Binghamton Press and Sun Bulletin*, Binghamton, New York.

Mary Moore, Bill's wife, reading his last letter home, March 25, 1963. Courtesy of *Binghamton Press and Sun Bulletin*, Binghamton, New York.

The house on Woodland Avenue in Binghamton, New York, where Bill Moore lived from 1937 to 1945. Courtesy of the author.

Bill's sister Louise's home on Carey Street in Binghamton, New York, where in 1955 he wrote *The Mind in Chains*. Courtesy of the author.

Floyd Simpson's grocery in Collbran, Alabama, as it looked in 2001. The house to the right is the residence of Gaddis Killian. Courtesy of the author.

Floyd Simpson, accused murderer of Bill Moore, shown flanked by attorneys William Beck (left) and Roy McCord (right) after his release on bail from Gadsden jail on April 29, 1963. Courtesy of the Collections of the Library of Congress.

The Freedom Walkers gather outside Chattanooga's Fairview Presbyterian Church before leaving for the Greyhound bus station, May 1, 1963. Left to right: Robert Gore, Sam Shirah, Richard Haley, Winston Lockett, Eric Weinberger (partially hidden), William Hansen, unidentified man, Bob Zellner (foreground), and Zev Aelony. Courtesy of Charles Moore.

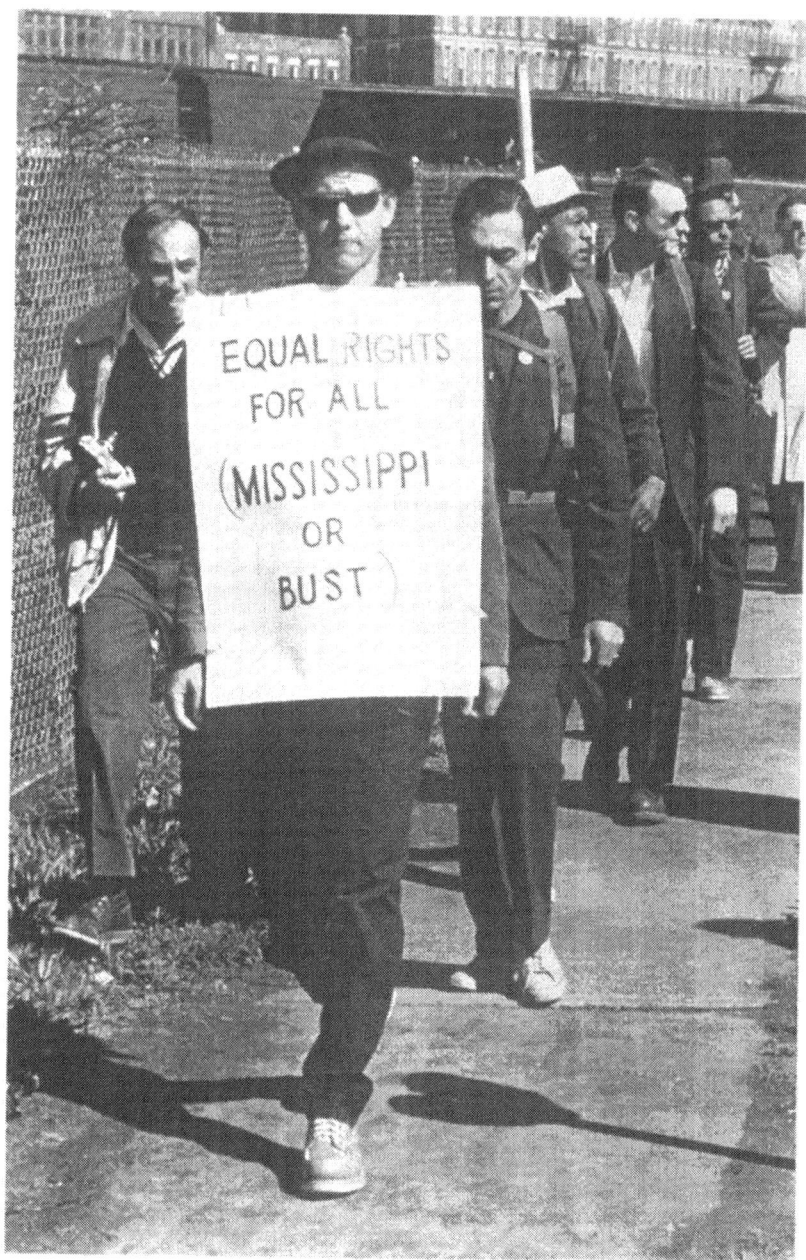

The Freedom Walkers march through an industrial area on the fringes of Chattanooga on their way to Lookout Mountain, May 1, 1963. Front to back: Sam Shirah, unidentified man, Eric Weinberger, Richard Haley, Bob Zellner, Winston Lockett, and unidentified man. Courtesy of Charles Moore.

Reverend Samuel Curtis Shirah, Sr. (Big Sam) and Oneita Shirah, the parents of Sam, Jr., Richard, and Sue. Courtesy of Dr. Sue Shirah-Sands.

Liz Khrone and Sam Shirah working with the White Folks Project in Biloxi, Mississippi, 1964 "Freedom Summer." Courtesy of Danny Lyon, Magnum Photos.

Sam Shirah in New Orleans, Louisiana, November 1964, shortly before the Waveland, Mississippi, SNCC conference. Courtesy of Danny Lyon, Magnum Photos.

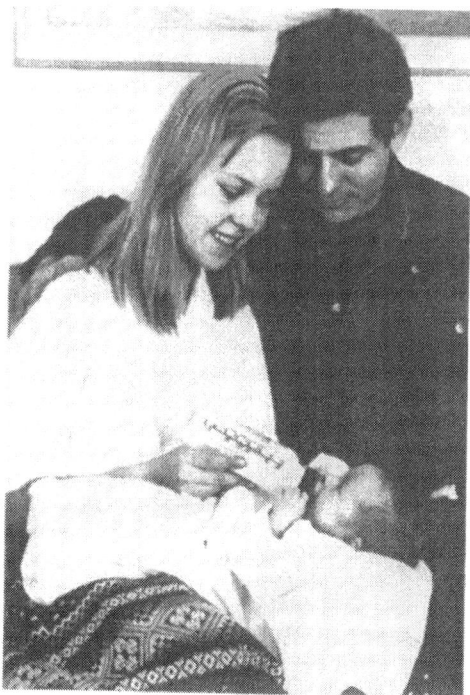

Liz, Sam, and Lisa Shirah, Grand Bay, Alabama, 1965. Courtesy of Dr. Sue Shirah-Sands.

Flyer used by Sam Shirah to promote the national Levis Jeans Boycott, Atlanta, Georgia, September 1967. Courtesy of Harlan Joye.

Sam Shirah and his daughters, Lisa (far left) and Rebecca (right) with his second wife, Benita Shirah in Dothan, Alabama, 1977. Courtesy of Dr. Sue Shirah-Sands.

The following day the Board of Christian Social Concerns submitted a resolution to the conference calling for all Christians to "uphold the law, repudiate racial hatred and violence, support freedom and equality for all, and apply compassion and understanding to those with whom we differ."[3] Big Sam voted for the resolution, which ultimately passed.

When the Shirahs returned home to the First Methodist Church of Defuniak Springs, Florida, news of their pastor's vote and his jailed son's confrontation with the governor had preceded them. A group of trustees accused Big Sam of plotting to integrate their church. Within a week Richard Shirah was picked up by the police and grilled about his brother's whereabouts. When he insisted that he didn't know where Sammy was, he was beaten by two officers who were members of Big Sam's congregation.[4]

The official board formally requested their pastor's resignation, but Big Sam refused to submit it. He wrote to Bishop Paul Hardin, Jr., that "because of my vote supporting the recommendations of the Conference Board of Social Concerns I have been labeled an integrationist and my son has been beaten. To some, I am no longer a minister of Christ but a messenger of Satan. Yet I *am* a Methodist minister appointed to serve this church and under no circumstances will I resign. God called me to this work, and I will not turn my back on it."[5]

Undeterred, the board passed a resolution that the congregation would not permit blacks to worship with them. Still, Big Sam refused to leave. He remained through June 1964 to complete his appointment.

A Slap on the Wrist

On June 3, 1963, the Freedom Walkers appeared before the regular session of Montgomery's circuit court. They were accompanied by Fred Gray, a black NAACP attorney. Colonel Al Lingo arrived in uniform to serve as a witness for the prosecution, but he also insisted on sitting at the prosecution table in his capacity as a criminal justice official. Although this was highly irregular, the judge overruled Gray's objection.

When James Forman, the first defendant, was acquitted (since he'd broken no law in driving across the Alabama state line), Lingo took out his service revolver and placed it on the table. When Landy MacNair, who'd been Forman's passenger, was also acquitted, he spun the gun barrel and glared at the judge. The seething Lingo was not mollified when the remaining ten Freedom Walkers were found guilty of "conduct calculated to provoke a breach of the peace." It was merely a misdemeanor—to Lingo's mind, a slap on the wrist.[6]

The Keener Freedom Walk

In deference to the mounting crisis on the streets of Birmingham, Baltimore CORE cancelled its June 14 Moore Memorial March, and substituted a prayer vigil in Keener, Alabama, on May 16. Participants were invited to continue Moore's walk after the service. Jim Peck flew in from New York City to represent the National Action Council, but this time Mary Moore did not accompany him.

As he was packing, Peck received a telephone call from Robert Shelton, Imperial Wizard of the United Klans of America.

"I understand you plan to come to Alabama," Shelton said. "In case you're interested, we are in a position to give you the same kind of publicity that Moore got."[7]

"I'm not particularly interested," Peck replied, and hung up on him.

Like William Joseph Simmons, the Alabama Methodist minister who'd founded the Georgia Knights of the Ku Klux Klan, Shelton considered himself a devout Christian. He despised Peck, an atheist born of Jewish parents.

During Klan rallies at Birmingham's Graymont Armory, Shelton often referred to the Klan as "a kind of religion." It was the kind which preached that white Christian Anglo-Saxons were God's chosen people.

"I don't hate niggers," Shelton told reporters, "but I do hate the Jews. The nigger's a child, but the Jews are dangerous people. . . . All they want is control and domination. . . ."[8]

CORE field secretary Mary Hamilton, a black woman, met Jim Peck's plane in Atlanta and took him to Birmingham on May 16 where they waited at the black-owned Gaston Motel for other activists to gather.

Forty-one-year-old actress Madeleine Sherwood was one of the first to arrive. She'd been following the Birmingham demonstrations on television from her Greenwich Village apartment in New York City. After watching repeated episodes of brutality, she and her friend Peter DeRome decided to go to Alabama. (Sherwood had appeared in the movies *Cat on a Hot Tin Roof*, *The Crucible*, and *Sweet Bird of Youth*, and would go on to play Mother

Superior on Sally Field's television series *The Flying Nun* from 1967 to 1970.)

Born in Montreal, Canada, the daughter of the dean of McGill University's school of dentistry, Sherwood had come to New York in 1949 to study at the Actors Studio. She'd marched with SANE in opposition to nuclear armament, and had tutored ex-convicts in Harlem with the Fortune Society. For years her friend Dotts Johnson, a black musician, had horrified her with stories about his uncles who'd been lynched. Johnson would never accept gigs further south than Baltimore, no matter how well they paid.

Sherwood and DeRome had contacted New York CORE while the staff was recruiting for the May 16 Moore Memorial. Sherwood learned that two cars were leaving immediately for Chattanooga, where a group was assembling to complete a walk against segregation which a murdered postman had begun.

"I'd never heard of William Moore," Sherwood recalled almost forty years later. "I didn't know if he was black or white or who had killed him. At first I thought it was the Alabama police. I just wanted to help, and people were going South to help, so Peter and I packed our suitcases."[9]

Sherwood and DeRome drove to Chattanooga with twenty-six-year-old Nelson Barr, who'd grown up in the white South, and a black volunteer from Chicago. They stopped at white activist George Doll's home, where they received two days of nonviolent resistance training before heading on to Birmingham to meet the others.

They traveled as far as Johnson City, Tennessee, before a trooper pulled them over and asked to see Barr's license. Shining his flashlight into the car the officer recognized Sherwood from her role as Miss Lucy in *Sweet Bird of Youth*, which had been released earlier that year. "My, my, lookie here, I know *you*, little lady," he said.

When Sherwood didn't answer, the trooper pulled out a pad. Barr was sure they'd be arrested. But the officer only handed his notebook to the actress. "Here, let me have your autograph for my missus. She's collectin' signatures from all you famous folks rushin' like fools down here. You make that out to 'Mert,' please."[10]

"Of course," Sherwood said, and got busy signing.

George Doll spent two days sensitizing the volunteers to what they might expect, cautioning them never to provoke anger or to get separated.

Then he shepherded them to the Alabama border. "Everybody go that's going," Doll shouted at the state line, "and those that's changed their minds come on along back with me."

They drove to Birmingham's A. G. Gaston Motel where they joined a thirty-car caravan. When they reached the small farm community of Keener, Alabama, at about 3:30 P.M., the lead driver had trouble locating the rest stop where Moore had been murdered. The picnic tables had been removed and all the trees cut down. The first four cars overshot and had to turn around. As they U-turned and pulled into the entrance, state troopers arrested the drivers.

"I could think of a million reasons not to come, and so could my friends," Sherwood told Michael Dorman of *Newsday*. "My agent didn't approve either. He felt this was not my fight. But I could think of a million and one reasons why I should come. I've come to the conclusion that this is the fight of every human being in this country."

When Dorman asked if she was afraid, she answered, "Yes. I'm scared stiff."

Twelve activists, including Sherwood and Lawrence Curry, who had driven the NAACP freedom canteen for the SNCC/CORE Freedom Walkers, pledged to continue Bill Moore's walk after the memorial service. Peter DeRome volunteered to serve as an observer.

The Rev. E. W. Jarrett, pastor of Gadsden's black Galilee Baptist Church, began the service at 4 P.M.

"We are gathered on this spot of ground to commemorate the gallant stand taken by William Moore, who died—but not in vain," he told the seventy-five mourners. "His death has shown the world the ugliness of segregation and the so-called Southern way of life. They shot William Moore. But his voice is still heard. It tells us and those yet unborn that we are determined to be free."[11]

Across the deserted stretch of Highway 11 a herd of cattle grazed peacefully as Nelson Barr told the group, "I've come to make amends for everything that's been going on down here for the last two hundred years. In Chattanooga I grew up under segregation. This system has destroyed both races. . . ."

Jim Peck climbed up on a tree stump to deliver the eulogy. He described his friend as a genuine idealist who worked for brotherhood all his life.

"Eighteen walkers have followed him," he said. "They have all been arrested. A dozen more are ready to follow in his steps today."[12]

A state trooper bellowing through a bullhorn nearly drowned Peck out. "You all at the rear are standing on private property," he warned.

Peck concluded by laying a wreath of fifteen yellow chrysanthemums on the ground.

After singing "Gonna Sit at the Welcome Table" and receiving the benediction, the new band of Freedom Walkers headed south. Madeleine Sherwood, wearing a white blouse, gray plaid culottes, and a straw sun hat, carried a sign reading "Human Rights Are the First Rights." She hadn't completed a hundred yards before a siren began blaring.

"Disburse now!" Patrolman R. P. Hooks thundered. "Cease and desist! If you walk that highway, we'll have to arrest you."

As the walkers crossed the white line, another trooper turned on his megaphone. "Desist. Desist. Walk back to the grass with your hands crossed behind your heads. You are all under arrest."

Some of the men cooperated, but Sherwood threw herself to the pavement beside four who had dropped to the ground just as George Doll had taught them to do. They were dragged into waiting patrol cars despite Nelson Barr's protest that "a man's got a right to walk the highways."

"You are arrested for violating the laws of the state of Alabama," the trooper told him.

"Can't you walk, little lady?" Officer Hooks asked Sherwood. When she shook her head, he and the other officer picked her up by the arms, her feet trailing, and placed her in the patrol car. The second officer was not so genteel. "Nigger lovin' whoring bitch," he growled as he pushed her into the back seat.[13]

Their incarceration in the Etowah County Courthouse brought the total of jailed Freedom Walkers to thirty.

The Etowah County Jail

Madeleine Sherwood, the only white woman arrested at the Keener memorial service, was placed in solitary confinement at Gadsden's Etowah County Courthouse to protect her from the other white female prisoners, who screamed obscenities at her.

Her cell was cold, and a harsh overhead light burned night and day.

Sherwood's bed was a steel frame with a filthy lumpy mattress. Her toilet was an open seatless hole, and she was often watched by the guards when she used it. "You're a nigger lovin' bitch, and you're goin' to hell. Straight to hell," the guard assured her.

"It was the singing—the gospel singing and freedom songs that kept me going," she remembered. "I didn't eat a thing for thirty-six hours. I was terrified, but determined not to let the guards see me cry."[14]

The Keener walkers agreed that no one would request bail except Sherwood, who pledged to refund it. She had to fly to Hollywood to complete an episode of the television series *The Fugitive*. After three days CORE posted her one-thousand-dollar bail, and Mary Hamilton drove her to the "colored drug store" where she met Fred Gray, the black attorney who represented all the Freedom Walkers.

When Sherwood finally returned to Hollywood, David Janssen, *The Fugitive*'s star, hugged her. "Boy, I admire you, honey," he said. "I could never do what you did."

"Janssen was a real human being," Sherwood recalled. "There was really no telling in those days who would support you and who would turn on you. After Alabama I made the sponsors nervous, and I lost a lot of TV roles. My publicist was embarrassed by what I'd done, and he got very angry. But my musician friend Dotts Johnson called me 'one brave hussy' and said he'd never fully trusted me or any other white person until I came back from Gadsden. And see, I'd always thought we were very close. . . ."

The reaction of actress Shelley Winters, Sherwood's New York Actors Studio colleague, however, shocked her. "If I expected anyone to understand how I felt it was Shelley," Sherwood said. "She was a committed activist herself. Still, the first thing she said to me was, 'Wow! Tough way to get publicity, honey.' That hurt very much."[15]

Freedom Now!

As Birmingham goes, so goes the South.
—Dr. Martin Luther King, Jr., 1963

After the SNCC/CORE Freedom Walkers were released from Kilby State Prison, James Forman sent Sam Shirah back to Gadsden to assist with the city's growing freedom movement. He dispatched Bob Zellner to Danville, Virginia, for the same purpose.

Suddenly the South was exploding. *Freedom Now!* was echoing everywhere. Cambridge, Maryland, was under threat of marshal law, and violence had erupted in Jackson, Mississippi, in Selma, Alabama, and in Savannah and Albany in Georgia. Zev Aelony had been arrested again in Americus, Georgia, and he faced the death penalty for inciting insurrection.

Aelony's arrest created an uproar in the European press. The German filmmaker who'd documented the final day of the Freedom Walk remembered the friendly young American who'd struggled with his high school German to answer questions, and led an outraged corps of English, Swedish, and German journalists. Their criticism embarrassed the Kennedy administration. Ultimately a federal court ruled that the Georgia statute under which Aelony had been arrested was unconstitutional. He was released after three months' incarceration.

By the end of 1963 SNCC had discontinued its campus coordination work, with the exception of Shirah's white student program. Middle-class black students were no longer carrying the weight of the movement. Teachers, cab drivers, barbers, maids, the employed and the unemployed were volunteering to work with SNCC. Some recruits were ready to battle in the streets for jobs, decent housing, and better schools. They were tired of waiting and felt they had little to lose.

The Gadsden Freedom Movement

Gadsden, Alabama, became a center of CORE activity after the Freedom Walkers and Diane Nash's Alabama Christian Movement for Human

Rights volunteers were incarcerated there. Mary Hamilton, CORE's only female field secretary, had been pressed into service to keep an eye on them.

A light-skinned black who refused to pass for white, Hamilton was a first-grade teacher in Los Angeles in 1961 and one of only two L.A. CORE members. The day after the Freedom Riders were beaten in Birmingham she registered two hundred new members.

"We were beside ourselves with joy," she remembered. "So many people finally fighting back! History had provided us with an opportunity, and I was not going to waste it."[1]

School ended Friday, and Hamilton boarded a train to Jackson, Mississippi, Monday morning. She was arrested for integrating the white waiting room of Jackson's Illinois Central railway station three days later and spent forty days at the Parchman penitentiary.

In 1962 Hamilton worked with Freedom Walkers Eric Weinberger and Winston Lockett in Lebanon, Tennessee, and in the spring of 1963 she was dispatched to Birmingham. Leaving the Sixteenth Street Baptist Church after a rally, she was arrested, placed in solitary confinement, and nearly raped by a white guard. Hamilton put up such a struggle that he told her she wasn't worth the trouble, and threw her back into the open holding pen.[2]

Mary Hamilton knew how dangerous county jails were, and she was very willing to leave her organizing work in Chattanooga to go to Gadsden and watch over the Freedom Walkers. She and Marvin Robinson, a Chattanooga coworker; Arlene Wilkes, who'd been arrested with Madeleine Sherwood and the Keener Freedom Walkers; and the SCLC's Bernard Lee mobilized the Gadsden freedom movement. Sam Shirah was one of six SNCC staffers assigned to help them.

Gadsden had always been a dangerous place for activists. The Goodyear Tire and Rubber Company had opened its first southern plant in Gadsden in 1929, and union organizers who were not willing to abide by Jim Crow were run out of town.

When Vice President Henry Wallace, the Progressive Party's 1948 antisegregationist presidential candidate, campaigned in Gadsden, Klansmen pounded his car with lead pipes and tried to pull him out of it. Wallace fled without making a single speech and declared that he'd "seen the eyes of fascism."

Throughout the 1950s and 1960s the Gadsden Klan sponsored tent revivals where hooded evangelists encouraged native-born Americans to accept Jesus and join the invisible empire. In 1959, the local Klavern erected a "Welcome to Gadsden" sign at the city limits. Just four years later Gadsden's black citizens were picketing segregated hotels, restaurants, schools, and parks. They conducted silent marches to demand employment opportunities in the downtown department stores, had sit-ins, blocked business entrances, conducted "snake dances" through the shopping district, and staged a lie-in on Main Street.[3]

Shirah worked with some local people who planned to finish Bill Moore's walk to Jackson. It was a much larger group than the SNCC/CORE band and was predominantly black.

On June 14 as they began their walk, Gadsden's mayor, Leslie Gilliland, obtained an injunction to stop *all* demonstrations within the city limits. Four hundred fifty activists, including the Freedom Walkers, were arrested.

The following day three hundred blacks standing outside the Etowah County Courthouse conducting a silent prayer vigil were attacked by fifty of Al Lingo's state troopers swinging wooden clubs and cattle prods. The Gadsden city police actually intervened to stop the blue-helmeted troopers as they viciously beat a black woman who had stumbled.[4]

On June 20 Shirah attended a mass meeting at the Galilee Baptist Church to hear Dr. Martin Luther King, Jr., offer words of encouragement. "Sometimes we hear, even from the lips of some of the highest officials in the land, that we ought to stop," King said. "The only way is for them to get rid of the conditions that brought these demonstrations into being. We will demonstrate until they integrate!"[5]

Five hundred twenty-three people had been jailed by June 23. Half were under sixteen years of age. When the mothers of the arrested children marched, fifty-two of them were also incarcerated. Gadsden seemed to be on its way to becoming another Birmingham.

In the midst of the rising tension, Shirah learned that Bob Zellner had been jailed in Danville, and that Forman wanted him to drive up to Virginia to help out there. Zellner, Avon Rollins (who'd been an observer on the Freedom Walk), and Ivanhoe Donaldson, a black SNCC field secretary from New York City, had been assisting Rev. Lawrence Campbell with Danville's "equity in public hiring" campaign, and all were charged under the state statute (the one used in the hanging of John Brown) of "inciting the colored population to acts of violence and war against the white population." A felony, it was punishable by up to ten years in prison.

Shirah left Gadsden for Danville just as Justice Department officials were arriving to negotiate a truce. Gadsden's public facilities were temporarily desegregated, but the demonstrations resumed on August 1. When a second group of activists assembled on August 3 to finish Moore's Freedom Walk, 683 people, including the walkers, were arrested.

CORE's executive secretary, James Farmer, and the actors Marlon Brando, Paul Newman, and Anthony Franciosa (husband of actress Shelley Winters) arrived in Gadsden to offer their support, but they decided not to defy the mayor's injunction by marching.

The NAACP's Legal Defense Fund appealed the injunction to federal court, but the Fifth Circuit refused to assume jurisdiction.[6] Without federal intervention, the Gadsden freedom movement was stalled, and state repression was effectively sanctioned. Historian Howard Zinn observed that "[the] demonstrations not only failed to elicit concessions, but appeared instead to solidify white resistance."[7]

Black and White Together

On June 6, 1963, James Farmer asked the harried Mary Hamilton to drive from Gadsden to Birmingham to meet actress Madeleine Sherwood's plane and bring her to the Etowah County Courthouse for a hearing.

Sherwood was terrified. "Mary," she whispered from under a blanket on the floor of Hamilton's 1959 Buick, "Mary, I think I'm going to vomit."

"Fine, vomit," Hamilton snapped. "Open up your purse and vomit. But don't move, and don't get anything on my upholstery. Now shut up! You white folks come down here to do good and just cause a heap more trouble than you're worth. Then you know what you do? No, you don't, do you? You *leave*. We stay cause we *live* here. Did you ever think of that, white lady? So go ahead and vomit." And Sherwood did.[7]

The assignment galled the exhausted Hamilton, who, like countless other black women, had spent months in southern jails without any of the attention that was being lavished on Sherwood. The actress didn't seem to understand how a white woman defended by a black attorney before a white judge could ignite white rage. The Etowah County Courthouse had recently been bombed, and Diane Nash's Alabama Christian Movement walkers were still locked inside. Hamilton believed that Sherwood's grandstanding put them at further risk.

When they arrived in Gadsden, Sherwood's hearing date was suddenly postponed. Ultimately, she flew from New York to Alabama four times. Each time Hamilton drove her the thirty miles to Gadsden and back, and each time Sherwood's hearing was rescheduled. The prosecution counted on her tiring of the expense and time. Her agent counseled her to drop the appeal and stay in the North to avoid prosecution, but she refused.

Yet Hamilton felt little sympathy for the actress, who, she believed, expected the thanks of Gadsden's blacks despite the fact that her repeated trips were of no practical help to them.

Hamilton had spent time in the Etowah County jail herself. She'd been sentenced for contempt of court when she refused to respond to cross-examination by a prosecuting attorney who addressed her as "Mary." White women were always respectfully addressed as Miss or Mrs., and Mary Hamilton insisted on being called "Miss Hamilton."

She appealed her conviction, and when the Alabama Supreme Court refused to hear the case, *Hamilton v. Alabama* went directly to the U.S. Supreme Court. Hamilton's conviction was reversed in 1964. The federal justices determined that the practice of addressing blacks by their first names amounted to establishing a racial caste system. Further, they deemed it unconstitutional to punish a black witness for refusing to respond when addressed by his or her first name. The NAACP's Legal Defense Fund considered the "Miss Mary Decision" a landmark ruling.[8]

Madeleine Sherwood's appeal dragged on until passage of the Civil Rights Act of 1964, when thousands of cases like hers were nullified. For her, it was a bittersweet victory.

"Mary was never completely convinced that I hadn't come South for a thrill or for some kind of therapy to deal with my white guilt," Sherwood remembered sadly. "It was a very tough time."[9]

Binghamton, New York

Late in August 1963, Bill Moore's widow, Mary Moore, was recalled to her job at the Transformers plant in Endicott, New York, and so was unable to make her trip to Alabama to confront accused murderer Floyd Simpson. Subsequently, CBS informed her that their plans for producing the documentary "Death of a Mailman" were cancelled.

Within four months of his brutal murder and after five failed attempts to finish his walk, the public memory of Bill Moore was dimming. Early in 1964 Robert Moore, Bill's father, suffered a fatal heart attack, and the following year Mary Moore married Courtland Birchard, a coworker at Transformers.

Jim Peck, standing in front of the Alabama state capitol representing CORE at the 1965 Selma voting rights march, tried to pay a final tribute to his friend Bill. He told the crowd of twenty-five thousand (including actress Madeleine Sherwood) that at long last Moore's Freedom Walk had been completed. Few knew who or what he was talking about.

Without Remorse

Do I not hate them, O Lord, that hate Thee?
—Psalm 139

To dismiss Floyd Simpson, the unindicted accused murderer of William Moore, as a redneck racist, a religious fanatic, or a social misfit would be to seriously misjudge him. Within his Ft. Payne, Alabama, community Simpson was a far more conventional figure than either Bill Moore or Sam Shirah were in theirs.

Simpson was a good family man, a good neighbor, and a proud member of the Ku Klux Klan. In 1963 the Klan operated so openly in Alabama that KKK welcome signs were posted outside the city limits of Gadsden, Montgomery, and Birmingham, right alongside the shields of the Rotary, Kiwanis, and chamber of commerce.[1]

At Klan meetings an American flag, a cross, an open Bible, and a sword were displayed to remind the Knights that they were soldiers in a war against the enemies of a Christian nation. Imperial Wizard Robert Shelton assured them that the civil rights movement was a plot by "beatniks, sex perverts, and tennis shoe wearing communists," to take over America.[2] As black churches exploded and burned and black men were lynched, Klan terrorists were often defended, and some even praised, from church pulpits.

Floyd Simpson had been baptized as a young man and was a member of the Gravel Hill Baptist Church in Collbran. Although he seldom attended services, he professed to be grateful that the Lord had spared him both in the Big War and in Korea. He'd returned whole, unlike his poor brother Carl who'd come back a cripple. Simpson respected the independent spirit of the Baptist Church: there were no bishops or cardinals, and every Baptist was encouraged to read the Bible and interpret the Word for himself.

The Bible, Simpson had been taught, was the final revealed word of God, and those who accepted Jesus through the ordinance of baptism were saved. Like his friend Gaddis Killian, who did attend church, Simpson knew that not *all* men were saved and not *everyone* could claim God's love. Only born-again Christians enjoyed that privilege.

Salvation, like faith, was a gift. Not until an individual was born again could he hope to be justified on biblical grounds. Frankly, those who were not saved did not deserve a better life. That was God's judgement. Thankfully, being saved was a once-and-for-all-time event, just like revelation of the Divine Word.

This uneven distribution of Divine Grace provided a basis on which men like Simpson and Killian understood how segregation could be acceptable in God's sight. God was selective. He might be the creator of all, but he didn't love all equally.

God intervened in human affairs through an ongoing war with Satan to win human souls. Those who disdained salvation were deceived by Satan and like him became the enemies of God.

Segregationists found biblical sanctions for separation of the races from the first chapter of Genesis, in which God brought forth living creatures each according to his own kind, to the cursing of Noah's son Ham, whose black descendants were enslaved, to the hard luck that the foreign wives of Moses, Samson, and Solomon brought. Passages in the Book of Leviticus forbade the breeding of animals of different kinds, the Book of Ezra warned the children of Israel not to intermarry among the Canaanites, and the New Testament declared that "[He] hath made of one blood all nations of men for to dwell on all the face of the earth, and hath determined the times before appointed, and the bounds of their habitation" (Acts 17:26).

God demanded segregation not just because blacks (like the Canaanites) were inferior, but because segregation preserved the purity of his chosen people—white Anglo-Saxon baptized Christians. When Israel proved unfaithful, God abandoned the Jews and transferred his promise of salvation to the Christians. Salvation was retained through obedience. God had withdrawn it from the unfaithful Jews, and he would remove it again if Christians proved unworthy.

Christian fundamentalists, therefore, could reasonably join forces with organizations like the white Citizens' Councils, and even the Klan, to preserve segregation.

The critical issue was personal salvation. One was either saved or he wasn't. Creation had been conceived in terms of good and evil. One either served God or served the Devil. One either cherished the Southern Way of Life or threatened it. It was the same ethic that Bill Moore's parents and grandparents had tried to instill in him, the one he'd abandoned for his teacher Gus Youngstrom's broader vision of the world.

Southern Christian fundamentalists believed that the earthly church was commissioned exclusively to save souls. Once a man was "washed in the Blood of the Lamb" he belonged to the eternal community. Change of any kind—religious or social—was suspect, since eternal truth was known to be unchanging. Jesus, the preachers said, was the same yesterday, today, and tomorrow. He had come not to abolish the law, but to fulfill it.

Episcopal bishop John Shelby Spong, who was raised in the Bible Belt, has observed that "when a fundamentalist Christian sees the Anti-Christ in someone who is disturbing his or her religious security it becomes not merely justifiable but downright righteous to utter words of condemnation and prayers for the early demise of that enemy." Known as "imprecations" these are prayers that God will curse his enemies. "Indeed," writes Spong, "you can even believe that you are God's anointed one chosen to rid the world of this demonic figure."[3]

Moore's atheism no doubt horrified Gaddis Killian, but Floyd Simpson's response was more complex. Simpson was an angry man, and Moore's atheism infuriated him. To Simpson's mind, atheists were communists, the same enemy he'd fought in Korea in 1950. In the American army he'd learned that communists were the sworn enemies of American democracy, religion, and culture. They were godless men, and in America they were mostly Jewish agitators who provoked blacks to insurrection.

Gary Thomas Rowe, an FBI informant who infiltrated Birmingham's Eastview #13 Klavern in 1963, described Ft. Payne's Kludd (chaplain), Rev. Willis Griffen, as "a particularly rabid Klansman" who believed in eternal damnation for communist race mixers. At an initiation rite, Rowe described Simpson's spiritual leader as "clamoring for violence."[4]

Floyd Simpson recognized in Bill Moore a walking, breathing threat to the Southern Way of Life. He was a blasphemer who not only broke God's laws but denied his very existence. Pagans were known to serve the devil, and Christians had a right and a duty to protect themselves against corruption. Simpson believed that Moore's repudiation of Christian faith had led to his heretical beliefs in communism and integration. Race *was* a religious issue. The enemies of racial separation were the enemies of God.

The Kingdom of God

Christian segregationists relegated Jesus' teachings about the inclusive nature of the Kingdom of God to the Afterlife. Christianity, they believed, was charged with calling the faithful *away* from the world rather than encouraging deeper involvement with it.

Black preachers—especially those involved in the civil rights movement—infuriated Christian segregationists with their notions of an *earthly* Kingdom. Some black clergy actually extended the hopes of Jesus' Kingdom to social justice!

White fundamentalists believed in a personal, not a social gospel. Soulwinning was the work that had been ordained by Jesus in his "Great Commission," recorded in the Gospel of Matthew. "Go ye therefore, and teach all nations, baptizing them in the name of the Father and of the Son, and of the Holy Ghost."[5]

Martin Luther King, Jr., an ordained Baptist preacher, talked about the Kingdom of God as if Jesus' intent had been to establish it on earth! The prophets, King argued, condemned oppression, and Jesus, in their tradition, turned both the social and economic orders upside down.

"Any religion," King said, "that professes to be concerned about a future good over yonder and is not concerned about the present evils over here is a spiritually moribund religion only waiting for the day to be buried."[6]

King's criticism was troubling enough, but when white people like William Moore came along denying God altogether and insisting that all men were created equal, they provoked an anger in men like Simpson that ran deeper than logic.

What Moore had experienced as a debate, possibly an argument, seems to have been an encounter of a far more serious nature for Simpson and Killian. Simpson became enraged by the arrogance of the outsider who threatened to drag the federal government, intermarriage, black rule, and religious upheaval into his ordered world.

Anthropologists use the term "pseudospeciation" to describe practices among primitive tribes whose isolation and cohesion become so strong that they are convinced that their customs are the standard by which everyone ought to live. As a result they often treat outsiders with a brutality they would never think of practicing among themselves.

Alabama Decides

On September 12, 1963, an Etowah County grand jury, with Judge Cyril L. Smith presiding, convened to review the People of Alabama's case against Floyd Simpson in the murder of William L. Moore. Circuit Solicitor William W. Rayburn demonstrated that on April 24, 1963, Moore's route had taken him past Simpson's grocery, that Simpson admitted speaking with Moore twice on that day, that the FBI had traced the bullets which killed Moore to Simpson's rifle, and that several witnesses had placed Simpson's black Buick near the murder site less than one hour before Moore's death.

But this was not enough to convince the panel of seventeen whites and one black man to indict Floyd Simpson, who was freed on September 12, 1963. Defense attorney William Beck said he'd been confident of the outcome all along. Beck was a resident of Ft. Payne, former speaker of the Alabama House of Representatives, and a close friend of Governor George Wallace.[7]

The message was clear. Not only would southern white juries refuse to indict a white man for killing a black man, they would not indict a white man for the murder of a race mixer and agitator who threatened the Southern Way of Life.

Danville

Bigotry tries to keep truth safe in its hand with a grip that kills it.
—Rabindranath Tagore

Sam Shirah arrived in Danville, Virginia, on Saturday, June 22, 1963, with Mary King, a white SNCC communications worker. When they reached SNCC headquarters in the High Street Baptist Church, King went to look for Dottie Miller, who was handling communications, and Shirah stayed in the basement to catch up with the staff. Suddenly four police officers kicked down the door and rearrested Bob Zellner, black field secretary Ivanhoe Donaldson, and white volunteer David Foss. A grand jury had indicted them in absentia for inciting to riot. White Danville had stopped laughing at the black freedom movement and had begun "handling it."

For three weeks Rev. Lawrence Campbell of the Bibleway Holiness Church and Rev. Alexander Dunlop of High Street Baptist Church had been leading demonstrators to city hall to demand integration of public facilities and establishment of a biracial school desegregation commission.

On June 5 the protesters had gathered on the steps of the municipal building to wait for Mayor Julian Stinson. At 5:30 P.M. Police Chief E. G. McCain told them that the mayor's office was closed. When the preachers replied that they were prepared to wait all night, McCain arrested them.

That evening Rev. Campbell used his one phone call to ask SNCC for help. "Danville," he told James Forman, "is becoming another Birmingham."[1]

Despite the incarceration of their leaders, the Danville activists continued to march to city hall every day until Judge Archibald Aitken issued a restraining order outlawing *all* demonstrations. On June 9 at a rally in defiance of Aitken's injunction, the activists called for a national boycott of Dan River textiles, specifically sheets and towels. Dan River Mills restricted the hiring of blacks to nonskilled and maintenance jobs.

Thirty-eight people were arrested and sixty-six more would be detained for conducting a prayer vigil at the jail that night. The following day, when nearly 150 people gathered outside the jail, McCain roared through his bullhorn, "I'm tired of you niggers feeding off this community like leeches!"[2] and ordered the fire department to turn its high-pressure hoses on them. The force of the hoses tore the dress off Gloria Campbell, the wife of Rev. Lawrence Campbell, as it knocked her down.

A freshly deputized white posse carrying table legs from a local furniture mill attacked the demonstrators. Heads were split open and bones were broken. Forty-seven people were injured seriously enough to require medical attention, and 105 (mostly teens) were arrested. Bob Zellner's fiancée, Dottie Miller, who'd been photographing the events, was hospitalized with a head injury.

The parents of Danville's young demonstrators were charged with "contributing to the delinquency of minors,"[3] and all the adult women who were arrested were required to undergo the humiliation of pelvic exams to check for venereal disease.[4]

City councilman John Carter defended the police response as appropriate to what he called "a Mau Mau riot."

"It put the fear of God in them," he said.[5]

Rev. Campbell called an emergency mass meeting at the Bibleway Church, and James Forman stood beside him as he begged his fellow black citizens not to lose heart despite the brutality.[6]

"Who is Mayor Stinson in the eyes of God?" Campbell thundered. "He was made from the dust of the earth. God blew breath in his nostrils, and God is able to trouble his mind and disturb his thinking."[7]

A Great Change

On June 11, 1963, responding to public pressure over the brutality of events in Birmingham, President John F. Kennedy sent a comprehensive civil rights bill to Congress. "[A] great change is at hand," he said, "and our . . . obligation is to make that revolution, that change, peaceful and constructive for all."

The following day, Medgar Evers, the NAACP's Mississippi field secretary, was murdered in Jackson by a member of the Greenwood white Citizens' Council. Evers had been leading a fair employment campaign similar to Danville's. When news of his assassination reached the mill town, angry black demonstrators filled the streets. Police carrying submachine guns set up roadblocks to keep people from gathering in their churches. Riot tanks roamed the city and helicopters hovered overhead. SNCC dispatched an additional twenty workers to Danville.

Dr. Martin Luther King, Jr., arrived two weeks later, and two thousand black citizens filled Danville's city armory to hear him speak.

"You have my full personal support and the support of the SCLC," King told them. "We're not afraid of jails. You've got to march and fill up the Danville jails. We've got to have strong, massive, non-violent demonstrations in Danville until the city engages in good faith negotiations with Negroes about their equal rights."[8]

But King didn't offer to lead the demonstrations as Rev. Campbell had hoped he would. When several CORE and SNCC activists bluntly asked him to march to city hall with them he politely refused. He explained that he was needed in New York City to plan for the March on Washington being organized to pressure Congress into passing President Kennedy's civil rights bill.[9]

It is evident that King understood that Danville would be a long siege. State courts were willing to accommodate the white segregationists with injunctions and remedies under the law.

The Danville City Work Farm

Shirah settled into Danville in the home of a black family and marched to city hall every day for two weeks carrying an American flag. On July 11 as he stopped to take direction from Matthew John, who was organizing the day's demonstration, a tall white man wearing a light suit and smoking a cigar came up behind him, shoved him, and ordered him to keep moving.

"Who are you?" Shirah asked.[10]

"Doesn't matter who I am," the man snapped. "I'm telling you to move on." A second well-dressed man wearing a large diamond ring grabbed Shirah's arm and told him he was under arrest.

"For what?" Shirah asked.

"Vagrancy."

Shirah went limp as they dragged him behind city hall into the police station. Once inside they threw him against the wall.

Captain Tower, the senior officer, stood over him. "Get your sorry ass up off that floor," he growled. When Shirah didn't move, Tower bent over and punched him in the stomach.

"I'm not cooperating," Shirah wheezed, "but I'm not resisting arrest."

The two plainclothesmen took turns beating him. "Get up, you nigger-loving bastard!" one bellowed as he twisted Shirah's right leg behind him. Shirah heard a pop and felt searing pain. He was sure that his leg was broken. When they finally stopped, Captain Tower warned him that they'd start again if he didn't get up.

Shirah dragged himself to the nearest chair. His shirt and jacket were torn in half and his face was bleeding badly. He limped to a desk where he was fingerprinted and charged with failure to comply with an officer's order to clear the street.

"Where are you staying?" Tower asked.

Shirah refused to give up the name of the black family who'd sheltered him.

"Why did you come to Danville?" the other officer demanded.

"I'm a folk singer from Montgomery, Alabama," he said. "I came here to sing."[11]

"You're an outside agitator is what you are," the officer charged.

"It's not up to me to prove my innocence," Shirah said. "It's up to you to prove me guilty."

At that point the man with the diamond ring hit him again.

Two and a half hours later Shirah was taken across the river to the city work farm. He was placed in a white cinder-block cell, and the guard told the other prisoners, "Here's one of 'em nigger lovers for ya." The prisoners took turns beating him. Two weeks later Shirah appeared before a judge and was fined fifty dollars, which SNCC paid.

On August 2, federal judge Thomas Jefferson Michie not only upheld but extended the city council's injunction barring mass demonstrations, and the Danville freedom movement sank into paralysis.

On August 11, 1963, the *New York Times* described the "Danville Method" of resisting civil rights activists which was being studied by segregationists all over the South. "Officials of other Virginia cities have traveled here to observe and learn in an unspoken compliment to a defense strategy that is the most unyielding, ingenious, legalistic, and effective of any city in the South."[12]

Martin Luther King returned three months after his successful March on Washington and announced that the SCLC would launch Operation Dialogue to confront Danville with the immorality of its racism. Should that fail, he said, he was prepared to lead a nationwide boycott of Dan River textiles. When a mass meeting was called at the High Street Baptist Church on November 15, fewer than five hundred citizens attended. A week later the president of the United States was assassinated, and Operation Dialogue was suspended indefinitely.[13]

Cognitive Dissonance

The falcon cannot hear the falconer;
Things fall apart; the centre cannot hold. . . .
—WILLIAM BUTLER YEATS

After his release from the city work farm, Sam Shirah remained in Danville, Virginia, until he was forced to flee with the remaining SNCC staff to evade a grand jury indictment for "inciting to acts of violence and war."

He returned to Defuniak Springs, Florida, to recuperate, but when he arrived at the parsonage it was clear that trouble had followed him home. News of his arrest had filled the local papers, and Big Sam's congregation was once again calling for their pastor's resignation. At the same time, Richard was getting ready to appear before the draft board to plead his case for conscientious objector status. The notoriety attached to his brother was not helping Richard's cause. Although Shirah still didn't have full use of his right leg, late in August he traveled back to Atlanta and moved into a large apartment on Peachtree Street with two roommates: Danny Lyon, a white SNCC photographer he'd met in Danville, and SNCC's black chairman, John Lewis.

Danny Lyon, raised in Forest Hills, New York, had volunteered with

SNCC in Albany, Georgia, during the summer of 1962 when he was a University of Chicago student. James Forman had put him to work as a staff photographer.

The Danville movement had a profound effect on Lyon. The son of a physician, he had never experienced segregated medical facilities before. He was horrified by the broken-down equipment and limited number of professional staff he encountered when he'd taken the injured Dottie Miller to the black Winslow Hospital.

Shirah enjoyed teasing Lyon about his baptism by fire in the rural South. SNCC veterans often counseled new white recruits to identify themselves as "colored" if they were stopped by the police, since white race mixers were despised. But when Lyon was detained for taking pictures at his first demonstration, he offered too much information. When he assured the sheriff that his grandfather was black, a deputy threatened to kill him. Lyon hadn't understood that his black grandfather would have to have had sex with his *white* grandmother to produce him. White activists were only safe if they claimed a black *grandmother*.[1]

Although they were men of very different temperaments, Lyon, Shirah, and Lewis became close friends. Future Georgia congressman Lewis flourished in the environment of marathon meetings and endless debate, while Shirah and Lyon often went off into the Georgia countryside to escape SNCC's intensity.

"You couldn't just get up and go to a movie," Lyon remembered. "*Everybody* went and you'd spend an hour debating which movie to see, who would drive, and where everyone would go afterwards. Sam was deeply committed to freedom and justice, but all that communal activity sometimes drove him crazy."

Years later John Lewis recalled Shirah as quiet but very intense. "You had the sense with Sam that he was battling the collective guilt of the entire White South," he said.[2] Ironically, Shirah and Lewis, both born in Troy, Alabama, could never have shared a meal there.

"That a black and a white from Alabama and a New York Jew were all close friends and actually lived together says something very important about the cross fertilization that was going on throughout the Movement," Lyon reflected years later.[3]

On August 26, Shirah and Mary King accompanied Big Sam to Chicago to attend the Second Methodist Conference on Human Relations, called to "bring about racial inclusiveness in the Methodist Church . . . and in the communities in which it serves." Big Sam had asked them to serve on a panel of college activists.

On Tuesday, August 27, Rev. Martin Luther King, Jr., addressed the conference. "Segregation," he said, "is on its deathbed, and the only question confronting the church and the nation is how costly and bloody they will make its funeral."[4] He received a standing ovation.

James Meredith, who had crossed the color line at Ole Miss, was the next speaker. He told the ministers that, while he believed everything that Christianity taught, he could not believe most of the things it condoned. Shirah was especially impressed by Meredith's calm yet bitingly critical manner.

He also enjoyed black comedian Dick Gregory's challenge to the preachers that "if religion had lived up to its responsibility every Negro would be saying thank God instead of thank the Supreme Court!"

The student activist panel was well received, although Shirah, King, and the other students felt like they were preaching to the converted. Rev. Jim Zellner had already circulated a paper entitled "Should Sympathy and Support Be Given to Young People Who Agitate and Demonstrate Against Racial Discrimination?"

How will we answer our young people, he asked, when, years down the road, they challenge us with questions such as these: "Where were you church people when we were being beaten in the streets? What happened to your voice when demagogues cried for our blood and called us dupes of the Communists? Did you visit us when they flung us in stinking jails and treated us like common criminals? When irresponsible politicians were using our crusade against racial discrimination to perpetuate their corruption and greed and the public press castigated us as troublemakers, some of you church people joined in with them. Where were you when we decided to do something positive, even if it was drastic, about what you taught us in Sunday School?"[5]

The white ministers endorsed the March on Washington, which was scheduled to begin the following Wednesday, August 28. Some flew directly to D.C. from Chicago to join the demonstrators at the Lincoln Memorial.

Shirah, however, anxious to finally begin his campus work, drove with Mary King back to Atlanta. He'd decided to begin at Birmingham-

Southern College, where he'd been expelled a semester before. Lyon went with him to photograph the initial campus meetings. While they were still in Birmingham, the Sixteenth Street Baptist Church suffered the shattering bomb blast that killed four black Sunday school children.

Lyon snapped a photograph of Shirah standing with a group of SNCC staff outside the Sixth Avenue Baptist Church, where three of the four funeral services were held. Doris Derby, the young black woman beside him, had represented the New York Friends of SNCC at William Moore's funeral almost five months earlier. They share a dazed expression. Shirah's eyebrows are furrowed and his shoulders slightly bent. He looks like he's bracing for a blow.

The SNCC field staff was anxious to organize demonstrations in Birmingham once the funerals were over. But the city was SCLC territory, and Dr. King insisted on maintaining calm. Despite the hope he expressed in his eulogy that "the innocent blood of these little girls may serve as the redemptive force that will bring new light to this dark city . . . ,"[6] many black activists had had their fill of redemptive suffering.

"Freedom Now" demonstrations had been replacing nonviolent direct action campaigns for months, and they were spreading beyond the South. Demands for improved housing, health care, education, police protection, and jobs were being heard in New York, Pennsylvania, Maryland, Missouri, Ohio, Nebraska, Rhode Island, Massachusetts, and New Jersey—261 cities in all. Activists carried banners declaring "We Won't Wait Another 100 Years," and "Birmingham Is Everywhere." Martin Luther King, Jr., had called it "the summer of our discontent."[7]

When Shirah attempted to organize a protest (against church bombings) on the Birmingham-Southern campus he was removed by the city police. Representatives from the BSC student union told him that, while they didn't want to affiliate with SNCC, they wanted to protest segregation. They asked for his help in contacting black student leaders from the nearby Miles College.

Whites had to create opportunities to meet blacks in Birmingham, they said, and they didn't know exactly how to go about it. Shirah renewed the contacts he'd made with Miles College's Anti-Injustice Committee during the boycott of the previous spring, and they set up a meeting. Dean Ralph Jolly threatened to expel anyone who attended, but when the students defied him and traveled to the black campus he did not move to discipline them.

While Shirah was in Birmingham he received a letter from his mother informing him that Big Sam's congregation was in turmoil again. On Sunday, September 22, Big Sam had prayed for the four murdered girls from his pulpit, saying, "Caution and timidity have governed our Christian concern. . . . Now we reap the bitter fruits of terror in our land, tears in our homes, and murder on our hands. . . . By Thy grace may we not be part of the world's problem, but may we let Thee use us to bring an answer to the prayers of all Thy people when they pray, Thy Kingdom come. Thy will be done."

Twelve elders walked out of the service. The following day the Pastoral Relations Committee, enraged by the accusation that there was blood on their hands, drafted another resolution to the official board to request a change of pastors.

One member said he blushed with shame to think that his pastor was part of "that movement." Another said, "If he can't preach from the Bible, then let him withdraw," while a third acknowledged that "while I don't agree with the pastor it isn't him so much as his family that's the problem."[8]

For a second time in as many months Big Sam wrote to Bishop Hardin requesting permission to complete his appointment in Defuniak Springs. He quoted the Methodist Social Creed, which states that "we believe that God is Father of all peoples and races . . . and that all men are brothers. . . ." and observed that "[p]erhaps it is a change of heart rather than a change of pastors that is needed here." Bishop Hardin did not argue the point, nor did he transfer Rev. Shirah.[9]

The Belated Beloved Community

While the Sixteenth Street Baptist Church bombing increased cynicism about nonviolent resistence on black campuses, it had a very different effect on many white southern campuses. When Governor George Wallace declared that the bombing was the work of outside "communist agitators," some white students became integrationists overnight.[10] Shirah was suddenly inundated with requests for help organizing campus demonstrations.

At the same time, however, white participation in the southern freedom movement was being seriously questioned by black activists. Hope for interracial cooperation had gradually turned into disillusionment. In the wider world, whites were retaliating against black demonstrators with increasing brutality, and the sight of white activists participating in civil rights demonstrations fed the segregationists' rage.

The dangers of organizing in black communities increased whenever white women assisted, and SNCC's black field secretaries complained bitterly that white males invariably tried to take over black political movements.

By the fall of 1963 SNCC's mission had evolved beyond campus coordination into grass-roots mobilizing. Amassing political power had become a primary goal. Many white students, on the other hand, were just beginning to appreciate the concept of the beloved community. White southern students were belatedly volunteering to fight segregation just as young black activists were identifying it as only one aspect of a totally corrupt system. More radical blacks favored separating from a white America they defined as hopelessly racist.

Shirah, however, was heartened by the enthusiasm that he found among middle-class white southern students. He traveled to the black campus of Claflin College in Orangeburg, South Carolina, to take part in an interracial meeting with students from the University of South Carolina at Columbia, forty miles away. When the group attempted to integrate a movie theater in Orangeburg, Shirah was arrested with them. He arrived in Tallahasse, Florida, in November and was arrested with white Florida State's Student Group for Equal Rights, which was demonstrating with the NAACP.

At the University of Louisville he helped organize Students for Peace and Freedom, and at the University of Southern Mississippi in Hattiesburg he worked with white student activists to produce an alternative newspaper. Throughout the fall of 1963 he encouraged countless white students to organize on and off campus, led demonstrations, and generally disrupted campus life at white southern colleges.

In Nashville, Shirah met with students from the white campuses of George Peabody, Skarritt, and Vanderbilt who'd opened an integrated campus grill and had organized a Joint University Council on Human Relations with black activists from Fisk, Meharry, American Baptist Seminary, and Tennessee A & I. All were involved with the Nashville Christian

Leadership Council (NCLC), a local SCLC affiliate. They asked for his help in organizing a regional conference to reach out to other white southern students.

Shirah complained to Anne Braden that he was having trouble keeping up with all the requests for support. In two months he'd visited twenty campuses in six states. He requested help, and she promised to get it for him.

Greenville, Mississippi

On November 14, 1963, Shirah met with seven white and thirty-five black SNCC field secretaries in Greenville, Mississippi, to plan for a massive Mississippi summer project. One thousand volunteers, mostly white college students, would be recruited to register black voters in the Delta for three months.

Inevitably the discussion turned to the merits of whites working in the black communities. Black staffer Ivanhoe Donaldson asked how SNCC could hope to develop black rural leadership through a project that depended heavily on whites.

"We don't have much to gain from Negroes meeting whites," MacArthur Cotton, a black Mississippi field secretary, observed, "we've got too much to lose if they come down here and create a disturbance and then leave."[11]

There was enough dissension to shelve the project, but Bob Moses, the black SNCC field secretary who'd conceived it, threatened to resign if SNCC voted to exclude whites. "If you want to run a racist organization, count me out," he said. "I always thought that the one thing we can do for the country that no one else can do is to be above the race issue."[12]

Although strong unresolved opposition remained, plans for the Mississippi summer project moved forward.

Another Direction

*In the fight for human dignity we have never underestimated our
opposition, but we have often overestimated our support.*
—AARON HENRY, MISSISSIPPI FREEDOM DEMOCRATIC PARTY

Sam Shirah hurried back to Atlanta when the news broke that President
John Fitzgerald Kennedy had been fatally shot in Dallas, Texas. At the
Raymond Street headquarters the SNCC staff was already gathered
around a borrowed television set speculating about what they might expect
from the new white southern president, Lyndon Johnson.

Most anticipated a crackdown on activism, but opinions were divided
about what SNCC's field secretaries should do until the national direction
became clear. Forman wanted to continue pressing Congress to move on
the civil rights bill which was stuck in the House Rules Committee.

"Whatever Kennedy did for civil rights he did because pressure groups
demanded action," Ivanhoe Donaldson said. "And we have to keep up that
pressure."[1]

Shirah agreed, and he encouraged SNCC's executive committee to call
for campus demonstrations to support the bill.

But others, fearing that mass demonstrations would endanger the Mississippi field staff, urged caution.

"They've already identified the assassin as a leftist," one argued, "and
the John Birchers will use [the assassination] as a club against the Movement."[2]

But Shirah was persistent. He believed that it was crucial to remain
proactive.

"While the country is still in shock we need to come up with a strong
offense," he pressed. "We can't risk losing momentum." Ultimately he,
Forman, and Donaldson prevailed.

The Howard Conference

On Thanksgiving weekend, seven days after the president's assassination,
Shirah headed to Howard University in Washington, D.C., for SNCC's

fourth annual conference. He was eager to take part in the Lincoln Memorial civil rights vigils and to meet Ed Hamlett, a white graduate student
from Jackson, Tennessee, who'd been recommended by Marion Barry to
help with the white southern student project. (Anne Braden, as good as
her word, had provided additional SCEF funding.)

Barry, SNCC's first chair (and later mayor of Washington, D.C.), had
served with Hamlett on the University of Tennessee's Human Rights Action Group, which had desegregated the school's cafeteria.

Shirah took one look at Hamlett's Stanley Blacker sports jacket and
buttoned-down shirt and uncharacteristically lashed out at Barry for nomi-
nating such an inappropriate candidate.

Hamlett was astounded. He could not believe the abuse that the
scruffy-looking Shirah felt free to hurl at Barry.

"I looked like a typical white college student," Hamlett remembered,
"and that enraged Sam."[3]

Shirah had been stung by black criticism of white insensitivity. Now
Barry, who was black, seemed to have gone out of his way to find a poster
boy for everything blacks found distasteful about white liberals.

But Barry argued that Hamlett would be effective in negotiating with
white college administrators. Ultimately he was appointed, over Shirah's
strong objections.

More than thirty years later, Hamlett recalled Shirah as a "mover and
shaker," so intensely driven by the pressure he put on himself that he had
little patience with those he judged less committed or less savvy.

"What I remember most was his courage," Hamlett said. "It was un-
shakable, almost foolhardy. And Sam had a big streak of southern sentimentality, too. The fact that he led the Freedom Walkers into Alabama
was no surprise to anyone who knew him. Bill Moore's willingness to risk
his life to end segregation appealed to Sam. He always admired raw courage, but he was less welcoming of whites who looked like they might be
dabbling in the movement and he could be real surly until he got to know
you."[4]

Where Do We Go from Here?

On November 29, 1963, James Forman welcomed three hundred SNCC
delegates, observers, and guests who'd assembled in the Howard Univer-

sity chapel basement and charged them to think about SNCC's future. He praised President Johnson's appeal to Congress for passage of strong civil rights legislation, but said that, despite Martin Luther King's announcement that the SCLC would observe a month-long mourning period for President Kennedy, "[W]e have to push hard for passage of the civil rights bill. We would be derelict in our duties to our people and to President Johnson if we declared a moratorium."[5]

Author James Baldwin followed with the keynote address. A black man, he speculated that President Kennedy had been killed because he broke the long-standing agreement between the North and South that "you do with your Negroes what you want to, and we'll do with ours what we want to."

Citing the ambivalent national mood, Baldwin compared white America's overwhelming grief for its late president with what he deemed muted responses to the murders of William Moore, Medgar Evers, and the four black children killed in Birmingham.

Sounding a very different note, fifty-one-year-old black pacifist Bayard Rustin, coordinator of the March on Washington, warned the delegates that the civil rights movement had reached an impasse. "The tactics of lying in, sitting in, and praying in are gimmicks which have gone about as far as they can go," he said.

He reiterated what many black leaders, including A. Philip Randolph, the seventy-four-year-old president of the Brotherhood of Sleeping Car Porters, had said at the March on Washington: that because blacks were economically disadvantaged and because any attempt to improve their status at the expense of the white poor would endanger blacks, an end to white *and* black poverty was a prerequisite to racial equality.[6]

Rustin quoted from a recent Harris Poll measuring growing fear among whites that blacks were moving too fast and that their demands for jobs would result in white unemployment.

"We can demand a seat on the bus and get it," he told them, "because the seats are available. We can demand a place at the lunch counter and get it, because the stools are already standing. But we won't get jobs, because there aren't enough jobs to go around."[7]

"Negroes can't make progress without new allies," he assured them. "If we don't expand our base, we will decline into a sectarian movement.[8]

Rustin recommended that SNCC advocate a Marshall Plan for *all* poor Americans.[9]

"Heroism and the ability to go to jail should not be substituted for an over-all social and political reform program," he said, and urged SNCC's whites to stop putting on blue jeans and running down to Mississippi. "Go to work and agitate in your own communities," he said. "Organize workers and the unemployed and build a foundation for an interracial economic alliance.

"When the day comes that the white unemployed adopt the spirit and tactics of the civil rights movement, we are on our way to a revolution in this country."[10]

Rustin's message resonated with Shirah, who was reminded of the popular song that was being sung all over the poor white South:

You have to be black to get a welfare check
And I'm broke
No joke
I ain't got a nickel for a Coke
I ain't black you see
So Uncle Sam won't help poor nigger-hating me.[11]

Shirah understood that as long as whites felt that they were competing with blacks for jobs and benefits they would react violently to any black advancement.

Other white SNCC field secretaries, however, did not appreciate Rustin's advice or their black colleagues' enthusiasm for it. By the end of 1963 almost one-fifth of the SNCC staff was white, and most preferred to continue working in black communities despite the fact that some black staff were asking, "How would *you* know what it's like to be black?"[12]

Shirah suggested that maybe it *was* time for whites to stop trying to force the issue of their value.

Hadn't SNCC begun by coordinating black campus demonstrations? he asked. Hadn't SNCC subsequently broadened its focus to include community organizing? He recommended following Rustin's advice and expanding the white southern student project from campus coordination to poor white community organizing. A majority of the black staff supported him.

Many of Shirah's white colleagues, however, accused him of being naive. "You're just helping them push us out," one told him.[13] But Forman asked Shirah to prepare a written report for the executive committee.

Carry It On

Shirah returned to Atlanta to write his report, which he called "A Proposal for Expanded Work Among Southern White Students: An Appalachian Project." He recommended that SNCC partner with the Students for a Democratic Society's Appalachian Committee for Full Employment, which was sponsoring summer volunteers in Hazard, Kentucky, to assist white coal miners who'd been on a year-long strike.

For more than a decade the demand for deep-mined coal in Perry County had been shrinking. Cheaper strip-mining operations were putting deep miners out of business. Because of layoffs, revenue from union dues dropped, and the United Mine Workers closed its hospitals. The miners struck over cancellation of their health insurance in the winter of 1962, but the UMW declared it a wildcat strike and refused to negotiate for them.

Demonstrations quickly became violent. The miners were accused of dynamiting coal trucks, bulldozers, and railroad bridges. UMW security guards brutally attacked and beat the picketers. Relief workers were needed to distribute donated food and clothing.

Shirah proposed that SNCC recruit white staff and volunteers to make the deliveries and to assist the miners in applying for unemployment insurance benefits and welfare.

"For too long we have attempted to bring white people into the Freedom Movement," he wrote. "I think we must reverse this process and take the movement into the white communities. We must help white people see that the Negro has gained strength by casting off fear and that the white man is still the slave to fear, but he can cast it off, too."[14]

Shirah also recommended that the white student project be assigned a meaningful role in the Mississippi summer project. Volunteers, he suggested, could register voters for the Mississippi Freedom Democratic Party (MFDP) in poor white communities just as others would be doing in the black communities of the Delta. His recommendations were adopted by SNCC's executive committee and ultimately by the Council of Federated Organizations (COFO), which was responsible for coordinating the summer project.[15]

SNCC's executive committee voted to hire Ed Hamlett as Shirah's assistant and to approve white student summer projects in Hazard, Kentucky, and in Jackson, Hattiesburg, and Biloxi in Mississippi. Shirah was authorized to form a steering committee for the Appalachian project.

Pleased with his progress, Shirah planned to go home to Defuniak Springs for Christmas. But when he returned to the Raymond Street headquarters he found singer/songwriter Bob Dylan camped out during an airport layover.

Shirah had met Dylan when they had both performed with the Freedom Singers at a SNCC benefit in Carnegie Hall. He admired Dylan for performing despite receiving death threats. Dylan often said that he felt a spiritual connection with SNCC.[16]

He and his girlfriend, CORE activist Suze Rotolo, had come to Mississippi in July with singers Pete Seeger and Theodore Bikel to perform in a Greenwood cornfield in support of the voter education campaign. There Dylan introduced "Only a Pawn in Their Game," a song he dedicated to Medgar Evers. In it Dylan described Evers's killer (a member of the white Citizens' Council) as a pawn of the racist society. He was the first American folk musician to depict poor whites as victims of segregation, and that appealed to Shirah.

Like Shirah's musical idols Woody Guthrie, Pete Seeger, and Jimmie Rodgers, Dylan romanced the outsider and the rebel. Shirah admired his music, but told Danny Lyon that he thought he could sing rings around him. Shirah stayed in Atlanta long enough to play guitar and sing with Dylan and to get himself arrested again. He never made it home for the Christmas of 1963.

The United Nations ambassador from Kenya, Oginga Odinga, minister of home affairs in the new Jomo Kenyatta government, passed through Atlanta on a U.S. State Department tour in December and asked to meet with members of SNCC, the American freedom fighters he'd heard so much about. A SNCC delegation met him at the Peachtree Manor, Atlanta's only integrated hotel, where the Freedom Singers performed for him in the lobby and chanted *Uhuru!* (freedom now!).

After the visit a few hungry SNCC staff members stopped for lunch at the Toddle House restaurant next to the hotel. Blacks in the group were refused service.

The lunch break quickly turned into a full-blown sit-in. Twenty-one SNCC staff members refused to leave the Toddle House and were arrested and charged with trespassing. The following day (December 22), ten SNCC activists including Shirah, John Lewis, former Freedom Walker Chico Neblett, and Danville activist Ivanhoe Donaldson continued the sit-in and were taken to Forrest County's Big Rock Jail.

An angry Jim Forman called for a national "Christmas in Jail" campaign, and requested that SNCC sympathizers picket Toddle House restaurants across the country. Comedian Dick Gregory flew to Atlanta to join the sit-ins, and two hundred demonstrators were ultimately arrested.

On December 31 forty SNCC activists picketed the New York Stock Exchange to protest the Toddle House chain's policy of integration in the North and segregation in the South.

Forman was so angry at the insult to the Kenyan ambassador that he convinced SNCC's executive committee to purchase stock in Dobbs Houses, Inc. (parent corporation of Toddle House) so that he could attend the next board meeting. Before that meeting, however, Toddle House agreed to serve black customers in the South.[17]

Civil rights activists were often bitterly criticized for embarrassing America on the international front, yet few white Americans seemed disturbed by shabby treatment of Third World diplomats. This was the same kind of injustice that had brought Bill Moore to Maryland's Highway 40 almost a year before. Although the Freedom Highways Project, like the Freedom Rides, had captured the nation's attention, it had not ended segregation. In 1964, that hope was transferred to the civil rights bill stalled in Congress.

The Fifth Circuit

In January 1964, the ten SNCC/CORE Freedom Walkers petitioned the U.S. Court of Appeals for the Fifth Circuit to overturn their conviction for breaching the peace in Alabama. Their appeal was based on repeated requests for injunctions (which federal judge Frank Johnson had denied) to prohibit Public Safety Commissioner Al Lingo and the Alabama State Police from interfering with their right to safe interstate travel.

"We are not going to have a federal union if citizens cannot go from one state to another without being arrested," Jack Greenberg of the NAACP Legal Defense Fund argued. He stressed that the walkers had experienced no trouble in Tennessee or Georgia.[18]

But on July 21, 1964, Judge Johnson's refusal to grant a federal injunction was upheld, and the walkers stood convicted.

Some of My Best Friends Are White

After his court appearance, Shirah drove to New York City with Anne and Carl Braden to attend the annual banquet of the Friends of the Southern Conference Education Fund (SCEF). Anne Braden asked him to report on his work with white southern students, and she encouraged him to raise funds for the Appalachian project.

On February 3, 1964, Shirah approached the dais of the Hotel Roosevelt ballroom in his jeans and work boots. He smiled out at the audience of over six hundred New Yorkers and said, "I am here to say that not only are some of my best friends Negroes, but some of my best friends are white." They laughed as he went on to explain that the southern freedom movement was generally misunderstood as being a black concern.

"Why have we forgotten the white man and his poverty?" Shirah asked. "Where is the movement that will help him handle his frustrations and help him to see that the goals of the white man are the same as those of the Negro? . . .Where is the movement that will say to us whites that we are slaves to fear, to hate, to guilt, and to an inferiority complex that the Negro has overcome. . . .We must catch up with him."[19]

There were more disenfranchised whites than blacks in the South, Shirah said, and more unemployed and uneducated whites than blacks in the nation. He asked the Friends of SCEF to take a step toward changing that by supporting the striking Hazard coal miners.

"Help us help the white poor before right wing groups get to them," he said. "We need your assistance in building an alliance of poor whites and poor blacks."[20]

As long as southern whites who want to end segregation are afraid to express their dissension, they are not free either, he said. The Friends of SCEF opened their hearts and their wallets to the charismatic young crusader.

In mid-February Shirah finally scheduled an Appalachian project steering committee meeting at the Highlander Folk School, then located in Knoxville. For years Highlander had hosted seminars for white unionists and civil rights activists. Myles Horton, Highlander's director, had agreed to train volunteers to work with the Kentucky miners. His school was one of the few places in the South where blacks and whites could meet together. Horton and Anne and Carl Braden were Shirah's senior advisors for the Appalachian project, and he'd recruited several Hazard miners and SDS field staff to attend the meeting.

Unfortunately, he also brought Jake Rosen, a white former City College of New York student and current Atlanta organizer for the Progressive Labor Party (PLP). Rosen lived in the same Atlanta housing project as Shirah and Danny Lyon, and they had become friends.[21]

The steering committee's task was to prepare a report of SNCC's program goals for a student/miner conference on poverty and unemployment to be held in Hazard on March 23. The conference was cosponsored by the National Committee for Miners and SDS. By this time the unemployed Hazard miners had established a "roving picket" movement attempting to organize small nonunion mines. Shirah wanted to send in southern white volunteers to join them in their fight and to establish a strong SNCC presence.

As the meeting began, Rosen, whom SNCC staffer Nelson Blackstock described as "a charming young '50's gangster type complete with pompadoured hair," became disruptive. When he encouraged the miners to arm themselves for guerilla warfare, Horton asked him to leave. Shirah, however, insisted that he stay. Horton ultimately refused to continue, and Shirah left with Rosen.

Each cooperating organization had been asked to make a presentation at the SDS conference on March 23. Since Shirah had not gotten his committee's input, his report was high on enthusiasm and low on specifics, and he was criticized. To make matters worse, Rosen followed him to Hazard, passed out PLP literature, and continued to encourage the miners to revolt. Rumors spread quickly that he was armed. When Shirah and Rosen returned to their room during a lunch break they found their bags packed and waiting for them on the sidewalk.

Before the weekend ended the *Hazard Herald* ran a story under the banner "Communism Comes to Kentucky" about communists infiltrating the miners' strike. The *Herald* accused communists (without specifically mentioning Rosen) of manipulating the striking miners to overthrow the government.

James Forman was livid. When Shirah returned to Atlanta Forman upbraided him for taking Rosen to Kentucky. SNCC was generally supportive of staff members and associates regardless of their political affiliations, but Rosen was advocating armed revolution. Publicity like that could push SNCC right into the arms of HUAC and permanently taint the organization as SCEF had been tainted.

"How would SNCC raise needed funds if word got out that it knowingly harbored communist revolutionaries?" Forman asked.

Shirah defended his political blunder by casting it as a philosophical issue.

"Isn't the movement about free association?" he retorted. "Isn't that what democracy is supposed to be about? Rosen's got lots of labor experience and he's a friend of mine. Don't give me any shit about Communists or Trotskyites and don't tell me who I can associate with."[22]

Many times he'd heard Anne Braden say that any white person in the South who worked against segregation was going to be labeled a communist. If you refused to work with them then who *was left* to work with?[23] When Shirah felt he was right he would not back down.

He was clearly becoming a problem for Forman. Shirah could generate enthusiasm and build community like nobody else, but he was disorganized, sometimes to the point of being self-destructive, and his lack of political savvy threatened to mire SNCC in unproductive controversy. In the end, SNCC would play only a minor role in the Hazard project, and Shirah was sent back to the campuses to recruit for the Mississippi summer project.

Early in April he packed a bag and joined Ed Hamlett for a tour of Alabama, Florida, and Georgia. Hamlett recalled that Shirah was agitated and restless during their trip. His moods swung wildly from enthusiasm to depression.

"Sam could go without sleep for days traveling from campus to campus nearly nonstop," Hamlett said, "but he could also become seriously depressed, and during those times he'd withdraw completely." Hamlett, who later trained as a psychiatric nurse, thought he recognized symptoms of manic-depressive illness in Shirah's behavior when he was under pressure.[24]

Shirah and Hamlett ended their trip in Nashville by working with a task force from Vanderbilt, Scarritt, and Peabody to plan a regional white southern activist conference that the Nashville group had requested back in September. Ed Hamlett was anxious for them to take a leading role in the Mississippi summer "White Folks Project." While Shirah returned to Atlanta, Hamlett stayed on in Nashville.

COFO's Mississippi summer project recruitment brochure was released late in April, and it included a capsule description of the "White Community Project," written by Scarritt's Sue Thrasher: "The effort to organize and educate Mississippi whites in the direction of democracy and decency can no longer be delayed. About thirty students, Southern whites who have recently joined the civil rights movement, will begin pilot projects in white communities. An attempt will be made to organize poor white areas to make steps toward eliminating bigotry, poverty, and ignorance."

The response was so overwhelming that the Nashville students appealed to both SNCC and SCEF to fund a white southern activist conference *before* Mississippi summer, and SNCC's executive council granted Hamlett nine hundred dollars. With assistance (and additional funding) from senior advisors Anne and Carl Braden, and with a steering committee consisting of Myles Horton, Ella Baker (a black founding advisor to SNCC), and Jane Stembridge (a white SNCC cofounder), Hamlett and Shirah got to work.

White Shadow of SNCC

Vows begin when hope dies.
—Leonardo da Vinci

"Many [of us] who came to the movement with a paternalistic and missionary attitude have advanced far beyond that stage, but most have still not found a place or a meaningful role," said Ed Hamlett, struggling to articulate the problem of white isolation in the freedom movement to the forty-five white southern student delegates who had assembled in Nashville on Easter weekend in 1964. The solution, he said, was to double SNCC's efforts to build a national interracial coalition for fair housing, full employment, and economic reform.

"Do you have the courage and vision that it takes to make a revolution?" he challenged them, closing with Norman Mailer's charge that "[w]e gave away our freedom a long time ago. We gave it away in all the revolutions we did not make, and in all the acts of courage we found a way to avoid."[1] With those words the Southern Student Coordinating Committee (SSOC) was launched on April 3, 1964.

James Forman, Marion Barry, and John Lewis attended the conference to confirm SNCC's support. Shirah was also present, but he kept an uncharacteristically low profile. He had not attended another conference planning session after the first steering committee meeting. This conference was clearly Ed Hamlett's.

The question of SSOC's relationship to SNCC arose almost immediately. Would SSOC be a SNCC project under black leadership or a white spin-off? The delegates were quickly moving toward the latter, but Shirah, Jim Forman, and Anne Braden argued against division. A separate white organization sounded too much like segregation to them.

Braden recommended that SSOC focus on the special needs of SNCC's white staff. "You're just avoiding the problem of racism if you split," she said.[2] Shirah argued that the responsibility for bringing the civil rights movement to white campuses should remain with SNCC.

By the end of the weekend, however, John Lewis was calling SSOC "a white shadow of SNCC" and said that it was one more indication of brewing racial tension.[3]

Two weeks later Robb Burlage, coauthor of the SDS Port Huron Statement, drafted SSOC's mission statement. "We, as young Southerners," he wrote, "hereby pledge to take our stand now together to work for a new order, a new South, a place which embodies our ideals for all the world to emulate, not ridicule. We find our destiny as individuals in the South in our hopes and our work together as brothers."

Claude Weaver, a black artist from Harvard who was on the SNCC staff, designed a coat of arms using as his model a photograph of white activist Archie Allen and John Lewis shaking hands in front of a confederate flag. Shirah liked the image, believing that it effectively represented their goal—to make war on poverty and racism in the South.[4]

"We have to reclaim the symbols of the Old South and use them in a new context," he explained. But others argued that using the rebel flag was offensive. Raising the battle flag claimed by white people who'd sought to keep blacks enslaved as a symbol of racial unity was questionable at best.

Shirah's enthusiasm for recycling the stars and bars suggests how conflicted he and many of the SSOC delegates were. While opposed to their ancestors' cause, they were proud to be descendants of such courageous fighters. Shirah insisted that there was no conflict between his determination to end the injustices of racism and his love of its perpetrators. He believed that the mission of SNCC's white arm, which he called the "White Folks Project," was to liberate white southerners, not to defeat them.

While verbalizing a connectedness with SNCC, SSOC continued to meet and behave as if it were a separate organization. Many southern white activists whose voices were no longer welcome in SNCC shifted their energies to the new committee. In May 1964 SSOC began publishing *The New Rebel* (later called *The New South Student*). Editor Sue Thrasher wrote of their mission: "The populist movement and the labor movement both failed to resolve the issue of race. It is the responsibility of the freedom movement, before the threat of the movement to the white poor further increases, to include them in our efforts."

No specifics were offered.

The Mississippi Freedom Democratic Party

A major objective of SNCC's 1964 Mississippi summer project was to support an insurgent party that would challenge Mississippi's regular Democratic Party for seating at the 1964 Democratic National Convention.[5] The regular Democrats excluded blacks.

During the winter of 1963 and spring of 1964, the Mississippi Freedom Democratic Party (MFDP) had filed the necessary papers for precinct, county, and state party conventions and had been barred at every level. This gave them a legal basis for a challenge. SNCC planned to register black voters and white voters with the MFDP, who would ultimately choose their own delegates to the national convention in August.

White Folks Project volunteers under the direction of SNCC would be assigned to register voters in the poor white communities of Biloxi and Jackson.

Shirah did not attend any of the project orientation sessions at either Western College for Women in Oxford, Ohio, or at the Highlander Center in Knoxville. He'd returned to Atlanta suffering through a period of despondency so severe that Bob Zellner, who was training recruits at Western, urged him to come north and speak with Harvard psychologist Dr. Robert Coles, who was working with the volunteers. Shirah refused.

Shirah's friend and white SNCC colleague Nelson Blackstock attributes Shirah's depression to the realization that, with the establishment of SSOC and the failure of the Hazard project, Shirah had lost both a campus and a community basis on which to build a permanent white folks project within SNCC.[6] His dream of expanding white campus recruitment into white community activism (using SNCC's model of moving from black campus organizing to community organizing) seemed doomed.

He had dropped the ball himself in Hazard, and now Ed Hamlett was running with white southern recruits to form a new organization. While he hadn't proved himself much of a leader, Shirah remained convinced that poor whites and southern blacks were natural allies. If their efforts to liberate themselves were kept separate, each group would remain weak. It behooved powerful forces who wanted to maintain the status quo to keep them separated. He believed that SNCC and SSOC, with all their talk about separatism, were actually playing into the hands of those forces.

Yes, racism flourished everywhere, but only the white South had turned it into an ideology. Without the movement, poor whites would continue to fight for segregation to their own detriment.

While Shirah was in Atlanta, SDS leaders Tom Hayden, Al Haber, and Todd Gitlin arrived at SNCC's Raymond Street headquarters. They were working on a community organizing project in Newark, New Jersey, and were looking for assistance.

At the SNCC office Hayden picked up on the staff's tensions, specifically the signs of racial animosity, and he asked Shirah, "What's really up with SNCC?"

"SNCC is a sinking ship," Shirah said, and flashed an ironic smile.

"That's profound, man," Hayden said.

"Yeah," Shirah mumbled and winked at Jane Stembridge, who had just returned to Atlanta from Greenwood, Mississippi. The petite blue-eyed North Carolinian was one of the first white SNCC volunteers.

"What was *that* about?" she asked Shirah when Hayden left.

"*Profound*. Profound, my ass," Shirah laughed. "We're all on an ego trip. There isn't a damn thing profound about any of it."

"Sam and I were in the struggle for emotional reasons," Stembridge explained, "and because of what we'd seen and experienced. We were committed pacifists. He had no patience with the rhetoric and moralistic mumbo jumbo of SDS."[7]

Freedom Summer

The cities of the South shall be shut up. . . .
Lift up your eyes and behold them that come from the North. . . .
—THE BOOK OF JEREMIAH

When her last class of the spring semester ended at the University of Illinois in Champlain, Elizabeth Khrone, a junior, packed her red Studebaker Lark, picked up her best friend, Carol Stevens, and headed for Jackson, Mississippi. Short and blonde, with a round angelic face and intense blue eyes, Liz was going to volunteer with SNCC's white student summer project. She'd met campus traveler Sam Shirah four months earlier at an SDS rally in Chicago where SNCC field secretary Casey Hayden was the featured speaker.[1]

"How y'all doin?" Shirah had asked the group. He introduced himself as "the man from L.A."—lower Alabama—and winked at Liz. They'd been writing letters to each other ever since. In April Shirah asked her to come south for the summer. She hadn't needed much convincing.

To Liz, an English major raised in Elmhurst, Illinois (a Chicago suburb), Sam Shirah, with his heavy-lidded eyes, thick Alabama drawl, and long curly brown hair, cut an exotic figure. He was handsome, rugged, playful, and completely dedicated to racial justice.

Shirah seemed to combine the best qualities of the two men Liz most admired—he had the intelligence and warmth of her father, who was a reporter, and the fierceness of her grandfather, who was a preacher. Shirah sang like Johnny Cash, and his charisma could raise any meeting to the level of a revival.

His disdain for politics also appealed to Liz. She was active in the campus SDS chapter, and Shirah's commitment to nonviolence made every guy she'd ever dated seem shallow by comparison. When he asked her to meet him in Jackson, Mississippi, she couldn't wait to start packing.

Liz read in *Newsweek* that Jackson's mayor, Allen Thompson, had ordered a thirteen-thousand-pound armor-plated riot tank with a submachine gun mounted on it. He also had a fleet of trailer trucks waiting to haul the summer volunteers to the state fairgrounds if he ran out of room in his jails.

"We're going to be ready for them," Thompson said. "They won't have a chance."[2] FBI director J. Edgar Hoover did little to relieve the tension when he announced that "we most certainly do not and will not give protection to civil rights workers. The FBI is not a police organization. It is purely an investigative organization, and the protection of individual citizens, either natives of the state or coming into the state, is a matter for the local authorities."[3]

Even though Liz and Carol had missed the Mississippi summer project orientation in Oxford, Ohio, Shirah told them they could manage with on-the-job training.

For three days the young women drove through flat countryside, past steamy cotton fields with hot wind blowing in their faces. Highway 61's two-lane monotony was broken only by crumbling shacks and weatherworn barns. They drove straight to Jackson's COFO headquarters at the ominous address of 1017 Lynch Street, where many other northern volunteers had also gathered.

Liz and Carol were assigned a room in a freedom house near the campus of Jackson State College, a black school, and were trained to protect themselves by lying in a fetal position and covering their heads with their arms. They quickly learned how to explain the significance of the Mississippi Freedom Democratic Party and how to register voters on freedom forms.

Using role-play they practiced approaching local people. Simply asking blacks to talk about voter registration was inviting them to risk their homes, their jobs, perhaps even their lives. Liz practiced inviting folks to come to a church meeting, to attend a voter registration class, or to go to the county clerk's office and ask for permission to register. If they were denied registration forms by the clerk, the volunteers would have to show them how to fill out affidavits which would be sent to the Justice Department's Civil Rights Division.

During the day local black churches served as freedom schools, where children were taught math, reading, music, art, and black history. In the evenings adults attended citizenship classes. Although Liz and Carol were encouraged to accept teaching assignments, Liz was determined to register voters.

The volunteers were cautioned never to travel alone and never to drive with whites and blacks in the same car after sunset. Their instructors, not much older than themselves, were SNCC and CORE staff members, black and white, mostly men, who were dressed in "bib overhauls," white T-shirts, and denim jackets.

Liz was surprised that there weren't more beatnik types among her fellow recruits, the kind that always seemed to get involved in the SDS demonstrations back on the Champlain campus. Most of the summer volunteers looked like members of the student council. The girls wore bright blouses and skirts or shorts, and the guys were in sport shirts. Some of the older ones were teachers, lawyers, psychiatrists, and social workers. They'd been trained in Ohio, and almost everybody was white.

Jackson, Mississippi, was also filled with men in business suits investigating the disappearance of three summer workers, Andrew Goodman, Michael Schwerner, and James Chaney. An FBI satellite office was scheduled to open in July, and Justice Department staff and reporters were everywhere, taking photos, asking questions, and making notes. Everyone was on edge. The week Liz and Carol arrived, a CORE field secretary was beaten in the Hinds County jail, a group of white volunteers were roughed up at the train station, and shots were fired into the black Henderson's Café near the COFO office.

After a day of canvassing and teaching, the volunteers would gather back at the office, and some would ruminate about their motives. One girl wondered if she was doing this thing for the wrong reason; a young man from California wanted to know if he was naive or neurotic. Many had been called impulsive, stubborn, uncompromising, or even spoiled by the folks back home. They'd been warned that they would instigate trouble in the South. A young man from Boston shrugged. Dissenters have always been called crazy, he assured them.

Sam Shirah arrived a few days after Liz and Carol. He'd been assigned to Biloxi to set up living arrangements for the volunteers and had to complete the job before he could pick Liz up. He was thinner than when she had seen him in the spring, and he appeared disheveled. Shirah spent most of his time in Jackson in the COFO office arguing with White Folks Project director Ed Hamlett. Liz kept busy helping out wherever she was needed.

Shirah and Hamlett agreed that their goal was to identify the issues that could be used to organize white southerners, but they disagreed about nearly everything else. Hamlett wanted to establish a school desegregation committee of middle-class Biloxi whites. Shirah argued that the involvement of poor whites was more critical.

Hamlett resented Shirah's eleventh-hour input. It felt like a repeat of the SSOC conference. Shirah had twice dumped organizing tasks into Hamlett's lap while Shirah retreated to Atlanta to lick his wounds.

With the project's target population still unresolved, Liz, Danny Lyon, and Lyon's girlfriend, Heidi Dole, piled into Liz's Studebaker and followed Shirah's VW bug to the Gulf Coast. (Lyon had accepted an assignment for Simon & Schuster to develop a photo essay entitled "The Movement." Playwright/activist Lorraine Hansberry would be providing the text.) They arrived in Biloxi just as the Civil Rights Act of 1964 became the law of the land.

Eighteen volunteers were assigned to Biloxi, a resort city often derided as "the Redneck Riviera." The city had a sizeable middle-class population, a flourishing tourist trade, and a large year-round population of working-class and poor whites. Blacks had periodically attempted to integrate the local beaches, and one such event had provoked a full-scale race riot four years earlier.

Point Cadet[4]

Tension continued to crackle between Hamlett, who remained convinced that the White Folks Project's best chance for success rested with Biloxi's white clergy, business, and professional leaders, and Shirah, who was adamant about developing grassroots leadership. The middle class would never commit, Shirah insisted, because they had too much to lose. He preferred to talk with the poor about what they had to gain.

Bruce Maxwell, a volunteer from Texas, agreed with Shirah. "The movement isn't encouraging poor [white] folks to fight for themselves," he said, "The less the movement does for them, the more they will be threatened by it."[5]

The only living accommodations Shirah had been able to book were at the once-grand Riviera Hotel, which overlooked Biloxi Bay. Shirah became friendly with the manager, Chris Maples, another amateur musician who leased him nine rooms on the third floor.

Robert Williams, a twenty-five-year-old Vietnam veteran who was honeymooning at the Riviera with his fifteen-year-old bride, Lois, also became Shirah's buddy. The tattoo-covered Williams had recently been released from prison, where he'd served a year for breaking a man's neck in a fight.

Williams became so friendly so fast that some of the volunteers wondered if he'd been planted by the Klan. Williams eventually confessed to Shirah that he *had* been sent to gather information, but that he'd become disgruntled with the Klan because it never seemed to accomplish anything. He told Shirah that if he could convince him that SNCC would help him more than the American Nazi Party, he'd register with the MFDP (instead of joining the ANP) and work to register other locals. Shirah did, and Williams became so dedicated that on August 6 when the state convention met in Jackson's Masonic Temple to choose its sixty-eight representatives to the 1964 Democratic National Convention Williams was selected to serve as one of only four white delegates.

Late in July, as Williams was registering voters among the oyster fishermen, a Biloxi policemen had bellowed, "What the hell do you think you are?"

"A goddamn Freedom Fighter!" Williams had bellowed back. Liz told Shirah, "Six more like him and Mississippi could be magnificent![6]

But Liz's optimism wasn't contagious. Many of the recruits away from home for the first time grumbled about the poor accommodations, the raging mosquitos, and the hostility of the townspeople.

Shirah complained to Hamlett that they were apathetic because they spent too much time strategizing and not enough time in the field. He tried, without success, to recruit more local leaders like Robert Williams to serve as role models.

When townspeople asked if the Mississippi Freedom Democratic Party was "that nigger party," Shirah instructed the volunteers to respond that MFDP was a party for people like themselves who weren't represented by the regular Democrats and that MFDP would work for jobs, decent schools, housing, and hospitals for both blacks and whites.

One older man, a self-identified Klansman, told a registration team that they were "damn fools."

"You don't understand Mississippi," he said. But as they left his front porch he called them back, picked a bouquet of roses from his garden, and gave it to one of the young women. "Good luck," he said. "But I still think you're crazy."[7]

Biloxi was only thirty-five miles from Grand Bay, Alabama, where Big Sam had been sent to the First Methodist Church with a substantial cut in pay. The Shirahs had been forced to vacate the Defuniak Springs parsonage so quickly that Sue had missed her high school graduation ceremony. Life was difficult for them in the summer of 1964. Shirah bought a secondhand motorcycle and made several trips to Grand Bay to see them. He and Liz sometimes brought Robert Williams, Nelson Blackstock, and other SNCC staff and volunteers home with them to swap stories with his father and enjoy his mother's cooking.

At the end of July, with Shirah and Hamlett still at odds about project goals, the dispirited White Folks Project volunteers met with Anne Braden and Myles Horton in nearby Gulfport to chart a course for the remainder of the summer.

"Why do we keep arguing this way?" Shirah asked in frustration. "What's more important, politics or people?"[8]

Some of the volunteers, however, considered *him* to be the problem. When they accused him of putting off middle-class whites because he looked like a beatnik he assured them it was no great loss. Clearly at an impasse, with neither Horton nor Braden able to bring the leaders to consensus, they agreed to form two task forces.

Shirah took nine volunteers, including Liz, Robert Williams, Bruce Maxwell, and Nelson Blackstock, to the Point Cadet district to concentrate on registering fisherman, day laborers, and taxi drivers, while Hamlett kept the rest downtown. Blackstock remembers that "Sam was always more of a visionary than a clear political thinker, but we got the feeling that he saw into things more deeply than the rest of us and that made us want to follow where he was headed."

By mid-August they'd registered twenty whites on MFDP freedom forms. They'd convinced some of the Point Cadet locals that joining forces with blacks could result in more jobs, better schools, stronger unions, and better health care. The South couldn't afford to maintain two separate sets of institutions, Shirah told them. If segregation continued, the poor of both races could look forward to second-rate services and broken-down equipment.

Trouble followed, however, when some oyster fishermen who had previously organized a union took an interest in MFDP. The corporate distributors who had broken their union began to exert renewed pressure.

In August rumors spread that the jobs and poverty programs that MFDP promised would all go to blacks. SNCC was a black organization, the agitators said, and the registration workers were funded by SNCC. The volunteers did not enhance their credibility when they displayed SNCC and COFO posters in the windows of the vacant store where the MFDP precinct meetings were held. The landlord told them that they would have to vacate the storefront, and finally even Chris Maples, the good-natured manager of the Riviera Hotel, evicted them. Since the summer was nearly over, many returned home, while others moved on to Jackson or Hattiesburg.

On August 20, Shirah and Liz waved goodbye to MFDP delegate Robert Williams and his wife, Lois, as they boarded the bus in Jackson for Atlantic City with high expectations. With the Civil Rights Act of 1964 the law of the land, the activists had real hope that local blacks could make the MFDP cause heard within the national Democratic Party.

The rules of the convention provided that a delegation could be challenged if it was not representative of the constituency it claimed. MFDP delegates planned to show the Democratic Party's Credentials Committee that the white Democratic Party regulars not only excluded blacks, but opposed much of President Johnson's domestic policy. Many openly supported Sen. Barry Goldwater's Republican candidacy.[9]

On August 22, 1964, the MFDP presented its case. While the Credentials Committee refused to seat them, it offered a compromise providing two at-large seats, "guest seats" for the rest of the delegation, and a promise that the 1968 convention would bar any delegation that discriminated against blacks.

The MFDP delegates refused the compromise since it would have required them to stand with the Democratic regulars, whose platform stated, "We oppose, condemn and deplore the Civil Rights Act of 1964. We believe in the separation of the races in all phases of our society."[10] It would mean conciliation to the forces that had murdered Goodman, Chaney, and Schwerner.

SNCC staffer Jean Smith later said, "In our hearts we knew our flawless arguments would fall on deaf ears . . . no group of white people was going to send some of its own packing in order to make room for us."[11]

Weighed in the Balances . . .

Evaluations of the White Folks Project differ, but most participants agreed that organizing poor whites proved much more difficult than organizing poor blacks. Bruce Maxwell, who remained in Mississippi after Freedom Summer, noted that poor blacks, despite their misery, had "a certain spirit" that he never found among poor whites. Blacks tended to develop a collective comradery which sustained hope, while whites seemed more suspicious of outsiders and more interested in lining up behind dema- gogues like George Wallace and Ross Barnett. They had to be reassured again and again that federal help for blacks would not harm their own chances of getting out of poverty.[12]

There were no institutions in poor white communities to parallel the black churches or grassroots leaders to match the black preachers who often headed local movements. White Christian fundamentalism in fact hindered interracial organizing. Some white Christians refused to join forces with black people, whom they believed God had cursed.

Shirah maintained, however, that the White Folks Project had demon- strated that working one-on-one in white communities permitted organiz- ers to get past the "mob mentalities" that threatened civil rights workers in other Mississippi cities. There was no violence in Biloxi, and school integration proceeded peacefully in August.[13]

Robb Burlage, a white southerner, cautioned that whites seldom orga- nized along racial lines except when they wanted to suppress other groups. They seemed to prefer protesting an issue over rallying in support of one. "We who want a democratic South," he said, "must organize white people not as white people but around their problems, and we must encourage them to see that they will never solve those problems until they can unite with black people."[14] Burlage believed that when whites and blacks orga- nized independently hostility always resulted. He strongly recommended that integration be resurrected as a central movement goal.[15]

At a 1989 Mississippi memorial service for Goodman, Schwerner, and Chaney, Georgia congressman John Lewis noted that, in retrospect, "we made a serious mistake when the Movement turned against its first princi- ple: integration. The seeds that were planted twenty years ago have borne very bitter fruit."[16]

Waveland, Mississippi

The strain of Freedom Summer and the bitterness of the Democratic National Convention threw the SNCC staff into crisis. The national press assailed MFDP's shortsightedness in rejecting the Democratic Party's compromise and called the Mississippi summer project "a camp for the privileged."

While summer project volunteers had established forty-one freedom schools serving two thousand students at twenty locations, seventeen churches had also been burned, two hundred fifty people arrested and countless beaten, and three volunteers had lost their lives.

While Mississippi NAACP president Aaron Henry (an MFDP delegate) said that the summer project's greatest contribution was showing blacks that some white people were interested in their problems, Bayard Rustin, angered by the intransigence of the MFDP delegates (who, he believed, should have moved beyond protesting to coalition building), congratulated them for "snatching defeat from the jaws of victory."[17]

Shirah and the Mississippi staff suffered the same criticism that had been applied to Bill Moore—that they were not realistic, but were "pitifully naive pilgrims" who didn't understand the political process and preferred martyrdom to compromise.

Fatigue, disappointment, and internal tensions threatened to overwhelm them. When the Mississippi staff gathered in Hattiesburg to evaluate the summer effort, they found themselves polarized around the same three issues which had been dividing them for over a year: the rejection of nonviolent protest, internal racial conflict, and disorganization.

A pattern of grouping, regrouping, and separating was tearing at the fabric of the organization. At times it manifested itself as black vs. white, at other times as white vs. white, and sometimes even as black vs. black.

Shirah was afraid that SNCC's executive committee would use the Hazard and Biloxi failures to justify scrapping the white southern student project. Agitated and unable to sleep, he was living on Jim Beam whiskey and peanut butter sandwiches. "I'm immobilized," he told Nelson Blackstock.

Personal problems also plagued him. He and Liz, who had worked so well together, had parted badly. He loved her in his way, but she had made the mistake of falling in love with him. When she told him that she was pregnant, he assured her that marriage was out of the question. In addition to his unwillingness to settle down, Shirah could barely support himself on his $9.64 weekly SNCC paycheck. But Liz refused to consider abortion and would not go back to Chicago.

She moved to Louisville, Kentucky, in early September and stayed with the Braden family. She'd met Anne Braden during the White Folks Project retreat in Gulfport, and Braden had offered her a job writing for the *Southern Patriot*.

Shirah visited a few times, but he could not shake her determination to have his baby with or without help. Jane Stembridge was also writing for the *Patriot* in Louisville that fall. She'd decided to take a hiatus from the movement and was heading to New Orleans, where many of the white SNCC staff were gathering. Shirah impulsively decided to go with her. Danny Lyon, who'd already left SNCC, was working there on a photo essay about the Free Southern Theater, the only integrated touring company in the South. New Orleans was one of the few southern cities where blacks and whites could associate freely.

White SNCC staffers Casey Hayden, Mendy Samstein, and Mary King all found their way to New Orleans in the fall of 1964. All except Samstein were white southerners, and all had become disheartened. Their constant fear of arrest and the strain of incessant danger, violence, and death in Mississippi had left them physically and mentally exhausted. Stembridge had written of the Delta that "the hatred is everywhere and there is no escape."[18]

Their futures with SNCC were also uncertain. Hayden had been harshly criticized for leaving Jackson at the end of the summer without authorization. She was sharing an apartment with Mary King, who had worked with Shirah in Danville. Both were learning photography and filmmaking skills from Matt Heron, who'd covered the Mississippi summer project for *Black Star*. They were struggling to figure out where to go and what to do if they were cut from SNCC.

Stembridge rented a big sunny apartment at 8740 Rue Royale Street, and Shirah moved in with her. Her father, like his (and Mary King's), was a white southern liberal clergyman, and Stembridge shared Shirah's moral fervor, disdain for politics, and sense of southern guilt. She'd written to a friend explaining that she'd joined the freedom movement "because I too needed to be free, respected, a person understood. Being white does not answer your problems, being able to go anywhere does not end your needs."[19]

Stembridge found a position as a waitress at a coffeehouse, and Shirah took odd jobs to help cover the rent. Their furnishings consisted of one large mattress and a coffee pot. They shared a deep love of music, especially gospel and country music, and often sang together.

Stembridge recalled that Shirah spent a lot of time drinking in the French Quarter bars. He'd decided that he was going to leave SNCC, but he wasn't sure what he would do with the rest of his life. "Sam was confused, lonely, and feeling very guilty," she said. "Some nights he'd just lay in my arms and cry."[20]

Shirah felt guilty about Liz and the baby, about his contribution to his father's shattered career, and about the failure of the White Folks Project. The old feeling of being on the right side of things which had sustained him during the Freedom Walk and through the Gadsden and Danville movements was gone.

Stembridge remembers that Shirah fell in love impulsively and intensely, like a soldier in wartime, and he had a number of affairs that summer.

Stembridge, a lesbian who'd never hidden her sexual preference, was comfortable living with him until he fell in love with her. Shirah asked Stembridge to marry him, and when she explained that she was exclusively attracted to women he assured her that it did not matter. They were soul mates, he said. No one would ever understand them the way they understood each other. They could marry, he explained, and keep seeing other people, but theirs would be a lasting bond.

Stembridge assured him that, although she loved him dearly, marriage was out of the question. Almost forty years later she remembers him as a playful spirit who was a lot like Bill Clinton—a good ole boy and a brilliant bad boy, whose restlessness, charm, and love of music drew people to him.

Shirah continued to drink and use drugs heavily and by September had contracted hepatitis. Big Sam drove from Grand Bay, Alabama, to pick him up and take him home.

The minister's disappointment was difficult to conceal. Big Sam neither smoked nor drank. While his religious faith had always sustained him, he was at a loss as to how to comfort his older son, who seemed to be sinking deeper and deeper into despair. Big Sam was also concerned about Liz, who was still living with and working for Anne Braden while awaiting the birth of his grandchild.

Shirah hadn't changed his mind about settling down with Liz, but during his recuperation his parents began pressuring him to get married. Big Sam told him that the very least he could do was be with Liz when his baby came.

In November Shirah pulled himself together to attend a SNCC staff retreat at the Gulfside Methodist Church in Waveland, Mississippi. While he still planned to resign, he felt obligated to attend the retreat to demonstrate his gratitude for being maintained on the payroll without an assignment for two months.

Shirah went back to New Orleans on his motorcycle, picked up Danny Lyon and his camera equipment, and drove on to Waveland.

The SNCC staff spent three days discussing their future in the small Gulf Coast town. With its decentralized structure SNCC no longer seemed capable of managing the political party and network of freedom schools and community centers that the summer project had spawned. SNCC had grown too big too quickly. Eighty-five staff members were hired over the summer, and many of the white volunteers refused to go home. To make matters worse, the Mississippi Freedom Democratic Party, after refusing the convention compromise, had decided to support the Johnson/Humphrey ticket anyway.

James Forman favored restructuring to create a more centralized organization focused on political activism, while Bob Moses sympathized with the overwhelmingly white faction of community organizers who rejected hierarchal structure.

Stokely Carmichael disparaged this group as ineffective "floaters," high on freedom, "Goin' where the spirit say go, and doin' what the spirit say do."

Shirah had functioned as a floater for his entire SNCC career. Forman had used him and Zellner in a variety of capacities because they understood the southern white code. He'd sent them to Gadsden and Danville to assess the nature of the resistence, to encourage potential white support, and to let blacks know that there were native southern whites willing to help.

Now Carmichael argued that those functions were no longer of any value. He maintained that SNCC had to concentrate on building strong political power bases and that white field secretaries hindered that process.

The debate kept breaking down as the "structure people" (hardliners) refused to talk about program until the question of structure was resolved, and the "program people" (floaters) refused to talk about structure until a program direction could be agreed on. Little was resolved.

The Waveland stalemate had ramifications in the field. Mississippi's freedom schools and community centers began to close. Within a year Bob Moses would resign, Stokely Carmichael would replace John Lewis as chair, and Ruby Doris Smith would succeed James Forman as executive secretary. The hardliners would prevail, and all the floaters would eventually be expelled.

Moving On

I have been ecstatic; but I have not been happy.
—EDNA ST. VINCENT MILLAY

Sam Shirah resigned from SNCC in December 1964. As the organization continued to move toward black exclusiveness, the executive council voted to discontinue the white southern student project, and all white community organizing programs defaulted to SSOC.

Although the council insisted that its goal was to encourage local blacks to build their own movement independent of whites, Shirah accused them of lumping working-class whites together with the white liberals who'd betrayed them in Atlantic City. Refusing to deal with individuals was racist, he argued. He reminded Jim Forman that SCEF had funded the white southern student project and that it could therefore continue without cost to SNCC. Forman contended that it had become redundant with the establishment of SSOC.

When Shirah proposed retaining a white presence in SNCC and using the SCEF funds to ease racial tensions within the organization, the council refused to support him. Ironically, it was just the kind of difficult work that SNCC had once asked the nation to undertake.

In the end Shirah accepted the need to separate. He'd grown frustrated by white southerners who could never seem to understand how segregation hurt them, and now, in 1965, SNCC's black nationalists were asking how working with poor whites could help them gain political clout. Neither side saw any value in coalition. Each was a millstone around the other's neck. Shirah felt like he'd come full circle, only to arrive at the place he'd joined SNCC to escape. He was not alone in his despair.

An exhausted black field secretary explained, "[Love] doesn't work. . . . I spent years loving the shit out of people, and nothing changed. The same people run things."[1]

Separation from SNCC was especially disorienting for whites who identified with blacks but unlike Shirah felt no affinity with southern whites. A white field secretary with four years in the movement reflected, "I never thought the day would come when I would begin to question the value of integration; but blacks in the movement talk more and more about pulling away from all contact with whites and building what life they can for themselves. It seems as if we're back where it all started, each of us keeping away from the other race. I don't know what more to say. Some things are too hard to put into words."[2]

Alcohol and drug use increased among the "floaters" as SNCC left them behind. For several years they'd worked in an underground resistance movement in Mississippi, Alabama, and Georgia. They'd tested and defied southern laws, and many faced the future with prison records. Liquor and narcotics had been used to blunt anxiety and fear, and some field workers had gotten hooked. Shirah was using peyote, amphetamines, and marijuana along with increasing quantities of bourbon to medicate his depression.

Negrophilia

The Southern Conference Education Fund had been founded in 1947 as an interracial effort to defeat segregation. By 1964 it was the major white southern voice for interracial coalition building. The Southern Student Organizing Committee, SCEF's heir apparent, had evolved in response to SNCC's increased focus on black nationalism.

SNCC's northern whites, however, never considered either SCEF or SSOC a full partner in the movement. The idea of working with poor southern whites (whom they defined as oppressors) did not interest them. Therefore, many white SNCC activists bypassed SSOC and transferred their political support to SDS, which was an organization of predominantly northern whites.

At the same time SSOC strengthened its fraternal ties with SDS, and in 1965 Ed Hamlett accepted a seat on the national council.

Shirah continued his association with SSOC, but cautioned against any full-fledged merger with SDS. He reminded Hamlett that SSOC had been founded as a white *southern* reform movement.

Tom Hayden, Al Haber, and Todd Gitlin were neo-Marxists, while Shirah continued to believe that SNCC's mission to abolish racism was compatible with the American protest tradition. He considered himself a pacifist and a social reformer, while their goal was to build an alternative society, violently if necessary. He bitterly resented their reference to all white southerners as "seggies" or "crackers."

SDS activists maintained that black culture was less hypocritical than white culture. Some field staff actually began to copy black diction and mannerisms to rid themselves of their white identity. Shirah considered that arrogant and condescending. Only the poor had virtue, they seemed to be saying. Only the poor and those, like themselves, who recognized virtue.[3] His advice was "You can't be black, so don't try."[4]

Writer Debbie Louis, who *is* black, would later identify this phenomenon as *Negrophilia*: the belief that black culture held all the answers for a totally bankrupt white culture.[5]

Ain't Made For Stoppin'

In December 1964 Shirah volunteered for SCEF's Southern Mountain Project in Kentucky. With the cooperation of SSOC, SDS, the SCLC, and District 65 of the Retail, Wholesale, and Distribution Workers Union, SCEF had formed an Appalachian Economic and Political Action Conference (AEPAC) and was sending volunteers into Pike County to organize against strip mining, to advise unemployed mountain people of their federal entitlements, and to assist them in accessing their benefits.

Coal company officials accused the interracial work teams of "stirring up the poor," and many SCEF volunteers were arrested for vagrancy. Local people who cooperated with them were also threatened by the police. Shirah was arrested several times.

Anne and Carl Braden hoped to link the unemployed white Appalachian miners with the black freedom struggle and to pilot an integrated poor people's movement which could be replicated in Mississippi and Alabama. This was very similar to the program Shirah had once hoped to lead. Overly optimistic about passage of the 1965 Appalachian Redevelopment Act, the Bradens perhaps organized too quickly. Within a year the Southern Mountain Project began sinking from the weight of internal disputes, inadequate funding, and an inexperienced staff.[6] The following year the Bradens and their remaining volunteers would be arrested and charged with conspiracy to overthrow the governments of Pike County and the state of Kentucky.

In February 1965, Shirah left Pike County on his motorcycle and arrived in Louisville one day after the birth of his daughter, Lisa Anne Shirah (Li for Liz, Sa for Sam, and Anne for Anne Braden). Lisa Anne had been premature and her difficult delivery left Liz very weak. Mr. and Mrs. Khrone, who were at the hospital, were anxious to hear about wedding plans. Shirah finally told Liz that Big Sam had made him an offer he couldn't refuse.

"Said he'd come up here and marry us for nothing, what do you think about that?"[7] It was as close to a proposal as he could manage. At first Liz refused, reminding him that she'd been taking care of herself since the summer. Ultimately, however, he convinced her of his sincerity. She still loved him, and, while he wasn't happy about settling down, he'd fallen in love with his daughter, Lisa.

Anne Braden was due back in Pike County on their wedding day, and, when she told Shirah she wouldn't be able to make the ceremony, the very nervous young man confided that he wasn't at all sure he'd get there himself.[8] But Big Sam married Liz and Sam, Jr., in the hospital chapel on February 26, 1965. After the wedding Shirah decided not to return to the Southern Mountain Project, and he took Liz and Lisa to the Grand Bay parsonage, where Liz recuperated.

It didn't take Shirah long to grow restless in Grand Bay. In May he, Liz, and Lisa returned to Louisville so that Liz could resume writing for the *Southern Patriot*. They moved back in with Anne and Carl Braden.

Bob Dylan summed up the feelings of many burned-out activists in the fall of 1965 when he told *Newsweek* magazine that he was withdrawing from politics. "Songs can't save the world," he said. "When you don't like something you gotta learn to just not need that something. . . . I'm not pessimistic. I don't think things can turn out, that's all, and I've accepted it. It doesn't matter to me. It's not pessimism, just a sort of sadness, sort of like not having no hope."[9]

While Shirah agreed in theory, it was impossible for him to "just not need" things. Marriage and family were separating him from everything he thought he needed most—friends and freedom. Home life was confining, and he knew that he could not be faithful to Liz. He escaped by spending increasing amounts of time away from her and the baby and by using drugs. When Anne Braden caught him smoking marijuana in her home she told him that they'd have to leave.

"I'm willing to go to jail for your freedom," she said, "but not for your right to smoke that stuff."[10]

In August 1966 the restless Shirah attended a labor organizing seminar at the Highlander School. He knew that labor unions were recruiting movement activists because of their community-organizing skills. At Highlander he met a representative from the Amalgamated Meat Cutters Union and applied for a project assignment to help organize a textile mill in Statesville, North Carolina. He was hired, and he and Liz rented a small home outside the manufacturing town sixty miles north of Charlotte. Two months later he returned to Highlander for an advanced labor seminar and reconnected with Casey Hayden, who'd been organizing a women's welfare recipients union for SDS in Chicago, and Mendy Samstein, who'd completed a Teamsters assignment in St. Louis.

Sympathetic to his old friends who were "between things," Shirah impulsively invited them to North Carolina to stay with his family. He gladly stretched his limited finances to include two more adults.

The three SNCC veterans spent their evenings drawing up plans for an interracial movement of the poor which they called the Southern Organizing Committee. Hayden and Samstein had become disillusioned with labor movement politics and were trying to determine how labor organizing could more directly benefit the poor.[11]

Shirah maintained that the labor movement could only be reformed from the inside, and that the Southern Organizing Committee would have a better chance for success if it found some issue besides labor to organize around. Experience had taught him that it was virtually impossible to compete with established unions for southern workers and fight white resistence to integration at the same time.[12] But Hayden and Samstein didn't agree. For three weeks they argued, and it felt very much like the old SNCC days.

When the much-ignored Liz discovered that she was pregnant, she told Shirah that the strain of providing for their guests was too much. In late December, Hayden and Samstein left for New York City to look for work. Plans for the Southern Organizing Committee were indefinitely placed on hold.

Shirah loved Statesville, North Carolina. It was near Union Grove, headquarters of the Old Time Fiddlers and Bluegrass Convention, and he spent a lot of time with the local musicians. In his jeans, boots, and flannel shirts with the sleeves rolled up, he looked like a working man, and his loud, hard-drinking lifestyle gave him credibility with the plant workers. He also achieved financial stability for the first time in his life and was able to afford a mortgage on the home he and Liz had been renting. It was as close to domestic bliss as they would come. Three months later, after weeks of feeling ill, he was told by a local doctor that one of his kidneys had stopped functioning. It was the result of the injuries he'd suffered from the beatings in Danville.

One-third of Shirah's damaged kidney had to be removed, and he required a long period of recuperation. Since he'd accepted the organizing job on a project basis, he was not entitled to benefits or sick leave pay. Ultimately he was unable to meet his mortgage payments and lost his home.

When he was able to work again, Shirah took a Greyhound bus to Atlanta and applied for a position with the International Ladies Garment Workers Union (ILGWU). Martin Morand, Atlanta's ILGWU regional director, met him at the station. When Morand asked where his bags were, Shirah pulled out a toothbrush and grinned.

Morand hired him on the spot, and Shirah moved Liz and his two daughters to the city that had once been the center of his life. He quickly demonstrated his worth as an organizer when he traveled with Morand to Hartsville, Tennessee, to intervene in a wildcat strike.

The Hartsville plant manager had accused several workers of stealing, but the shop steward charged management with framing the union members. Shirah had known John Sigenthaler, editor of the *Nashville Tennessean*, when he had worked as an aide to Attorney General Robert Kennedy. He asked the editor to assign a photographer to try to obtain irrefutable proof of who was stealing. The photographs proved embarrassing to management and brought everyone to the bargaining table. Violence was avoided, and the strike was ultimately settled.

Shirah always shone in volatile situations. The day-to-day work of contract management, however, held little fascination for him. Unions are organizations of compromise, and Shirah always preferred the role of crusader. He'd led an unstructured life as a SNCC floater and on his return to Atlanta resumed some bad habits. He began sitting up all night with friends, playing his guitar and singing, then found it difficult to keep regular daytime hours.

Blue Ridge

Just as Shirah was growing bored with the ILGWU, a wildcat strike at a Levi Strauss plant in Blue Ridge, Georgia, captured his attention. A year before, the all-female piece-worker staff had contacted the ILGWU to request representation.

Their first contract was a sweetheart arrangement in which management was required to sign off on all grievances.

"It was a joke," shop steward Darlene Davis said.[13]

Blue Ridge employees were forbidden to speak with each other during working hours and were not paid for sick time without a doctor's note. The last straw came when management violated the contract's seniority clause and hired new workers at a piece rate above the union wage.

Four hundred fifty women walked off their jobs on August 10, 1966, and began around-the-clock picketing.[14] When Levi Strauss charged the union with conspiracy to deprive the corporation of profits, the ILGWU declared the strike action illegal. Shirah and his fellow organizers were ordered to stay away from the picket lines.

Levi Strauss recruited 290 scabs (many of whom were previously fired piece workers) to replace the strikers, and several women on the picket lines were beaten up.[15]

"Why do the colored people in any part of the country have more rights and get treated better than we do at Levi?" one of the strikers asked reporters. "All we ask," she said, "is to be treated as well as the colored people."[16] Shirah's knee-jerk response was to throw himself back into organizing poor whites.

He drove to Fannon County on his motorcycle and assisted an SDS group planning a national boycott of Levi's jeans. He also got the Atlanta SSOC chapter involved. SSOC's Harlan Joye worked with Shirah to establish the Southern Labor Action Movement, or SLAM, a special unit of SSOC assigned to the Blue Ridge strikers. When SSOC's executive committee refused to fund SLAM, Shirah argued that labor organizing was the kind of work students *ought* to be doing. He and Joye developed a strong following on the Atlanta campuses.

On August 12, 1967, Shirah led thirty students and the husbands, brothers, and boyfriends of the strikers as they pulled off their Levi's in Atlanta's Piedmont Park and threw them into a bonfire. The women carried banners and shouted, "Down with Levi's." The "burn-in" kicked off the national boycott campaign.

"Levi's have been the uniform of the college student, the civil rights worker, the young radical and the hippie," Shirah told the crowd. "We ask you to show your support for the four hundred brave women [who have been] on strike for over a year in Blue Ridge by giving up your uniform."[17]

Shirah was warned that continued public support of the strikers would cost him his job, but the threats only made him bolder. He was convinced that if the Blue Ridge action failed, labor organizing in the mountains would be set back for years. Unions like the ILGWU, he said, spent too much time persuading management to put the union label on their products and not enough time negotiating for the things workers really needed.

The strike dragged on for fifty-six weeks, and Shirah picketed, organized rallies, and wrote a song about the strike. "*It ain't just a matter of pay, Mister. It ain't just a matter of pay. We want to be treated like people, Mister, and the strike will be over today.*"

In August 1967 he was fired. Already a hero, he became a martyr to the Atlanta students, who called SLAM "a SSOC with balls." But veteran activists considered him one of SNCC's "walking wounded." He was often drunk, unreliable, and argumentative. In 1967 few people understood that activists could suffer anything like "shell shock," but in 1969

Dr. Robert Coles, the Harvard psychiatrist who'd w̲
volunteers during the Mississippi summer project, refle
some civil rights workers in whom long and hard exposu
of their kind of work has produced more than a temporary
fatigue.' Fixed anger and suspicion plague them. They lo̲ ̲o̲t only perspective and humor, but they begin to distrust the intentions and aspira-
tions of others, so that fewer and fewer people, even among their own coworkers, can be trusted. Hate and its moral and psychological equivalents
appear: scorn for newcomers in civil rights, distrust of anyone, black or
white, connected ever so slightly or innocently with the 'power structure.'"[18]

Some former colleagues accused Shirah of pressuring SSOC to fund
SLAM in order to create a job for himself, but, despite powerful objections, the executive committee ultimately voted to fund his program on a
project basis.

"That Shirah was able to interest people in SLAM," one movement
scholar observes, "was testimony to his tremendous powers of persuasion.
He attracted the support of young white Southerners wherever he went,
and regardless of the particular cause [he advocated], SNCC, SSOC or
SLAM, he was able to reach people through the sheer force of his personality."[19]

Both SLAM and the Levi Strauss boycott ended badly, however. On
September 1, 1967, the Blue Ridge contract expired, and Levi Strauss
called for an election. The replacement workers decertified the union on
September 13.

Instead of continuing the boycott campaign which was finally attracting
national attention, the strike leaders opted to focus their energies on creating an independent sewing cooperative. With a four-thousand-dollar loan
from SCEF, Appalachian Enterprises leased a factory in Mineral Bluff,
Georgia, and contracted to sew a thousand dresses each week on fifty
leased sewing machines.

Shirah suspected that the strike leaders had been co-opted. He believed
that Levi Strauss had encouraged clothing manufacturers to temporarily
subcontract to the cooperative until all interest in the boycott disappeared.
That is exactly what happened.

Shirah tried to keep the boycott campaign alive as a SLAM project, but

August 24, 1967, SSOC's executive committee voted to discontinue financial support for SLAM, and Shirah was once again unemployed.

Despite his hard work, complete dedication, and the loss of his job, Shirah had actually accomplished very little. At twenty-four he began to be haunted by his unrealized dreams: the college education he'd thrown away, the career in music that had never gotten started, and the lost opportunities in Hazard, Biloxi, and Statesville.

Yet he took no action. He was, as he had told Nelson Blackstock, "immobilized." He spent most afternoons playing guitar, writing songs, and discussing revolution with Ernie Marrs, an old socialist musician friend of Pete Seeger's.

At the same time, Alabama governor George Wallace's political star was rising. He had become a national symbol of white resistence. Making a second run for the presidency, he vowed to "shake the eyeteeth of the liberals of both national parties." When Shirah heard him, he got drunk and began to talk wildly about bombing the Atlanta Federal Building. Although he never followed through, he succeeded in alienating most of his remaining associates. His erratic behavior contradicted everything he'd ever committed himself to or worked for.

In the meantime, his brother, Richard, who'd been denied conscientious objector status and classified 1-A by the Defuniak Springs, Florida, draft board, had moved to Atlanta and was staying with Sam and Liz.

No longer eligible for a student deferment, Richard had not been successful in appealing the draft board's decision, and his lottery number was coming up. In Atlanta he became involved with SSOC's conscientious objector counseling program and with the Committee to End the War in Vietnam.

Shirah's inability to find work created hardships for Liz and their daughters, and Richard presented an added burden. As his relationship with Liz deteriorated, Shirah encouraged her to start having affairs. He enjoyed a number of liaisons while they lived in Atlanta and had always advocated free love. While Liz tried to make allowances, the hippie lifestyle was not what she wanted for herself or her daughters. When Shirah proposed moving to a commune on a farm outside Atlanta, Liz refused. In the spring of 1969, after completing a teaching certificate program at Atlanta University, she packed up four-year-old Lisa and two-year-old Rebecca and moved to Wisconsin. Shirah relocated to the commune by himself.[20]

He lived in the Georgia countryside for a few months, playing his guitar, writing songs, smoking marijuana, and selling herbs to support himself. In late spring he fell in love with another musician and traveled north with her, where they performed together at a few coffeehouses in New York City's East Village before breaking up.

While he was in New York he contacted Casey Hayden, who'd left Atlanta three years earlier because she said she didn't know which side of town to live in anymore. By 1966 she wasn't welcome in the black community, but she couldn't live among "southern liberals" either. She'd settled in Sullivan County, New York, with her boyfriend, Donald Boyce, and encouraged Shirah to come visit them for the Woodstock Music and Arts Festival. Boyce, a skilled carpenter, was helping the Santa Fe Hog Farm Commune set up camp kitchens and first-aid stations, and Hayden assured Shirah that there was plenty of work available.

Shirah would have welcomed any excuse not to return to Atlanta in 1969. After Liz and his daughters left, his brother, Richard, was drafted and ordered to report to Montgomery's Maxwell Air Force Base. Unable to conform to the pressures of military life, Richard suffered a serious schizophrenic break and had to be hospitalized. He would spend most of the next ten years in and out of mental hospitals.

At the same time, Big Sam was transferred from Grand Bay, and Oneita, who'd finally finished her bachelor's degree in social work, was forced to give up her first professional position because of the transfer. Big Sam would be relocated every two years from 1969 until he retired in 1984. A furious Sue Shirah placed the blame for her family's troubles squarely on her brother Sam's shoulders and refused to speak to him.

Peace, Love, and Music

Sam Shirah was captivated by the bohemian community of Woodstock, New York, nestled in the shadow of Overlook Mountain. With its old clapboard houses, weeping willow trees, and thick pine forests, Sullivan County looked like it was lifted right out of the rural South. At the music festival, held forty miles away in Bethel, Shirah felt like he was among kindred spirits again. With a quarter of a million others he coped with rain, heat, hunger, and crowded conditions for three blissfully nonviolent days.

Shirah felt a familiar spirit stirring as people spoke of a Woodstock nation, of being reborn, and of "coming home." The redemptive vision of the beloved community seemed alive again in the company of long-haired hippie freaks. Antiwar activist Abbie Hoffman (who had taught at a Mc-Comb, Mississippi, freedom school in the summer of 1965) called Woodstock "a nation of the alienated."

After the festival Shirah decided to remain in the North. He'd been saddened by what white Mississippi chaplain Ed King called "the power of hate and the weakness of love."[21] Coping with the gulf between the South's professed religious beliefs and its cultural practices, with lost causes, and with social injustices had left him emotionally drained.[22]

Southern historian Fred Hobson has observed that the movement "had always been for participating whites in part about saving their own souls—about willing themselves back into a religion they could believe in—and their feelings of rejection within the movement in its latter days suggested they were not worthy after all."[23]

The white South had remained unmoved by SNCC's moral claims, and Shirah had clearly overestimated the reservoir of white southern good will. Those white activists who'd taken a stand had simply been too few and too late. The blacks who were leading SNCC and catching the media's attention in 1969 wanted no part of them.

The counterculture seemed to offer another opportunity for nonpolitical organization, personal liberation, and chemical euphoria. He was willing to search the Woodstock nation for what he hadn't been able to sustain in SNCC.

Leaving the South, however, felt like an abandonment of Big Sam, who had been grappling with betrayal, isolation, and disappointment for almost thirty years. He'd lost nearly everything but his determination not to be driven out of Alabama. Between May of 1968 and May of 1969, thirty-five of Big Sam's colleagues resigned from the Alabama–West Florida Conference. Feeling unsupported by their bishop and disillusioned by the impotence of the church, they had just walked away.[24] But Big Sam stayed, insisting that God had called him to minister to white segregationists. Shirah had lost that kind of faith.

In the fall of 1969 Shirah accepted a job with the War on Poverty's

Comprehensive Education and Training Act (CETA) program in Wood-stock. For the next ten years he lived his life as his ancestors had. He became an avid fisherman and hunter and grew his own food, trying to the best of his ability to remain independent. He focused his energies on local politics and seriously pursued his interest in music.

"Sam was a dreamer," Anne Braden remembered, "but he had good dreams."[25]

A March against Fear

The harvest is past, the summer is ended, and we are not saved.
—JEREMIAH 8:20

As it turned out, the pilgrimage to Jackson ended just as it had begun, with one man walking. On June 5, 1966, James Meredith, the black hero who had inspired Bill Moore in 1962 and impressed Sam Shirah at the 1964 Chicago clergy conference, began a one-man, 220-mile March against Fear from Memphis, Tennessee, to Jackson, Mississippi.

Meredith, a native of Kosciusko, Mississippi, had returned home only once after integrating the University of Mississippi. Three years later he wanted to inspire Mississippi blacks to register to vote and help them conquer the fear that they (and he) still felt living and traveling in the Magnolia State.

"If I can walk through Mississippi without harm," he told reporters, "other Negroes will see that they can, too."[1]

Meredith, like Moore, was a loner. He didn't seek endorsements for his march and he didn't ask anyone to walk with him. After two days and twenty miles on the highway, he was shot near Hernando, Mississippi, and rushed to Bowld Hospital in Memphis, where he remained for a week.

Once again SNCC and CORE mobilized to finish a one-man pilgrimage, but the 1966 activists were very different from the ones who'd gathered in 1963. Stokely Carmichael, SNCC's new chair, and CORE's Floyd

McKissick were not interested in either nonviolent protest or white participation. Dr. Martin Luther King, Jr., walked with them this time, but he failed to overshadow either one.

Meredith had plotted a course straight down Highway 51 through the racially troubled counties of Panola, Holmes, and Madison. The marchers began from the site where Meredith had fallen, but chose to weave through the Delta, visiting small communities on their way and encouraging black citizens to register to vote. Willie Ricks, who had served as a SNCC observer on the Freedom Walk, led the effort to mobilize voter registration teams. Meredith became concerned that the march was promoting SNCC. From his Memphis hospital bed he complained that the focus on voter registration was becoming diluted, and he was not pleased. From that point on, the march was plagued by internal squabbles, competition, and factionalism.

External opposition fed the combative spirit. All along Highway 51 the marchers were denied use of rest stops and camping facilities. When they entered Greenwood on June 16 local police informed them that they would need the school board's permission to camp in the yard of the Stone Street Negro Elementary School. Carmichael, who was well known in Greenwood, argued that the yard was public space, and he was taken into custody. He told the crowd, "This is the twenty-seventh time I have been arrested. I ain't going to jail no more. We've been demanding our freedom for six years and have gotten nothing. What we gonna start saying now is *Black Power!*"[2] Those two words gave fifty anxious reporters their page-one story.

After a rally that evening Willie Ricks informed Carmichael that he had "left the people hollering *Black Power* and they're still screaming."

By June 21 the number of marchers had increased to three hundred. When they stopped at Philadelphia, Mississippi, they were attacked by a white mob. Deputy Sheriff Cecil Price (who would be convicted of conspiracy in the 1964 murders of Goodman, Schwerner, and Chaney) refused to permit his deputies to intervene until the activists fought back. Carmichael and McKissick (who'd permitted the militant Deacons for Defense to march with them) refused to restrict the demonstrators to nonviolent protest.

Martin Luther King, Jr., tried to reason with the angry marchers. "We cannot win with violence," he said. "We are ten percent of the population of this nation," and it would be foolish for anyone to think that black people could "get our freedom by ourselves. There's going to have to be a coalition of conscience, and we aren't going to be free in Mississippi or anywhere in the United States until there is a committed empathy on the part of the white man."[3]

McKissick and Carmichael dismissed him. They were tired of white segregationist rage, black compromise, and white liberal betrayal.[4]

When SNCC's John Lewis attempted to speak he was shouted down with chants of "black power!"

"That night I felt like the uninvited guest," Lewis said. "It's hard to accept when something is over even though you know things have to change. In the beginning, with the sit-ins and Freedom Rides, things were much simpler. . . . People just had to offer their bodies for their beliefs and it seemed like that would be enough, but it wasn't. By that time nobody knew what would be enough to make America right."[5]

Three years earlier ten SNCC/CORE Freedom Walkers had sung, "Keep on a-walkin', keep on a-talkin', walkin' on to Freedom Land." In 1966 the marchers chanted, "Too much love, too much love. Nothing kills a nigger like too much love. . . ."

On June 23 the Canton, Mississippi, police sprayed the marchers with tear gas. "The attack," Martin Luther King, Jr., said, "was one of the best expressions of a police state I have ever seen."[6]

Meredith arrived in Canton to rejoin the march the following day but found that the procession had already moved on. He was furious that the demonstrators would approach Jackson without him, and he threatened to take a group back to Canton to lead a splinter march to Jackson's Tougaloo College.

The leaders spent Saturday night, June 25, on the Tougaloo campus arguing about who was authorized to speak for the group, who would be allowed to sit on the dais, and who was prepared to support the new rallying cry, "black power."

An uneasy peace was negotiated before the procession entered the capital city. Meredith acknowledged the internal strife to the crowd of nearly twenty thousand standing before the capitol.

"You might assume that I was shot by a Negro since all you've been hearing about is Negroes being divided," he said. "But from this day on, our focus is going to be on the issue of freedom."[7] He made it clear that he personally supported black power.

Carmichael advised the crowd that "Negroes must build a power base in this country so strong that we will bring them [whites] to their knees every time they mess with us."[8]

Three years earlier Bill Moore had attempted to deliver a message of tolerance to Governor Ross Barnett at 300 East Capitol Street, right around the corner from where the crowd chanted, "Black power!" There was a new governor now, Paul B. Johnson, who, unlike Barnett, was not a member of the white Citizens' Council, and there were new leaders and a new mood.

Moore's plea that Mississippi would "be gracious, and make certain that when the Negro gets his rights and his vote that he does not in the process learn to treat the white man with the contempt and disdain that, unfortunately, some of us now treat him" had never reached the governor's mansion.

The kind of hope and unity that had sustained the Freedom Walkers, black and white, was never evident during the March against Fear. The earlier walkers had identified a single enemy, while the Meredith marchers experienced enemies all around them and even among themselves.

Dr. Richard Haley, a Freedom Walker who by 1966 had been appointed CORE's southern regional director, also walked with the Meredith marchers. In 1963 he'd told the crowd gathered in front of Chattanooga's Greyhound bus station that the Freedom Walkers intended to walk across Alabama. "We will not be appeased," he'd said, "but we intend to present, if anything, a perfect picture of peace. We hope to impress the people we meet not with our uniqueness, but with our humility. . . ."[9] Three years and many bitter experiences later he told a *New York Times* reporter in Pope, Mississippi, that "[t]he white has moved only from a position of greater paternalism to a position of lesser paternalism and in fighting to move him all the way we're going to swing wildly at times and hit somebody who doesn't deserve to be hit. It is inevitable. It is part of the process of finding our identity."[10]

That inevitability had not been apparent to Bill Moore or to Sam Shirah in 1963. Both believed that the white South had the will to forestall it, because they understood that oppressors not only destroy others but ultimately themselves.

I pray that the eyes of your heart may be enlightened.
—EPHESIANS 1:18

Sam Shirah and Bill Moore might reasonably be called prophetic dreamers. Their notions about social justice echo the concerns of the biblical prophets Jeremiah, Isaiah, and Amos. Justice was a moral issue for all of them. Both Moore and Shirah believed that when a powerful majority denies human rights to a minority the moral fiber of society is weakened. Their insistence that every American was entitled to the promises and protections of the Constitution was a message that many Americans found distasteful. Like Amos and Isaiah, who charged their leaders with being "oppressors of the poor and crushers of the needy," Moore and Shirah were social irritants.

The activist rabbi Abraham Joshua Heschel has observed that one of the greatest contributions of the biblical prophets was their exposure of the evil of indifference. They were not tolerant of wrongs done to others, he said, but resented other people's injuries. Their most important activity was interference—remonstrating about wrongs inflicted on people and meddling in affairs which were seemingly neither their concern nor their responsibility.[11]

Both Moore and Shirah believed that change began with the individual and that the human heart was the engine of change. Mass movements might educate, motivate, and bond people, but, without the engagement of hearts, momentum could never be sustained. If individual hearts couldn't change, the South would merely trade active segregation for the de facto northern variety. Both men despised hypocrisy and were not afraid to point out that white liberal hearts had to change just like white segregationist hearts. Like the clergy who often denounced them, Moore and Shirah believed that they also had a mission to redeem the souls of white southerners.

As with the biblical prophets, however, it is unwise to confuse the seer with his revelation. Shirah and Moore were hardly exemplary men. They were neither good husbands nor good fathers. It was their willingness to live their values in the face of overwhelming opposition that makes them exceptional.

Sue Shirah-Sands says that it's difficult to articulate the kind of burning idealism that drove her brother Sam in the early years of SNCC, because so little of it has survived his generation.

Floyd Simpson, the man who linked Shirah's and Moore's lives with a bullet, was a better socialized and more economically productive individual than either of them. He was a good husband, a good father, a good neighbor, and a good Baptist. It appeared that he was comfortable with the world around him, and the world seemed more at ease with him than with either Moore or Shirah. The intersection of their lives in March 1963 raises troubling questions about the relativity of American values and the fragility of good intentions.

The history of the 1960s freedom movement is filled with white southerners like Bill Moore, Sam Shirah, and Floyd Simpson. They and thousands like them with impossible ideals, mixed motives, and raging anger once struggled with others in a massive tug of war over whether to move the nation forward or hold it in place.

Epilogue: Highway 11 Revisited

Mystery, I read somewhere, is not the absence of meaning, but the presence of more meaning than we can comprehend.
—Dennis Covington, *Salvation on Sand Mountain*

In the spring of 2000 I drove to Chattanooga, Tennessee, and down Highway 11 through Georgia and northeast Alabama to follow the trail of William Moore, Sam Shirah, and Floyd Simpson. I fully expected to travel through Dogpatch, and, as with most of the assumptions I had made when I set out to write this book, I was completely and absolutely wrong.

Hamilton County, Tennessee, Dade County, Georgia, and Dekalb and Etowah counties in Alabama, while still very isolated, are prosperous boroughs containing some of the most voluptuous farmland in America. There are no junkyards, no whitewashed truck tires filled with flowers in front yards, and no washing machines on front porches.

Floyd Simpson's grocery still stands in Collbran, Alabama, but its gas pumps have dried up, and a sign in front reads "Gad's Antiques." An old man working outside looked puzzled when I pulled up in my rented car with New York plates. In a moment of panic I asked if he had any glass drawer pulls. He rubbed his chin and said he'd gotten some a while back but had sold them, and, since he was going out of business, suggested that I try the Mountain Top Flea Market on 287 near Attalla.

I asked if he'd been in business long. He shook his head. "Not *this* business." My heart pumped. "Owned this building more'n forty years though," he said. He told me that he'd lived nearby for all his eighty-three years.

I could not believe that I was looking into the face of Gaddis Killian, Floyd Simpson's landlord. He was a good-looking, kindly, grandfatherly type who wore eyeglasses and was hard of hearing. Broad-shouldered and strong, he was far from the sickly character I'd envisioned. Killian looked rather prosperous. He was wearing new jeans, a red baseball cap advertising some local mill, and a McGovern/Shriver campaign button which I never recovered sufficiently to ask him about.

I am not proud to say that I lost my courage that afternoon on the empty highway. I did not take the golden opportunity to ask Gaddis Killian about Floyd Simpson, William Moore, or the Freedom Walkers. I was afraid, terrified by an old man who by all outward appearances wished me no harm. I cannot imagine how Bill Moore stood in front of that same store forty years ago fielding questions from four angry young men.

What might Killian have told me? With all the belated indictments of civil rights–era murderers, I've been assured that most men of his generation refuse to talk about any of it anymore. But that's hardly the point.

Assuming our business was finished, Killian returned to sorting his inventory, and I drove on to Ft. Payne. I learned that Floyd Simpson had died in a nursing home in 1998 at the age of seventy-five. After Moore's murder he'd left the grocery on Highway 11 and leased another on Route 6. Three years later he'd abandoned the grocery business entirely and worked at a series of mill jobs until he retired. He learned to live with a local reputation of being "the man who'd gotten away with murder," a dubious distinction which caused him to be admired by some of his neighbors and avoided by others.

Simpson advanced in the Ft. Payne Klan and became a Klokan, or investigator, responsible for conducting background checks on recruits. In 1965, the FBI questioned him about his role in a series of bombings around Birmingham as activists were gathering there on their way to the Selma voting rights march. Simpson told the investigators that he did not believe in violence and he did not want to discuss the Klan or segregation except to say that he was a segregationist.

Three years later he abruptly stopped attending Klan meetings. By then hundreds of FBI informants had infiltrated the organization, and Imperial Wizard Robert Shelton was in jail for tax evasion. Simpson remained a member of the Gravel Hill Baptist Church, however, and was buried in its yard in an unmarked grave next to his old store. He was mourned by Lucille, his wife of over fifty years, five surviving children, nine grandchildren, and nine great-grandchildren.

When I arrived in Gadsden, Alabama, District Attorney James E. Hedgspeth agreed to review the Simpson case file with me at the old Etowah County Courthouse. He explained that, although Gadsden was never a bastion of liberalism, it was, and is, a live-and-let-live town. Unlike most of the South, Gadsden had industries that were unionized, and good wages and benefits were available at the Goodyear tire plant. When I asked about Floyd Simpson's connections to the Ft. Payne Klan, he brushed the subject off as speculation. Besides, the Klan wasn't all bad, he told me, especially back in the twenties and thirties when it concentrated on reforming people who were less than upstanding: men who beat their wives, drank too much, or abandoned their children. White or black, they were taken for a ride, and by the time that ride was over they'd achieved a change of heart.

Hedgspeth said that his own grandmother had been active in the Klan. "Your grandmother?" I asked.

"Yes, indeed. It wasn't until the sixties when a lot of no-accounts began bombing churches that all the decent folks left the Klan."

I knew then that I wouldn't get anything more from the D.A. than what the public record contained, what he was compelled by law to give me. He said that Public Safety Commissioner Al Lingo, a man worse than Bull Connor, died in 1969 and good riddance. That didn't compute. How could Hedgspeth be proud of his Klan granny and trash Al Lingo, the best friend the Alabama Kluxers ever had?

"Look, he was no damn good," he assured me, apparently amazed that I could ask such a question.

Hedgspeth suggested that I visit William W. Rayburn, who'd been Alabama's circuit solicitor (state district attorney) in 1963. Rayburn was the man who'd convinced Governor George Wallace to offer a thousand-dollar reward for information leading to the arrest of Moore's killers. "Bill and Helen are always on their porch," Hedgspeth said. "Just drive on over there and have a chat with him."

Rayburn was walking to his car carrying dry cleaning over one arm as I pulled up. Thirty-seven years had passed, and he rightly wanted to know what interest I had in the Floyd Simpson matter. His wife opened their screen door and demanded to know whom he was talking to. When he told her who'd sent me she moaned, "Oh, Jim Hedgspeth!" and let the door slam.

Rayburn, a contemporary of Gaddis Killian, was also hard of hearing, but he seemed more fragile.

"I'm sorry, I'd like to help you," he said, "but I can't. It was too long ago. I don't remember."

"What did you think when the grand jury refused to indict Simpson?" I asked.

His eyes flashed and I got a momentary sense of what he must have been like as a prosecutor. "I had no way of knowing what they were thinking," he snapped. "Grand jury deliberations are privileged. How *would* I know?"

"Did you get the feeling that the jury was angry, or maybe afraid?"

He reached for his car door. "Look, I'm sorry. I don't remember. It was my job to present the evidence, and there wasn't enough to indict."

I was politely dismissed. Nearly four decades earlier Rayburn had demonstrated to a grand jury that Bill Moore's route had taken him past Floyd Simpson's grocery, that Simpson admitted speaking with Moore twice on the day of his murder, that the bullets which killed Moore had been traced to Simpson's rifle, and that numerous witnesses placed Simpson in Keener, Alabama, less than one hour before the killing. The jury wasn't charged with determining reasonable doubt, only probable cause, and they refused.

But Rayburn had given me something of great value despite himself. He helped me understand just why Bill Moore, Sam Shirah, and all other white southern activists had been considered crazy. Not only were they up against men like Killian and Simpson who believed so strongly in white supremacy that they suffered no remorse over the murder of race mixers, but they had to count on the fidelity of men like Rayburn who were required to run for office to keep their jobs—men who were in a position to change things but were often co-opted or chose not to rock the boat. Still, who was I to judge Rayburn? Hadn't I folded just hours before? Hadn't I backed away from Gaddis Killian because I wasn't sure I could handle the consequences of taking a chance when I felt alone and unprotected?

Moore and Shirah, knowing the odds as they did, took public stands against segregation anyway. By most definitions, that's crazy.

White privilege is so deeply embedded in our society that most white Americans unconsciously believe that the benefits their skin color brings are entitlements. Often we (both black and white) are at a loss as to how to respond to whites who repudiate privilege. In 1963 we called them crazy, disloyal, even blasphemous.

Many white activists *did* come from society's fringes, and, if they did not begin there as Bill Moore had, their activism often rendered them permanent outsiders, as was the case with Sam Shirah. Later, after the March on Washington, when integrated cocktail parties became fashionable, privileged white activists who had risked position and reputation were celebrated as heroes, while working-class activists who'd lost what little they had, bringing the wrath of family, neighbors, coworkers, and friends on themselves, were remembered as crazy.

By 1975 Sam Shirah had married Benita Crow, a "northern liberal" with two teenagers, and moved to Bearsville, New York. They lived in a renovated barn just outside the Woodstock art colony. Benita was dark-haired, self-assured, and energetic, and she shared Shirah's love of fun.

Shortly after his marriage he entered local politics and organized the Woodstock Independent Party (WIP) with the hope of getting the locals and hippies (who despised each other) to work together. He put a group to work on his mayoral campaign, which he ran as if he were an old southern populist, calling for governmental reform and civic improvement. When he lost the election and was still unable to get the warring factions to work together, he decided that what they needed was to learn to play together first. He planned a two-hundredth-birthday bash in celebration of New York State and organized a parade through the town. The day, complete with frog-jumping contests, long-rifle tournaments, bake-offs, and colonial costumes, was a resounding success.

"He was a wild mixture of corny patriot and social critic," Benita recalled. "After that party everyone called him 'Uncle Sam,' and he was elected chairman of the Woodstock Bicentennial Planning Committee. Sam had a real talent for bringing people together."

On January 11, 1980, twenty-three-year-old Martin (Mojo) Wattel, a newcomer to Bearsville whom Shirah and Benita had befriended during the Christmas holidays, became convinced that Shirah had raped his wife. Wattel forced his way into Shirah's home waving a .22 rifle.

"I know I'll go to jail for this, but Jesus told me to do it," Wattel said, and shot Shirah through the chest. As Shirah fell, Wattel screamed, "Oh, my God! What have I done?"

Sobbing with remorse, Wattel helped Benita Shirah carry her mortally wounded husband to the car. They drove to Benedictine Hospital, where Shirah was pronounced dead. He was thirty-six years old.

The Bearsville community mourned "Uncle Sam," and an editorial in the *Woodstock Times* noted that "like all activists, Sam Shirah had his share of ardent friends and severe critics. But he was widely regarded as a man who would fight hard and work hard to change things for the better as he saw them."

At his memorial service in Dothan, Alabama, Rev. Thomas Lane Butts told the mourners that "Samuel was one of the children of the parsonage who frightened us by taking what he heard in church more seriously than we ever dreamed that he might."

William Moore, the white activist who first stirred my curiosity, had also been murdered by a white man with a .22 rifle in his thirty-sixth year. More than twenty years later his name was put on the roll of forty martyrs remembered at the Civil Rights Memorial in Montgomery, Alabama. When the memorial was dedicated in 1989, Mary Moore Birchard, Moore's widow, told the staff, "If they don't stop calling him an atheist I think I'll croak. It makes my blood boil. He was a Christian. If he had not believed in God he couldn't have undertaken his final mission. It was God's love that helped him go."

Forty-year-old Danny Weyant, Moore's stepson, said, "I'm glad he's remembered. I think he made as much of a contribution as the others did, but I have big feelings about what he could have done if he was alive. . . . The kind of man he was, he could have done more alive."

Moore was also honored by the Birmingham Civil Rights Institute and by the establishment of the William L. Moore Memorial Chapter of CORE, which was established in Endicott, New York, shortly after his death.

Jim Peck continued to edit the War Resisters League newsletter and went to work for Amnesty International after he was fired from CORE in 1965. Like SNCC, CORE became a black nationalist organization. In a 1983 interview he said, "My life has been dedicated to nonviolent direct action to try to make this a better world. It is my philosophy that the struggle has to be a nonending one, because I am not one of those idealists who envision a utopia." He suffered a massive stroke later that year and died at Walker Methodist Nursing Home in Minneapolis in 1993.

Four years after James Meredith graduated from Columbia University

Law School he unsuccessfully campaigned for the 1972 Republican nomination for U.S. senator from Mississippi. Meredith had become critical of black dependence on the federal government, and he endorsed conservatives Ronald Reagan and George Bush, Sr. In 1989 he joined the public relations staff of white North Carolina senator Jesse Helms, who had bitterly resisted the civil rights movement in the 1960s. A year later Meredith joined the public relations staff of former KKK grand dragon David Duke.

Governor George Corley Wallace died peacefully on September 13, 1998, in his seventy-ninth year. He had run for president four times, always portraying himself as the champion of the "little man" fighting against the tyranny of the big federal government. "The instincts of a common-sense Alabamian," he once said, "are better than the brains of any New York intellectual moron." In the 1968 Democratic primaries he received almost as many votes as Hubert Humphrey. Black voters supported him in 1982 for a fourth term as Alabama's governor after he said he'd been wrong about segregation and asked their forgiveness.

Near the end Wallace tried to make amends for all the pain he'd caused. He publicly apologized on many occasions and in 1991 declared on national television that "what I did was wrong." It was reported that as he got older he grew increasingly fearful of dying with the weight of his sins on his soul. In a 1993 interview with the *Boston Globe* he explained, "I'm not a bad man. I'm all right with the Lord."

I warned early on that there were no happy endings to these stories. They are chapters of shadow history, that chronicle of rejected events that have been declared better forgotten. These narratives are complex and frustrating. What is the point, we ask? They seem to resonate only for those who believe that we get essentially what we ask for and pretty much what we deserve. But there is another lesson offered by the complicated lives of these men, one which is captured insightfully by Lillian Smith, a white Georgia writer and student of human nature.

Smith observed in 1962 that "we [always] need someone to blame. We cannot bear our anguish if we know that it springs from our own hearts."

There is a spirit abroad in life of which the Judeo-Christian ethic is but one expression. It is a spirit that makes for wholeness and for community; it finds its way into the quiet solitude of a Supreme Court justice when he ponders the constitutionality of an act of Congress which guarantees civil rights to all its citi-

zens; it settles in the pools of light in the face of a little girl as with her frailty she challenges the hard frightened heart of a police chief; it walks along the lonely road with the solitary protest marcher and settles over him with a benediction as he falls by the assassin's bullet fired from ambush; it kindles the fires of unity in the heart of Jewish Rabbi, Catholic Priest, and Protestant Minister as they join arms together, giving witness to their God on behalf of a brotherhood that transcends creed, race, sex and religion; it makes a path to Walden Pond and ignites the flame of nonviolence in the mind of a Thoreau and burns through his liquid words from the Atlantic to the Pacific; it broods over the demonstrators for justice and brings comfort to the desolate and forgotten who have no memory of what it is to feel the rhythm of belonging to the race of men; it knows no country and its allies are to be found wherever the heart is kind and the collective will and the private endeavor seek to make justice where injustice abounds, to make peace where chaos is rampant, and to make the voice heard on behalf of the helpless and the weak. It is the voice of God and the voice of man; it is the meaning of all the strivings of the whole human race toward a world of friendly men underneath a friendly sky.

—Howard Thurman, *The Luminous Darkness: A Personal Interpretation of the Anatomy of Segregation and the Ground of Hope,* © HarperCollins, 1965

Appendix 1

The Walks and the Walkers

The SNCC/CORE Freedom Walk

From CORE:
Dr. Richard Haley, black, 46, Portsmouth, Ohio
Robert Gore, black, 31, Hickory, North Carolina
Winston Lockett, black, 22, New Haven, Connecticut
Eric Weinbeger, white, 31, Great Neck, New York
Zev Aelony, white, 24, Minneapolis, Minnesota

From SNCC:
Bill Hansen, white, 23, Cincinnati, Ohio
Carver "Chico" Neblett, black, 22, Carbondale, Illinois
Jessie Harris, black, 21, Jackson, Mississippi
Bob Zellner, white, 24, Slocum, Alabama
Sam Shirah, white, 20, Troy, Alabama

Observers:
Landy McNair, black, Jackson, Mississippi
Avon Rollins, black, Knoxville, Tennessee
Eric Rainey, white, Chicago, Illinois
Willie Ricks, black, 19, Chattanooga, Tennessee
James Forman, black, 35, Chicago, Illinois
Casey Hayden, white, 23, Victoria, Texas
Dorothy Miller, white, 23, Queens, New York

The Alabama Christian Movement for Human Rights (Birmingham) Freedom Walk

Diane Nash, black, 21, Chicago, Illinois
Rev. Ennis Knight, black, 22, Birmingham, Alabama
Addie Harris, black, 23, Birmingham, Alabama
David Darling, black, 24, Birmingham, Alabama
Robert E. Jones, black, 21, Birmingham, Alabama
Mary Ann Thomas, black, 24, Birmingham, Alabama
Wavelyn Holmes, black, 19, Birmingham, Alabama
Paul Brooks, black, 24, St. Louis, Missouri

The Keener, Alabama, Walk

Madeline Sherwood, white, 41, Quebec, Canada
Lawrence Curry, black, Chattanooga, Tennessee
Bene Luchion, black, 22, New Orleans, Louisiana
Don Johnson, black, Cleveland, Ohio
Johnny Jackson, black, Cleveland, Ohio
Vardwick Johnson, black, Cleveland, Ohio
Nelson Barr, white, Chattanooga, Tennessee
Gordon Harris, white, Rochester, New York
Al Urie, white, Glen-Gardner, New Jersey
Bob Kachnowski, white, New York, New York
Arline Wilks, black, 16, Highpoint, North Carolina
Claudia Edwards, black, 17, Forrest City, Arkansas

Observers:
Peter De Rome, white, 35, New York, New York
Mary Hamilton, black, 25, Los Angeles, California
Marvin Robinson, black, 23, Baton Rouge, Louisiana

The Gadsden, Alabama, Walks

Two more attempts to complete Bill Moore's Freedom Walk were made by an unknown number of black citizens from Gadsden, Alabama, who were beaten and jailed, and whose names have been lost.

Appendix 2

Timeline

1962

January

The Voter Education Project (endorsed by the Kennedy administration and funded by private foundations in the North) begins with a joint voter registration campaign administered by the Mississippi chapters of SNCC, CORE, and the NAACP.

March

Bill Moore joins Baltimore CORE's Highway 40 Freedom Ride to protest discrimination in hotels and restaurants on Maryland's Route 40.

The FBI begins surveillance of Martin Luther King, Jr., and the SCLC for evidence of communist influence.

April

The Committee for Nonviolent Action (CNVA) sponsors a peace walk from Nashville, Tennessee, to Washington, D.C. Eric Weinberger and Robert Gore, two peace activists (and later Freedom Walkers), march with them.

June

SNCC, CORE, SCLC, and local activists demonstrate against the segregated public facilities in Albany, Georgia.

New World Review publishes Bill Moore's review of Erich Fromm's *Man May Prevail*.

Secretary of Defense Robert McNamara visits South Vietnam and declares that the forces of democracy are winning.

11–15. SDS schedules its first national convention.

July

CORE's Freedom Highways Campaign extends to North Carolina.

10–12. Martin Luther King, Jr., is jailed during Albany, Georgia, demonstrations.

August

New World Review publishes Bill Moore's article "My Friend in Viet Nam."

September

3. Federal district court orders University of Mississippi to admit James Meredith, a black man.

13. President Kennedy denounces the burnings of black churches in Georgia, where black voter registration training is being conducted.

24. Mississippi governor Ross Barnett blocks the admission of James Meredith to the Ole Miss campus.

October

1. "The Battle of Oxford." Three hundred twenty federal marshals are dispatched to Oxford, Mississippi, to enroll James Meredith at Ole Miss. Two people are killed, and 166 marshals and 210 demonstrators are injured.

9. The African republic of Uganda wins its independence from Great Britain.

11. Vatican II convenes in Rome.

12. Bill Moore joins activist Jim Peck on a peace sail to protest the sentencing of black reporter Bill Worthy for reentering the United States after an unauthorized trip to Havana, Cuba.

22. President John Kennedy announces a naval blockade of Cuba in response to evidence that the Soviets are constructing missile installations on the island. The world braces for nuclear war.

28. The Soviet Union agrees to withdraw its Cuban missiles, and the United States pledges not to invade Cuba.

November

17. Bill Moore accepts a post office transfer and moves to Baltimore, Maryland.

Bill Moore joins the Maryland Council for Democratic Rights and becomes active with MCDC's Committee to Abolish HUAC.

December

8. Bill Moore invites Attorney General Robert F. Kennedy to a meeting of MCDR's Committee to Abolish HUAC at his home.

31. Ho Chi Minh, president of North Vietnam, vows to outlast American aid to South Vietnam and to wage guerilla warfare for ten years if necessary.

1963

January

1. An act of Congress proclaims the centennial year of the American Emancipation Proclamation.

4. Pope John XXIII is named *Time* magazine's "Man of the Year."

7. Maryland Council for Democratic Rights and its Committee to Abolish HUAC vote to dissociate themselves from Bill Moore.

14. Governor George C. Wallace is inaugurated in Montgomery, Alabama.

14–17. Interfaith National Conference on Religion and Race convenes in Chicago, Illinois.

February

U.S. Civil Rights Commission releases the "Centennial Report on Civil Rights" noting that, while gains in equal rights in the South are slow, they appear to be inevitable, while northern bias is proving more subtle and harder to eliminate.

17. Bill Moore joins a stand-in with Morgan State College students to desegregate Baltimore's Northwood Theater.

The FBI commences an investigation of Bill Moore's activities with MCDR and his suspected ties with the Communist Party.

23. Jimmy Travis, a black SNCC voter registration volunteer, is shot on Highway 82 near Greenwood, Mississippi.

27. U.S. Supreme Court hears *Murray v. Curlett*, which challenges the practice of using the Lord's Prayer and Bible readings for opening exercises in the Baltimore public schools.

The Alabama Supreme Court upholds a permanent injunction prohibiting the NAACP from operating in Alabama. The NAACP appeals to the U.S. Supreme Court.

March

6. Shotgun blasts are fired into the Greenwood, Mississippi, home of the father of Dewey Green, after Green, a black student, makes an unsuccessful attempt to register at the University of Mississippi.

24. Field offices of the Greenwood, Mississippi, Voter Education Project are gutted by fire.

27. Daily voter registration marches to the Greenwood, Mississippi, courthouse begin. A federal suit against voting discrimination practices in Leflore County is brought against the state of Mississippi.

28. Billie Sol Estes is convicted of federal mail fraud.

29. Greenwood, Mississippi, voter registration activists are attacked by state police who use riot guns and German shepherd dogs.

Bill Moore joins Baltimore CORE's anti–Jim Crow demonstration in Westminster, Maryland. The Baltimore Colts football team threatens to move its training camp if segregation continues.

April

3. Martin Luther King, Jr., arrives in Birmingham, Alabama.

Bill Moore walks from Baltimore to Annapolis with a letter for Maryland's governor, Millard Tawes, requesting him to press the state legislature for an equal accommodations bill.

5. Sam Shirah joins SNCC staff after being expelled from Birmingham-Southern College for encouraging white students to join black Birmingham protesters.

12. Martin Luther King, Jr., leads fifty demonstrators through Birmingham and is arrested.

14. SNCC/SCLC activist Diane Nash arrives in Birmingham from Greenwood, Mississippi.

16. Martin Luther King, Jr., writes "Letter from a Birmingham Jail."

20. Bill Moore leaves Washington, D.C., on a Greyhound bus bound for Chattanooga, Tennessee.

21. Bill Moore arrives in Chattanooga, Tennessee.

22. Bill Moore crosses northern Georgia and enters Etowah County, Alabama.

23. Bill Moore is murdered on Highway 11 outside Attala, Alabama, in the community of Keener.

24. Rev. Fred Lee Shuttlesworth preaches at a mass meeting at the St. James Baptist Church in Birmingham, where Sam Shirah learns of Moore's murder.

25. Floyd Simpson is arrested for the murder of Bill Moore. Bill Moore's funeral is held in Binghamton, New York.

29. Floyd Simpson is released on a five-thousand-dollar bond pending grand jury action.

May

1. Ten SNCC/CORE volunteers leave Chattanooga, Tennessee, for the "William Moore Memorial Trek" to Jackson, Mississippi.

Eight black activists led by Diane Nash meet in Gadsden, Alabama, and attempt to complete Bill Moore's walk to Jackson, Mississippi. All are arrested.

2. Six thousand children between the ages of six and sixteen, Birmingham's Children's Crusade, march from the Sixteenth Street Baptist Church to downtown Birmingham. Nine hundred fifty-nine are arrested.

SNCC/CORE Freedom Walkers spend the night in Rome, Georgia.

3. The SNCC/CORE Freedom Walkers are arrested as they cross the Alabama state line and are incarcerated at the DeKalb County jail in Ft. Payne, Alabama.

Fire hoses and dogs are turned on teens and children marching in Birmingham.

Journalists abandon the Freedom Walkers and the Greenwood Voter Education Project and rush to Birmingham to cover the Children's Crusade.

4. Freedom Walkers are transferred from Ft. Payne jail to Etowah County Courthouse (Gadsden city jail).

7. Justice Department officials are dispatched to Birmingham to facilitate negotiations between city managers and the SCLC.

10. Birmingham Accord is reached.

11. A Klan rally is held in Bessemer, Alabama. The home of Rev. A. D. King, brother of Martin Luther King, Jr., and King's room at the Gaston Motel in Birmingham are bombed. Charles Arnie Cagle, a cousin by marriage of Bill Moore, is implicated. Downtown Birmingham erupts in rioting.

12. President Kennedy dispatches federal troops to bases near Birmingham.

15. Ten SNCC/CORE Freedom Walkers are transferred from Gadsden, Alabama, to Kilby State Prison in Montgomery and housed on death row.

16. A third attempt to complete Bill Moore's walk from Keener, Alabama, to Jackson, Mississippi, results in the arrest of eleven marchers, including Broadway actress Madeleine Sherwood.

18–19. As President Kennedy tours the South, the Jackson, Mississippi, Citizens' Council passes a resolution urging whites and blacks to repudiate "professional agitators" and their "invidious doctrine of genocide."

20. Martin Luther King, Jr., addresses a rally of three thousand in Harlem. Demonstrators jeer and chant, "We want Malcolm."

The U.S. Supreme Court voids convictions of blacks for demonstrating against segregation in four southern states, ruling that all had acted lawfully in exercising rights guaranteed by the Constitution.

A memorial service for Bill Moore sponsored by the Baltimore CORE is held at the First Unitarian Church of Baltimore.

25. Leaders of thirty African nations establish the Organization for African Unity.

31. The Danville Christian Progressive Association begins an "equality in public hiring" campaign in Danville, Virginia.

June

3. Pope John XXIII dies in Rome at the age of eighty-one.

4. Ten SNCC/CORE Freedom Walkers are convicted of breaching the peace in Montgomery, Alabama, fined two hundred dollars each, and released on two-hundred-dollar bonds pending appeal.

5. Danville, Virginia, activists sit in on the steps of the municipal building. Their leaders are arrested.

7. Sam Shirah arrives in Gadsden, Alabama.

10. The Gadsden freedom movement's campaign begins.

11. Alabama governor George Wallace stands in a doorway at the University of Alabama to prevent the registration of black students James Hood and Vivian Malone.

President John Kennedy announces that he will send a comprehensive civil rights bill to Congress.

A Buddhist monk immolates himself in South Vietnam to protest abuses of the Catholic Diem administration.

13. NAACP field secretary Medgar Evers is assassinated in Jackson, Mississippi.

14. Marshal law is declared in Cambridge, Maryland.

Gadsden, Alabama, mayor Leslie Gilliard obtains an injunction against the freedom movement demonstrators.

The Danville, Virginia, city council adopts an ordinance limiting picket lines to six people.

15. The U.S. Supreme Court declares in *Murray* v. *Curlett* that state

laws requiring Bible reading and prayer in the public schools are unconstitutional.

18. Gadsden activists make a fourth attempt to finish Bill Moore's walk from Gadsden to Jackson, Mississippi. Four hundred fifty people are arrested.

19. President Kennedy sends Congress the broadest civil rights bill any president has endorsed since Reconstruction.

Mississippi governor Ross Barnett welcomes Governor George Wallace to a rally in Jackson, Mississippi, dedicated to preventing the reelection of President Kennedy.

20. Justice Department officials are dispatched to Gadsden, Alabama, to negotiate a settlement of the eleven-day racial crisis. Dr. Martin Luther King, Jr., goes to Gadsden to offer moral support.

22. Sam Shirah arrives in Danville, Virginia.

July

5. Bob Dylan, Pete Seeger and Theodore Bikel perform in Greenwood, Mississippi, to raise funds for the Voter Education Project.

11. Sam Shirah is arrested and brutally beaten in Danville, Virginia.

Rev. Fred Shuttlesworth is elected chair of the Southern Conference Education Fund.

August

2. Virginia federal court upholds the Danville City Council's ordinance against mass demonstrations.

3. The fifth and final attempt is made to complete Bill Moore's walk from Gadsden. Six hundred eighty-two people are arrested. The Gadsden freedom movement falters.

Former Freedom Walker Zev Aeloney is charged with inciting insurrection in Americus, Georgia, and is threatened with the death penalty.

7. Patrick Bouvier Kennedy, infant son of President John Kennedy, dies.

12. Actress Madeleine Sherwood is sentenced to six months at hard labor for breaching the peace in Gadsden, Alabama.

Sam Shirah is released from the Danville City Work Farm and moves to Atlanta, Georgia.

15. Governor Ross Barnett, in an attempt to delay the graduation of James Meredith from the University of Mississippi, requests an inves-

tigation to determine if Meredith violated a university directive against inflammatory speech.

18. Wearing an upside-down button that says "Never" on his robe, James Meredith graduates from Ole Miss with a bachelor's degree in political science.

27. Peace walkers going from Quebec to Guantánamo, Cuba, arrive in D.C. and join the March on Washington.

28. Two hundred fifty thousand Americans march on Washington to support passage of the civil rights bill. Dr. Martin Luther King, Jr., delivers his "I Have a Dream" speech.

September

12. An Alabama grand jury refuses to indict Floyd Simpson for the murder of Bill Moore.

15. Four black girls at Sunday school are killed in the bombing of the Sixteenth Street Baptist Church in Birmingham, Alabama.

18. SNCC petitions the United Nations to probe civil rights violations in the South.

October

2. Sam Shirah is arrested in Columbia, South Carolina, for entering a movie theater with four black students from Benedict College.

5. The Alabama State Legislature passes an act to create the Alabama State Sovereignty Commission, which is charged with safeguarding the rights of the state from the encroachment of any agencies of the federal government.

November

22. John Fitzgerald Kennedy, president of the United States, is assassinated in Dallas, Texas.

24. The accused assassin of President Kennedy, Lee Harvey Oswald, is murdered in Dallas, Texas.

SNCC's fourth annual conference is held at Howard University in Washington, D.C.

December

5. The Warren Commission opens an inquiry into the Kennedy assassination.

10. The African republic of Zanzibar wins its independence from Great Britain.

12. The East African Republic of Kenya gains its independence from Great Britain. African nationalist leader Jomo Kenyatta is declared the first president.

23. Sam Shirah is arrested in Atlanta for sitting in at a Toddle House restaurant.

1964

January

8. President Lyndon Johnson declares "unconditional war on poverty in America" in his State of the Union address.

14. Jack Ruby is sentenced to death for the murder of Lee Harvey Oswald.

Sam Shirah attends the Friends of the Southern Conference Education Fund's twenty-fifth anniversary banquet in New York City.

February

4. The Twenty-fourth Amendment to the U.S. Constitution, prohibiting the use of a poll tax in the election of federal officials, is ratified.

Mississippi summer project recruitment flyers flood northern college campuses requesting students, teachers, nurses, artists, lawyers, and ministers to volunteer to help register black voters in Mississippi.

7. A Mississippi jury trying Byron De La Beckwith for the murder of Medgar Evers is deadlocked. A mistrial is declared.

March

5. Governor George Wallace announces his candidacy for the Republican nomination for president of the United States.

8. Malcolm X splits from Elijah Muhammad's Nation of Islam and considers forming a black nationalist party of his own.

12. Ten thousand New York City residents march on the board of education to protest busing proposal.

12. Malcolm X resigns from the Nation of Islam.

26–29. One hundred students and delegates from SNCC, SCLC, SCEF, and SDS meet with miners in Hazard, Kentucky, to organize an Appalachian miners' project.

April

3. Inaugural meeting of Southern Students Organizing Committee (SSOC) in Nashville, Tennessee.

7. Governor Millard Tawes signs Maryland's first public accommodations act.

21. Pope Paul VI is elected in Rome.

22. New York World's Fair opens in Flushing Meadow Park.

26. Plans for Mississippi Freedom Democratic Party are finalized.

African republics of Zanzibar and Tanganyika unite to form the Republic of Tanzania.

May

9–10. Follow-up SSOC planning conference with forty students held in Atlanta to strengthen ties with SNCC.

June

1. Governor Ross Barnett calls anticipated Mississippi summer project an invasion.

U.S. Supreme Court overturns the ban on NAACP activity in Alabama.

14. South African nationalist leader Nelson Mandela is sentenced to life in prison on a charge of treason.

15. First three hundred Mississippi summer project volunteers gather in Oxford, Ohio, for training.

Elizabeth Khrone drives from Champlain, Illinois, to Jackson, Mississippi, to volunteer with the White Folks Project.

21. Mississippi summer project workers James Chaney, Andrew Goodman, and Michael Schwerner disappear in Philadelphia, Mississippi.

White Folks Project begins in Mississippi, under the directorship of Ed Hamlett, in the cities of Biloxi and Jackson.

Rev. Samuel C. Shirah, Sr., is transferred from his parish in Defuniak Springs, Florida, and sent to a small congregation in Grand Bay, Alabama, as a result of the publicity generated from his antisegregation activities and those of his son Sam, Jr.

July

2. Sam Shirah arrives in Biloxi, Mississippi.

Urban rioting spreads to cities outside the South.

2. The Civil Rights Act of 1964 becomes the law of the land.

10. The FBI opens a field office in Jackson, Mississippi.

15. Barry Goldwater wins the Republican nomination for president.

18. In New York, Harlem and Brooklyn explode in rioting.

21. The U.S. Court of Appeals for the Fifth Circuit in New Orleans rejects an appeal from SNCC that the federal courts enjoin Alabama from prosecuting the ten SNCC/CORE Freedom Walkers for breach of the peace.

August

1. The Christian Crusade names Alabama governor George C. Wallace "Christian Patriot of the Year."

4. The bodies of civil rights workers Schwerner, Goodman, and Chaney are found in Philadelphia, Mississippi.

6. The state convention of the Mississippi Freedom Democratic Party is held in Jackson, Mississippi.

7. The Gulf of Tonkin Resolution authorizes President Johnson to "take all necessary measures to repel any armed attack against forces of the U.S. and to prevent further aggression."

16–17. Chicago, Illinois, erupts in racial rioting.

20. President Johnson signs the Economic Opportunity Act, the "war on poverty" bill.

25. Former attorney general Robert Francis Kennedy enters the New York state senate race.

26. The National Democratic Convention is held in Atlantic City. Lyndon Johnson is nominated. The Mississippi Freedom Democratic Party is denied a seat.

28–30. Philadelphia, Pennsylvania, erupts in racial rioting

September

14. Whites boycott New York City public schools to protest forced busing.

Sam Shirah travels to New Orleans, Louisiana.

October

15. Nikita Khrushchev is replaced by Leonid Brezhnev as premier of the Soviet Union.

24. Northern Rhodesia becomes the African Republic of Zambia, ending seventy-three years of British rule.

November

3. Lyndon Johnson defeats Barry Goldwater in a landslide to become the thirty-sixth president of the United States.

5. SNCC retreat is held at Waveland, Mississippi. Interracial future of SNCC is questioned.

13–15. One hundred fourteen white students from forty-six colleges gather in Atlanta for the first annual conference held by SSOC.

24. R. Sargent Shriver announces three new Great Society programs: the Job Corps, VISTA, and the Neighborhood Youth Corps.

December

10. Martin Luther King, Jr., receives the Nobel Peace Prize.

CORE requests that its white national leaders, including Jim Peck, step down from positions of responsibility.

Sam Shirah resigns from SNCC.

Notes

Part I
The Postman's Walk

Walker

1. William Moore's journal, April 21, 1963; *Binghamton Evening Press*, April 25, 1963. (In part I all incidents cited and all individuals encountered by Bill Moore are actual. Conversations which were not recorded have been reconstructed.)

2. *Binghamton Evening Press*, April 25, 1963.

3. Ibid.

4. *New York Herald Tribune*, April 25, 1963.

5. *New York Post*, April 24, 1963.

6. William Moore's journal, April 20, 1963; *Binghamton Evening Press*, April 25, 1963.

Student

1. William L. Moore, *The Mind in Chains: Autobiography of a Schizophrenic* (New York: Exposition Press, 1955), 67–72.

2. Ibid., 66.

3. Ibid., 31.

4. Ibid., 24–27.

5. Ibid., 79.

6. Ibid., 56–57.

7. Ibid., 119.

8. Ibid., 140–41.

9. Ibid., 135.

10. Ibid., 134–36.

11. Ibid., 146.

12. Ibid., 159–60.

Outsider

1. William Moore's journal, April 22, 1963; *Binghamton Evening Press*, April 25, 1963.

2. Drew Pearson, "Washington Merry-Go-Round," *Washington Post*, April 30, 1963.

3. Murray Kempton, "Pilgrimage to Jackson," *The New Republic*, May 11, 1963, 15.

4. William Moore's journal, April 23, 1963; Jack Mendelsohn, *The Martyrs: Sixteen Who Gave Their Lives for Racial Justice* (New York: Harper & Row, 1966), 57.

5. Moore, *The Mind in Chains*, 67–68, 78.

6. Thom Wilkerson, "Tom's Thumb," *Gadsden Times*, April 24, 1963.

7. *New York Herald Tribune*, April 25, 1963; *Birmingham News*, April 25, 1963.

8. William Moore's journal, April 22, 1963; *New York Herald Tribune*, April 25, 1963.

Patient

1. Elliot S. Valenstein, *Great and Desperate Cures: The Rise and Decline of Psychosurgery and Other Radical Treatments for Mental Illness* (New York: Basic Books, 1986), 107.

2. Moore, *The Mind in Chains*, 195–207, 298.

3. Valenstein, *Great and Desperate Cures*, 52.

4. Walter J. Coville, Timothy W. Costello, and Fabian L. Rouke, *Abnormal Psychology* (New York: Barnes and Noble, 1960), 257.

5. Moore, *The Mind in Chains*, 210.

6. Ibid., 183.

7. Ibid., 186.

8. Ibid., 177.

9. Ibid., 60.

10. *Atlantic Monthly*, January 1962.

11. Moore, *The Mind in Chains*, 184.

12. Ibid., 191.

13. Ibid., 186.

14. Ibid., 188.

15. Ibid., 223–24.

16. Ibid., 287.

17. Ibid., 260.

18. Ibid., 221.

19. Ibid., 238–39.

20. Ibid., 190.

21. Ibid., 192.

Activist

1. *Binghamton Sunday Press*, April 1, 1956.

2. Ibid.

3. J. Angus Johnson, interview by author, August 16, 2000.

4. Phyllis Garland, *Pittsburgh Courier*, May 4, 1963.

5. *Jacksonville Times Union*, December 17, 1956.

6. *Binghamton Sunday Press*, January 11, 1957.

7. Federal Bureau of Investigation, William L. Moore file. Memo dated February 13, 1963.

8. *Binghamton Sun Bulletin*, March 27, 1962.

9. Ibid., May 2, 1962.

10. Wyn Craig Wade, *The Fiery Cross: The Ku Klux Klan in America* (New York: Oxford University Press, 1987), 314.

Crusader

1. William Moore's journal, April 22, 1963; Mendelsohn, *Martyrs*, 58.

2. Michael Eric Dyson, *I May Not Get There with You: The True Martin Luther King, Jr.* (New York: The Free Press, 2000), 240.

3. Mendelsohn, *Martyrs*, 50–51.

4. James Peck, *We Who Would Not Kill* (New York: Lyle Stuart, 1958), 94.

5. Ibid., 91.

6. James Peck, *Underdogs vs. Upperdogs* (Canterbury, New Hampshire: Greenleaf Books, 1969, p. 53; reprint, New York: AMP & R Publisher, 1980).

7. *Binghamton Sun Bulletin*, May 28, 1962.

8. James Farmer, *Lay Bare the Heart: An Autobiography of the Civil Rights Movement* (New York: Penguin Books, 1985), 240.

9. Johnson, interview.

10. FBI, William L. Moore file. Memo dated February 13, 1963.

11. Richard K. Scher, *Politics in the New South: Republicanism, Race, and Leadership in the Twentieth Century* (New York: Paragon House, 1992), 291.

12. FBI, William L. Moore file. Memo dated December 27, 1962.

13. FBI, William L. Moore file. Memo dated December 13, 1962.

14. Mendelsohn, *Martyrs*, 52.

15. *Liberation*, May 25, 1961.

16. Maurice Isserman, *If I Had a Hammer: The Death of the Old Left and the Birth of the New Left* (Chicago: The University of Illinois Press, 1993), 127–28.

17. *Binghamton Press and Sun Bulletin*, February 9, 1986.

Native

1. William Moore's journal, April 23, 1963; Drew Pearson, "Washington Merry-Go-Round," *Washington Post*, April 29, 1963.

2. Moore, *The Mind in Chains*, 43.

3. *Binghamton Evening Press*, April 25, 1963.

4. *Chattanooga Times*, May 25, 1963.

5. William Moore's journal, April 24, 1963; Mendelsohn, *Martyrs*, 58.

Agitator

1. Gadsden district attorney James Hedgspeth, interview by author, June 2, 2000; FBI, William L. Moore file.

2. William Moore's journal, April 24, 1963; *Gadsden Times*, April 25, 1963.

3. Drew Pearson, "Washington Merry-Go-Round," *Washington Post*, April 29, 1963.

Mixer

1. Hedgspeth, interview.

2. *Gadsden Times*, April 26, 1963.

3. Ibid., April 27, 1963.

4. FBI, William L. Moore file. Memo dated April 24, 1963.

5. *Birmingham Post Herald*, April 25, 1963.

6. *Chattanooga News–Free Press*, April 24, 1963.

7. Hedgspeth, interview.

8. William Moore's journal, April 24, 1963; Mendelsohn, *Martyrs*, 60.

9. *Gadsden Times*, April 24, 1963.

10. *Birmingham News*, April 26, 1963.

Victim

1. *Birmingham Post Herald*, April 25, 1963.

2. *Binghamton Evening Press*, April 25, 1963.

3. Greenville (Mississippi) *Delta Democrat Times*, April 25, 1963.

4. *Washington Evening Star*, April 25, 1963.

5. Kempton, "Pilgrimage to Jackson," 15.

6. *Birmingham News*, April 25, 1963.

7. Mendelsohn, *Martyrs*, 60.

8. *Birmingham Post Herald*, April 25, 1963.

The Suspect

1. *Gadsden Times*, April 26, 1963.

2. *Birmingham News*, April 26, 1963.

3. *Gadsden Times*, April 26, 1963.

4. Kempton, "Pilgrimage to Jackson," 16.

5. *Time*, May 10, 1963, 19.

6. *Gadsden Times*, April 29, 1963.

7. Hedgspeth, interview.

8. Ibid.

9. FBI, Floyd L. Simpson file. Memos dated April 9, 1965, and April 21, 1967; Bill Stanton, *Klanwatch: Bringing the Ku Klux Klan to Justice* (New York: Grove Weidenfeld, 1991), 213; Gary Thomas Rowe, Jr., *My Undercover Years with the Ku Klux Klan* (New York: Bantam Books, 1976), 12.

10. Plaintiff's exhibits in *Beula Mae Donald, et al. v. United Klans of America*, Mobile, Alabama, 1983. United Klans Knights of the Ku Klux Klan of America, Inc., oath of allegiance and diagram of klavern.

11. Alabama special investigator Bob Eddy, communication with author, July 3, 2000.

12. Elizabeth Cobbs and Petric J. Smith, *Long Time Coming: An Insider's Story of the Birmingham Church Bombing That Rocked The World* (Birmingham: Crane Hill Publishers, 1994), 101–102.

13. Rowe, *My Undercover Years*, 22.

White Americans React

1. *Binghamton Evening Press*, April 25, 1963.

2. Sheila Michaels, interview by author, January 10, 2001.

3. *Binghamton Evening Press*, April 24, 1963.

4. *Binghamton Sun Bulletin*, April 25, 1963.

5. *Chicago Sun-Times*, "Murder Most Foul," April 26, 1963.

6. Stephan Lesher, *George Wallace: American Populist* (New York: Addison Wesley, 1994), 180.

7. Moore, *The Mind in Chains*, 1.

8. Ibid., 211.

9. York (Pennsylvania) *Daily Gazette*, May 6, 1963.

10. Jerry Handte, *Binghamton Evening Press*, April 25, 1963.

11. *Binghamton Evening Press*, April 25, 1963.

12. Kempton, "Pilgrimage to Jackson," 16.

13. Murray Friedman, "The White Liberals' Retreat," *The Atlantic Monthly*, January 1963, 42–46.

14. Erle Johnston, *Mississippi's Defiant Years, 1953–1973: An Interpretive Documentary with Personal Experiences* (Forest, Mississippi: Lake Harbor Publishers, 1990), 133.

15. Anne Braden, interview by Lenore Bredeson Hogan, Columbia University Oral History Project, June 11, 1980.

16. *Binghamton Evening Press*, April 25, 1963.

17. Ibid., April 26, 1963.

18. Mendelsohn, *Martyrs*, 45.

19. *Birmingham Post Herald*, April 30, 1963.

20. *Time*, May 10, 1963.

21. Kempton, "Pilgrimage to Jackson," 16.

Black Americans React

1. *New York Times*, June 7, 1964.

2. *Pittsburgh Courier*, April 25, 1963.

3. *Binghamton Evening Press*, April 25, 1963.

4. *Birmingham Post Herald*, April 25, 1963.

5. Inge Bell, *CORE and the Strategy of Non-Violence* (New York: Random House, 1968), 20.

6. *Philadelphia Afro-American*, May 4, 1963.

7. *New York Post*, April 24, 1963.

8. *Philadelphia Afro-American*, May 4, 1963.

The Civil Rights Establishment Reacts

1. Taylor Branch, *Parting the Waters: America in the King Years, 1954–63* (New York: Simon & Schuster, 1988), 750; Stephan Lesher, *George Wallace: American Populist* (New York: Addison Wesley, 1994), 179.

2. *Los Angeles Times*, April 25, 1963.

3. *New York Times*, April 29, 1963.

4. *Chattanooga Times*, May 1, 1963.

5. Claude Sitton, *New York Times*, April 29, 1963.

6. Pat Watters, *Down to Now: Reflections on the Southern Civil Rights Movement* (New York: Pantheon Books, 1971), 250.

Part II
The Freedom Walk

Passing the Torch

1. Branch, *Parting the Waters*, 749.

2. Andrew Manis, *A Fire You Can't Put Out: The Civil Rights Life of Birmingham's Reverend Fred Shuttlesworth* (Tuscaloosa: University of Alabama Press, 1999), 365.

3. *New York Times*, May 26, 1963.

4. Frank T. Adams, *James A. Dombrowski: An American Heretic* (Knoxville: University of Tennessee Press, 1992), 259.

5. Background information on Sam Shirah was provided by Dr. Sue Shirah-Sands in a series of interviews by the author, January 22–24, 2001.

6. Donald Collins, *When the Church Bell Rang Racist: The Methodist Church and the Civil Rights Movement* (Macon, Georgia: Mercer University Press, 1998) 18, 58.

7. Adams, *James A. Dombrowski*, 281.

Day One

1. Watters, *Down to Now*, 243.
2. *Mobile Register*, May 9, 1963; *Chattanooga News–Free Press*, May 9, 1963.
3. Watters, *Down to Now*, 244.
4. Oneita Shirah, letter to Ralph Jolly, dean of students, Birmingham-Southern College, April 25, 1963. Collection of Dr. Sue Shirah-Sands.
5. Winston Lockett, interview by author, March 6, 2001.
6. *Chattanooga Times*, April 30, 1963.
7. *Chattanooga News–Free Press*, May 1, 1963.
8. Zev Aelony, interview by author, September 19, 2000.
9. *Mobile Register*, April 30, 1963.
10. *Newsweek*, May 13, 1963.
11. *Chattanooga Daily Times*, May 2, 1963.
12. *New York Times*, April 28, 1963.
13. Text of telegrams taken from the *Chattanooga Times*, May 1, 1963, and the *Birmingham Post Herald*, April 29, 1963.
14. Watters, *Down to Now*, 251.
15. Howard Zinn, *SNCC: The New Abolitionists* (Boston:Beacon Press, 1964), 177.

Day Two

1. James A. Wechsler, "A Long Walk," *New York Post*, April 30, 1963.
2. *New York Times*, May 4, 1963.
3. *Newsweek*, May 13, 1963.
4. *Chattanooga Times*, May 3, 1963; *New York Times*, May 3, 1963.
5. *New York Times*, May 4, 1963; *New York Post*, May 4, 1963.
6. *Chattanooga Times*, May 3, 1963.
7. Zinn, *SNCC: The New Abolitionists*, 178.
8. *Chattanooga Times*, May 3, 1963; FBI, William L. Moore file. Memo dated May 3, 1963.
9. Greenville (Mississippi) *Delta Democrat Times*, May 3, 1963.
10. Eric Weinberger, interview by author, March 4, 2001.
11. Howard Thurman, *The Luminous Darkness: A Personal Interpretation of the Anatomy of Segregation and the Ground of Hope* (New York: Harper & Row, 1965), 57–58.
12. Weinberger, interview.
13. *New York Times*, May 3, 1963.
14. Seth Cagin and Philip Dray, *We Are Not Afraid: The Story of Goodman, Schwerner and Chaney and the Civil Rights Campaign for Mississippi* (New York: Macmillan, 1988), 221.
15. Pat Watters and Reece Cleghorn, *Climbing Jacob's Ladder: The Arrival of Negroes in Southern Politics* (New York: Harcourt, Brace and World, 1967), 61–62.

Day Three

1. William Bradford Huie, *He Slew the Dreamer* (New York: Delacorte Press, 1968; reprint, Montgomery, Alabama: Black Belt Press, 1997), 191.
2. *Chattanooga News–Free Press*, May 4, 1963.
3. Shirah-Sands, interview, January 23, 2001.
4. *Jackson Daily News*, May 3, 1963.
5. *Birmingham News*, May 4, 1963.

6. Robert Gore, interview by author, November 20, 2000.

7. James Forman, *The Making of Black Revolutionaries* (Seattle: University of Washington Press, 1972), 309.

8. *New York Times,* May 1, 1963.

9. Forman, *Making of Black Revolutionaries,* 312.

10. Zinn, *SNCC: The New Abolitionists,* 180–81.

11. Shirah-Sands, interview, January 24, 2001; FBI, Samuel Curtis Shirah, Jr., file, #4422674. Memo dated May 19, 1963.

12. Forman, *Making of Black Revolutionaries,* 308.

13. Aelony, interview.

14. Gore, interview.

15. John Hayman, *Bitter Harvest: Richmond Flowers and the Civil Rights Revolution* (Montgomery: Black Belt Press, 1996), 17.

16. Greenville (Mississippi) *Delta Democrat Times,* May 5, 1963.

17. FBI, Samuel Curtis Shirah, Jr., file, #4422674. Teletype dated May 3, 1963.

18. Sam Shirah, letter to his parents, May 16, 1963. Collection of Dr. Sue Shirah-Sands. The quotation is II Kings 6:16.

19. Gore, interview.

20. Sam Shirah, letter to Oneita Shirah, May 23, 1963. Collection of Dr. Sue Shirah-Sands.

21. Juan Williams, *Eyes on the Prize: America's Civil Rights Years, 1954–1965* (New York: Penguin Books, 1987), 175.

22. Sam Shirah, letter to his parents, May 23, 1963. Collection of Dr. Sue Shirah-Sands.

23. *The Southern Patriot,* June 1964.

Alabama Reacts

1. Bob Zellner, interview by author, August 28, 2000.

2. Ibid.

3. Collins, *When the Church Bell Rang Racist,* 79.

4. Shirah-Sands, interview, January 23, 2001.

5. Rev. Samuel Shirah, letter to Bishop Paul Hardin, June 1963. Collection of Dr. Sue Shirah-Sands.

6. Zellner, interview.

7. Peck, *Underdogs vs. Upperdogs,* 144–45 (reprint edition).

8. Wade, *Fiery Cross,* 314.

9. Michael Dorman, *We Shall Overcome: A Reporter's Eye-Witness Account of the Year of Racial Strife and Triumph* (New York: Dell Publishing Company, 1964), 165.

10. Madeleine Sherwood, interview by author, July 30, 1999.

11. Dorman, *We Shall Overcome,* 165.

12. Ibid., 166.

13. Sherwood, interview.

14. Ibid.

15. Ibid.

Freedom Now!

1. Mary Hamilton, interview by author, June 30, 1999.

2. Ibid.

3. August Meir and Elliot Rudwick, *CORE: A Study in the Civil Rights Movement, 1942–1968* (Chicago: University of Illinois Press, 1975), 215–16.

4. *Baltimore Afro-American*, June 29, 1963.

5. *New York Times*, June 21, 1963.

6. Adam Fairclough, *To Redeem the Soul of America: The Southern Christian Leadership Conference and Martin Luther King, Jr.* (Athens, Georgia: University of Georgia Press, 1987), 148.

7. Sherwood, interview.

8. Mary Hamilton, interview by author, June 30, 2000.

9. Sherwood, interview.

Without Remorse

1. Benjamin Muse, *Ten Years of Prelude* (New York: The Viking Press, 1964), 261.

2. David M. Chalmers, *Hooded Americanism: The History of the Ku Klux Klan*, 3rd ed. (Durham: Duke University Press, 1987), 388.

3. John Shelby Spong, *Rescuing the Bible from Fundamentalism* (San Francisco: Harper, 1991), 4.

4. Rowe, *My Undercover Years with the KKK*, 21.

5. Matthew 28: 19–20.

6. Mathew Ahmann, ed., *Race: Challenge to Religion* (Chicago: Henry Regney Company, 1963), 158.

7. Johnston, *Mississippi's Defiant Years*, 133.

Danville

1. Mary King, *Freedom Song* (New York: William Morrow, 1987), 86.

2. Rev. Lawrence Campbell, sermon, recorded in Danville, Virginia, 1963. Produced by Smithsonian Folkways, 1997: *Voices of the Civil Rights Movement: Black American Songs 1960–1966*.

3. Fairclough, *To Redeem the Soul of America*, 145.

4. Anne Karro, "Friends of Danville," *America*, May 9, 1964, 634.

5. *New York Times*, August 11, 1963.

6. *Birmingham News*, June 12, 1963.

7. Campbell, sermon.

8. Len Holt, *An Act of Conscience* (Boston: Beacon Press, 1965), 208.

9. Ibid., 207.

10. FBI, Samuel Curtis Shirah, Jr., file, #44-22674. Memo dated July 15, 1963.

11. Harlan Joye, memorial broadcast for Sam Shirah. Recorded at WRFG, Atlanta, November 3, 1980.

12. William Kunstler, *Deep in My Heart* (New York: William Morrow, 1966), 232.

13. David Garrow, *Bearing the Cross: Martin Luther King, Jr., and the Southern Christian Leadership Conference* (New York: Random House, 1989), 305–6.

Cognitive Dissonance

1. Danny Lyon, interview by author, July 1, 2000.

2. John Lewis, *Walking with the Wind: A Memoir of the Movement* (New York: Simon and Schuster, 1998), 244.

3. Danny Lyon, "Ain't Gonna Let Nobody Turn Me Round! Use and Misuse of the Southern Civil Rights Movement," *Aperture* 115 (summer 1989):75.

4. Collins, *When the Church Bell Rang Racist*, 80.

5. Rev. James A. Zellner, *Should Sympathy and Support Be Given to Young People Who Agitate and Demonstrate Against Racial Discrimination? A Challenge to the Church and the Older Generation by a Representative of Both*, Century, Florida, August 1963.

6. Spencie Love, *One Blood: The Death and Resurrection of Charles R. Drew* (Chapel Hill: University of North Carolina Press, 1996), 71.

7. Stephen B. Oates, *Let the Trumpet Sound: The Life of Martin Luther King, Jr.* (New York: New American Library, 1982), 247.

8. Minutes, Pastor–Parish Relations Committee Meeting, Defuniak Springs Methodist Church, Defuniak Springs, Florida, September 23, 1963.

9. Rev. Samuel Shirah, letter to Bishop Paul Hardin, September 1963. Collection of Dr. Sue Shirah-Sands.

10. Anne Braden, *HUAC: Bulwark of Segregation*. Pamphlet published by National Committee to Abolish HUAC, Los Angeles, California, 1963.

11. Nicolaus Mills, *Like a Holy Crusade: Mississippi 1964—The Turning of the Civil Rights Movement in America* (Chicago: Ivan R. Dee Publishing Company, 1992), 58.

12. Ibid., 60–63.

13. Clayborne Carson, *In Struggle: SNCC and the Black Awakening of the 1960s* (Cambridge: Harvard University Press, 1981), 99.

Another Direction

1. Danny Lyon, *Memories of the Southern Civil Rights Movement* (Chapel Hill: University of North Carolina Press, 1992), 119–20.

2. Ibid., 119.

3. Ed Hamlett, interview by author, March 8, 2000.

4. Ibid.

5. *New York Times*, December 2, 1963.

6. Arthur I. Waskow, *From Race Riot to Sit-In, 1919 and the 1960s: A Study in the Connections Between Conflict and Violence* (New York: Anchor Books, 1966), 237.

7. Anne Braden, interview by author, July 16, 2000.

8. *New York Times*, December 2, 1963.

9. *Washington Post*, December 2, 1963.

10. *The Student Voice*, December 9, 1963.

11. Jerome H. Skolnick, *The Politics of Protest* (New York: Ballantine Books, 1969), 224.

12. Allen J. Matusow, *The Unraveling of America: A History of Liberalism in the 1960's* (New York: Harper & Row, 1984), 350.

13. Sheila Michaels, interview by author, January 11, 2001.

14. Braden Files, University of Wisconsin, Madison, Wisconsin, Box 45.

15. COFO had been organized by former Mississippi NAACP director Medgar Evers in 1962 and was reactivated by SNCC's Bob Moses and David Dennis of CORE as a statewide coalition of Mississippi rights organizations in an effort to prevent conflict and duplication of effort among groups working on voter education projects. CORE's Michael Schwerner, who would later lose his life along with James Chaney and Andrew Goodman, proposed establishing a white project site in Meridian.

16. Nat Hentoff, *The New Yorker*, October 24, 1964.

17. Steven Kasher, *The Civil Rights Movement: A Photographic History*, 1954–1968 (New York: Abbeville Press, 1996), 4.

18. *The Southern Patriot*, November 1963.

19. Text of Shirah's remarks, "White Youth Seek Liberation," reprinted in *The Southern Patriot*, November 1963.

20. Ibid.

21. Background information on the Hazard Project was provided by Nelson Blackstock in a communication with the author, July 28, 2001, by Steve Max in a communication with the author, September 9, 2001, and from Greg Michel's interview with Nelson Blackstock, August 8, 1995.

22. Ed Hamlett, interview by author, January 21, 2001.

23. Lynne Olson, *Freedom's Daughters: The Unsung Heroines of the Civil Rights Movement from 1830 to 1970* (New York: Scribner, 2001), 178.

24. Hamlett, interview, March 8, 2000.

White Shadow of SNCC

1. *The Southern Patriot*, April 1964.

2. Braden, interview by Hogan.

3. Lewis, *Walking with the Wind*, 244.

4. Ed Hamlett, interview by author, March 16, 2002.

5. Lewis, *Walking with the Wind*, 242–45.

6. Nelson Blackstock, interview by author, January 10, 2001.

7. Jane Stembridge, interview by author, November 1, 2000.

Freedom Summer

1. Shirah-Sands, interview, January 23, 2001.

2. *New York Times*, February 24, 1964.

3. *Eyes on the Prize*, video series I, part 5, "Is This America?" Blackside Productions, Boston, 1987.

4. Background information on the Biloxi White Folks Project was provided by Ed Hamlett, Danny Lyon, Nelson Blackstock, and Jim Williams in interviews by the author; much additional information came from Len Holt's *The Summer That Didn't End: The Story of the Mississippi Civil Rights Project of 1964* (New York: William Morrow, 1965), 129–48.

5. Carson, *In Struggle*, 118.

6. Holt, *The Summer That Didn't End*, 134.

7. Ibid., 129–48.

8. Stembridge, interview.

9. Floyd Barbour, *Black Power Revolt* (Boston: Porter Sargent Publishers, 1968), 214.

10. Mary Aickin Rothschild, *A Case of Black and White: Northern Volunteers and the Southern Freedom Summers, 1964–1965* (Westport, Conn.: Greenwood Press, 1982), 65.

11. Irwin Klibaner, *Conscience of a Troubled South* (Brooklyn: Carlson Publishing Company, 1989), 219.

12. Ibid., 211.

13. *Washington Post*, August 23, 1964.

14. *The Southern Patriot*, June 1967.

15. Klibaner, *Conscience*, 209–20.

16. Mills, *Like a Holy Crusade*, 192.

17. Johnston, *Mississippi's Defiant Years*, 257; Jervis Anderson, *Bayard Rustin: Troubles I've Seen* (New York: Harper Collins, 1992), 279.

18. Olson, *Freedom's Daughters*, 201.

19. Ibid., 166.

20. Stembridge, interview.

Moving On

1. Watters, *Down to Now*, 404.

2. Robert Coles, *Farewell to the South* (Boston: Little, Brown, 1972), 349.

3. Carson, *In Struggle*, 102.

4. Zinn, *SNCC: The New Abolitionists*, 185.

5. Debbie Louis, *And We Are Not Saved: A History of the Movement as People* (New York: Doubleday, 1970), 50.

6. Klibaner, *Conscience*, 223.

7. Zellner, interview.

8. Braden, interview.

9. *Chicago Daily News*, November 27, 1964.

10. Braden, interview.

11. Mendy Samstein, interview by author, September 21, 2000.

12. Samstein, interview; Braden, interview.

13. *The Movement*, May 1967.

14. Background information on the Blue Ridge strike and the organizaton of SLAM was provided by Ed Hamlett, Harlan Joye, Barbara Joye, Nelson Blackstock, and Martin Morand in interviews by the author, and by Gregg Laurence Michel's "We'll Take Our Stand: The Southern Student Organizing Committee and the Radicalization of White Southern Students 1964–1969" (Ph.D. diss., University of Virginia, 1999), 386–402.

15. *The Movement*, May 1968.

16. Harlan Joye reporting on the Blue Ridge Levi Strauss strike and interviewing the strikers. Hosted by Mike O'Dell, Pacifica Radio Broadcast, Atlanta, 1967. Collection of Harlan Joye.

17. *SLAM Newsletter*, vol. 1, no. 1, August 22, 1966.

18. Coles, *Farewell to the South*, 253.

19. Michel, "We'll Take Our Stand," 376.

20. Harlan Joye, interview by author, March 20, 2001.

21. G. McLeod Bryan, *These Few also Paid a Price: Southern Whites Who Fought for Civil Rights* (Macon, Ga.: Mercer University Press, 2001), 24.

22. Stembridge, interview.

23. Fred Hobson, *But Now I See: The White Southern Racial Conversion Narrative* (Baton Rouge: Louisiana State University Press, 1999), 17.

24. Collins, *When the Church Bell Rang Racist*, 98.

25. Braden, interview.

A March against Fear

1. *New York Times*, June 6, 1966.

2. Carson, *In Struggle*, 209–10.

3. Garrow, *Bearing the Cross*, 484.

4. Carson, *In Struggle*, 210.

5. *New York Times*, June 25, 1966.

6. Garrow, *Bearing the Cross*, 486.

7. *New York Times*, June 27, 1966.

8. Ibid.

9. *Montgomery Advertiser*, May 1, 1963.

10. *New York Times*, June 12, 1966.

11. Mathew Ahman, ed., *Race: Challenge to Religion* (Chicago: Henry Regnery Co., 1963), 62, 63.

Bibliography

Adams, Frank T. *James A. Dombrowski: An American Heretic.* University of Tennessee Press, Knoxville, 1992.

Ahmann, Mathew, ed. *Race: Challenge to Religion.* Henry Regnery Company, Chicago, 1963.

Anderson, Jervis. *Bayard Rustin: Troubles I've Seen.* Harper Collins, New York, 1997.

"Attalla and the Huns." *America,* 108:658, May 11, 1963.

Barbour, Floyd, ed. *The Black Power Revolt.* Porter Sargent Publishers, Boston, 1968.

Bartley, Numan V. *The Rise of Massive Resistance: Race and Politics in the South During the 1950's.* Louisiana State University Press, Baton Rouge, 1969.

Bawer, Bruce. *Stealing Jesus.* Crown Publishers, New York, 1997.

Beers, Clifford Whittingham. *A Mind That Found Itself.* 1908. Reprint, University of Pittsburgh Press, Pittsburgh, 1981.

Belfrage, Sally. "Danville on Trial." *The New Republic,* November 2, 1963.

Bell, Inge. *CORE and the Strategy of Non-Violence.* Random House, New York, 1968.

Bennett, Lerone, Jr. *The Negro Mood and Other Essays.* Johnson Publishing Company, Chicago, 1964.

Boyle, Sarah Patton. *The Desegregated Heart: A Virginian's Stand in Time of Transition.* William Morrow & Company, New York, 1962.

Braden, Anne. "House Un-American Activities Committee: Bulwark of Segregation." Pamphlet published by National Committee to Abolish HUAC, Los Angeles, 1963.

———. Interview by Lenore Bredeson Hogan. Columbia University Oral History Project, New York, June 11, 1980.

———. *The Wall Between.* Monthly Review Press, Nashville, 1958. Reprint, University of Tennessee Press, Knoxville, 1999.

Branch, Taylor. *Parting the Waters: America in the King Years, 1954–63,* Simon & Schuster, New York, 1988.

Brisbane, Robert H. *Black Activism: Racial Revolution in the United States, 1954–1970.* Judson Press, Valley Forge, Pennsylvania, 1974.

Browning, Joan C. "Invisible Revolutionaries: White Women in Civil Rights Historiography." *Journal of Women's History,* fall 1996.

Bryan, G. McLeod. *These Few also Paid a Price: Southern Whites Who Fought for Civil Rights.* Mercer University Press, Macon, Georgia, 2001.

Bullard, Sara. *Free at Last: A History of the Civil Rights Movement and Those Who Died in the Struggle.* Oxford University Press, New York, 1993.

Burner, David, and Thomas R. West. *The Torch Is Passed: The Kennedy Brothers and American Liberalism.* Athenaeum, New York, 1983.

Cagin, Seth, and Philip Dray. *We Are Not Afraid: The Story of Goodman, Schwerner and Chaney and the Civil Rights Campaign for Mississippi.* Macmillan, New York, 1988.

Carson, Clayborne. *In Struggle: SNCC and the Black Awakening of the 1960s.* Harvard University Press, Cambridge, 1981.

———, ed. *The Student Voice 1960–1965: A Periodical of SNCC.* Meckler Press, Westport, Connecticut, 1981.

Carter, Hodding. *The South Strikes Back.* Doubleday & Company, New York, 1959.

Cash, W. J. *The Mind of the South.* Alfred A. Knopf, New York, 1941.

Caudill, Harry M. *Night Comes to the Cumberlands: A Biography of a Depressed Area.* Atlantic Monthly Press, Boston, 1962.

Chalmers, David M. *Hooded Americanism: The History of the Ku Klux Klan.* 3rd ed. Duke University Press, Durham, 1987.

Chappell, David L. *Inside Agitators: White Southerners in the Civil Rights Movement.* Johns Hopkins University Press, Baltimore, 1994.

Cobb, James C. *The Most Southern Place on Earth: The Mississippi Delta and the Roots of Regional Identity.* Oxford University Press, New York, 1992.

Cobbs, Elizabeth H., and Petric J. Smith. *Long Time Coming: An Insider's Story of the Birmingham Church Bombing That Rocked The World.* Crane Hill Publishers, Birmingham, 1994.

Coles, Robert. *Farewell to the South.* Little, Brown and Company, Boston, 1972.

Collins, Donald E. *When the Church Bell Rang Racist: The Methodist Church and the Civil Rights Movement in Alabama.* Mercer University Press, Macon, Georgia, 1998.

Columbus, Sally, and Ronald Behm. *Your God's Too White.* Inter-Varsity Press, Downers Grove, Illinois, 1970.

Cone, James H. *For My People: Black Theology and the Black Church.* Orbis Books, Maryknoll, New York, 1984.

Coville, Walter J., Timothy W. Costello, and Fabian L. Rouke. *Abnormal Psychology.* Barnes and Noble, New York, 1960.

Covington, Dennis. *Salvation on Sand Mountain.* Addison-Wesley, New York, 1995.

Cuninggim, Merriman, ed. *Christianity and Communism: An Inquiry into Relationships.* Southern Methodist University Press, Dallas, 1958.

Curry, Constance, et al. *Deep in Our Hearts: Nine White Women in the Freedom Movement.* University of Georgia Press, Athens, 2000.

Dabbs, James McBride. *Who Speaks for the South?* Funk & Wagnalls, New York, 1967.

Dickerson, James. *Dixie's Dirty Secret.* M.E. Sharpe Publishers, Armonk, New York, 1998.

Dorman, Michael. *We Shall Overcome: A Reporter's Eye-Witness Account of the Year of Racial Strife and Triumph.* Dell Publishing Company, New York, 1964.

Durham, Michael S. *Powerful Days: The Civil Rights Photography of Charles Moore.* Stewart, Tabori & Chang, New York, 1991.

Dykeman, Wilma, and James Stokeley. *Neither Black nor White.* Rinehart and Company, Inc., New York, 1957.

Dyson, Michael Eric. *I May Not Get There with You: The True Martin Luther King, Jr.* The Free Press, New York, 2000.

Egerton, John. *Speak Now Against the Day: The Generation Before the Civil Rights Movement in the South.* Alfred A. Knopf, New York, 1994.

Eskew, Glenn T. *But for Birmingham: The Local and National Movements in the Civil Rights Struggle.* University of North Carolina Press, Chapel Hill, 1997.

Evans, Sara. *Personal Politics: The Roots of Women's Liberation in the Civil Rights Movement and the New Left.* Vintage Books, New York, 1980.

Fairclough, Adam. *To Redeem the Soul of America: The Southern Christian Leadership Conference and Martin Luther King, Jr.* University of Georgia Press, Athens, 1987.

Fariello, Griffin. *Red Scare: Memories of the American Inquisition.* W.W. Norton & Company, New York, 1995.

Farmer, James. *Lay Bare the Heart: An Autobiography of the Civil Rights Movement.* Penguin Books, New York, 1985.

Feldman, Glenn. *Politics, Society and the Klan in Alabama 1915–1949.* University of Alabama Press, Tuscaloosa, 1999.

Forman, James. *The Making of Black Revolutionaries.* University of Washington Press, Seattle, 1972.

Frady, Marshall. *Wallace.* New American Library, New York, 1968.

Fraser, Ronald, ed. *1968: A Student Generation in Revolt.* Pantheon Books, New York, 1988.

Friedman, Murray. "The White Liberal's Retreat." *Atlantic,* January 1963, 42–46.

Gaillard, Frye. *The Heart of Dixie: Southern Rebels, Renegades and Heroes.* Downhome Press, Asheboro, North Carolina, 1978.

Garrow, David J. *Bearing the Cross: Martin Luther King, Jr., and the Southern Christian Leadership Conference.* Random House, New York, 1988.

———, ed. *Birmingham, Alabama 1956–1963: The Black Struggle for Civil Rights.* Carlson Publishers, Inc., Brooklyn, New York, 1989.

Golden, Harry. *Mr. Kennedy and the Negroes.* The World Publishing Company, Cleveland, Ohio, 1964.

Goldfield, David R. *Black, White and Southern: Race Relations and Southern Culture, 1940 to the Present.* Louisiana State University Press, Baton Rouge, 1990.

Greenberg, Cheryl Lynn, ed. *A Circle of Trust: Remembering SNCC.* Rutgers University Press, New Brunswick, New Jersey, 1998.

Hanns, Lilje. *Atheism, Humanism and Christianity.* Augsburg Publishing House, Minneapolis, 1964.

Hansberry, Lorraine. *A Matter of Colour: Documentary of the Struggle for Racial Equality in the USA.* Penguin Books, New York, 1965.

Haselden, Kyle. *The Racial Problem in Christian Perspective.* Harper & Brothers, New York, 1959.

———. *Mandate for White Christians.* John Knox Press, Richmond, Virginia, 1966.

Hayden, Tom. *Reunion: A Memoir.* Random House, New York, 1988.

Hemphill, Paul. *Leaving Birmingham: Notes of a Native Son.* Penguin Books, New York, 1993.

Hentoff, Nat. *The New Equality.* Viking Press, New York, 1964.

Hill, Samuel S., Jr. *Southern Churches in Crisis.* Holt, Rinehart & Winston, New York, 1966.

Holt, Len. *An Act of Conscience.* Beacon Press, Boston, 1965.

———. "Eyewitness: The Police Terror In Birmingham." *National Guardian,* May 16, 1963.

———. *The Summer That Didn't End: The Story of the Mississippi Civil Rights Project of 1964.* William Morrow, New York, 1965.

Hough, Joseph C., Jr. *Black Power and White Protestants.* Oxford University Press, New York, 1968.

Hudson, Winthrop S. *Religion in America.* Charles Scribner's Sons, New York, 1965.

Huie, William Bradford. *He Slew the Dreamer.* Delacorte Press, New York, 1968. Reprint, Black Belt Press, Montgomery, Alabama, 1997.

"In Bill Moore's Footsteps." *Time,* May 10, 1963.

Isserman, Maurice. *If I Had a Hammer: The Death of the Old Left and the Birth of the New Left.* University of Illinois Press, Chicago, 1993.

James, William. *The Varieties of Religious Experience.* University Books, New York, 1963.

Johnston, Erle. *Mississippi's Defiant Years, 1953–1973: An Interpretive Documentary with Personal Experiences*. Lake Harbor Publishers, Forest, Mississippi, 1990.

———. *I Rolled with Ross: A Political Portrait*. Moran Publishing Corporation, Baton Rouge, Louisiana, 1980.

Joye, Harlan E. "Dixie's New Left." *Trans-action*, September 1970, 50–56, 62.

Karro, Anne. "Friends of Danville." *America*, May 9, 1964, 633–35.

Kempton, Murray. "Pilgrimage to Jackson." *New Republic*, May 11, 1963.

Klibaner, Irwin. *Conscience of a Troubled South*. Carlson Publishing Company, Brooklyn, New York, 1989.

King, Mary. *Freedom Song: A Personal Story of the 1960s Civil Rights Movement*. William Morrow, New York, 1987.

King, Richard. *Civil Rights and the Idea of Freedom*. Oxford University Press, New York, 1992.

Kunstler, William. *Deep in My Heart*. William Morrow, New York, 1966.

Lacroix, Jean. *The Meaning of Modern Atheism*. Macmillan, New York, 1965.

Layman, Richard, ed. *American Decades, 1960–1969*. Gale Research, Inc., Detroit, 1995.

Lazenby, Marion E. *History of Methodism in Alabama and West Florida*. A publication of the North Alabama and Alabama–West Florida Conferences of the Methodist Church, 1960.

Lesher, Stephan. *George Wallace: American Populist*. Addison Wesley, New York, 1994.

Levy, Charles J. *Voluntary Servitude: Whites in the Negro Movement*. Appleton-Century-Crofts, New York, 1968.

Lewis, Anthony. *Portrait of a Decade: The Second American Revolution*. Random House, New York, 1964.

Lewis, John. *Walking with the Wind: A Memoir of the Movement*. Simon and Schuster, New York, 1998.

Lincoln, C. Eric. *Race, Religion and the Continuing American Dilemma*. Hill and Wang, New York, 1984.

Lomax, Louis E. *The Negro Revolt*. Signet Books, New York, 1962.

Long, Margaret. "The Imperial Wizard Explains The Klan." *New York Times Magazine*, July 5, 1964.

Louis, Debbie. *And We Are Not Saved: A History of the Movement as People*. Doubleday & Company, New York, 1970.

Lukas, J. Anthony. *Don't Shoot—We Are Your Children!* Dell Publishing Company, New York, 1968.

Luker, Ralph E. *Historical Dictionary of the Civil Rights Movement*. The Scarecrow Press, Lanham, Maryland, 1997.

Lynd, Staughton, and Alice Lynd, eds. *Nonviolence in America: A Documentary History*. Revised edition. Maryknoll, New York, Orbis Books, 1995.

Lyon, Danny. *Memories of the Southern Civil Rights Movement*. The University of North Carolina Press, Chapel Hill, 1992.

McCord, William. *Mississippi: The Long Hot Summer*. W. W. Norton & Company, New York, 1965.

McKenzie, John G. *Nervous Disorders and Religion: A Study of Souls in the Making*. New York, Crowell-Collier, 1962.

McMillen, Neil. *The Citizens' Council: Organized Resistence to the Second Reconstruction, 1954–64*. University of Illinois Press, Urbana, 1971.

McWhorter, Diane. *Carry Me Home: Birmingham, Alabama: The Climactic Battle of the Civil Rights Revolution*. Simon & Schuster, New York, 2001.

Manis, Andrew. *A Fire You Can't Put Out: The Civil Rights Life of Birmingham's Reverend Fred Shuttlesworth*. University of Alabama Press, Tuscaloosa, 1999.

Marable, Manning. *Race, Reform and Rebellion: The Second Reconstruction in Black America*. University Press of Mississippi, Jackson, 1984.

Martin, John Bartlow. *The Deep South Says Never*. Ballentine Books, New York, 1957.

Matusow, Allen J. *The Unraveling of America: A History of Liberalism in the 1960's*. Harper & Row, New York, 1984.

Meier, August. "The Growth of Negro Influence." *Current*, August 1963, 35–41.

Meier, August, and Elliot Rudwick. *CORE: A Study in the Civil Rights Movement, 1942–1968*. University of Illinois Press, Chicago, 1975.

Meier, August, Elliot Rudwick, and John Bracey, Jr. *Black Protest in the Sixties: Articles from the New York Times*. Markus Wiener Publishing Co., New York, 1991.

Mendelsohn, Jack. *The Martyrs: Sixteen Who Gave Their Lives for Racial Justice*. Harper & Row, New York, 1966.

Miller, Dorothy, and Danny Lyon. *Danville, Virginia*. Pamphlet published by the Student Nonviolent Coordinating Committee, Atlanta, Georgia, August 1963.

Miller, William Robert. *Martin Luther King, Jr.* Avon Books, New York, 1968.

Mills, Nicolaus. *Like a Holy Crusade: Mississippi 1964—The Turning of the Civil Rights Movement in America*. Ivan R. Dee Publishing Company, Chicago, 1992.

Moore, William. *The Mind in Chains: Autobiography of a Schizophrenic*. Exposition Press, New York, 1955.

———. "An Ex-Patient's Heartening Plea: How You Can Keep Thousands Like Me Out of Mental Hospitals." *Parade*, April 26, 1959.

———. "My Friend in Viet Nam." *New World Review*, August 1962.

Newfield, Jack. *A Prophetic Minority*. New American Library, New York, 1967.

"No Place to Walk—A Tribute to William Moore." *Newsweek*, May 13, 1963.

Oates, Stephen B. *Let the Trumpet Sound: The Life of Martin Luther King, Jr.* New American Library, New York, 1982.

Olson, Lynne. *Freedom's Daughters: The Unsung Heroines of the Civil Rights Movement from 1830 to 1970*. Scribner, New York, 2001.

Paper, Lewis H. *The Promise and the Performance: The Leadership of John F. Kennedy*. Crown Publishers, New York, 1975.

Paris, Peter J. *The Social Teaching of the Black Churches*. Fortress Press, Philadelphia, 1985.

Payne, Charles M. *I've Got the Light of Freedom: The Organizing Tradition and the Mississippi Freedom Struggle*. University of California Press, Berkeley, 1995.

Peck, James. *Freedom Ride*. Simon & Schuster, New York, 1962.

———. *Underdogs vs. Upperdogs*. Greenleaf Books, Canterbury, New Hampshire, 1969. Reprint, AMP & R Publisher, New York, 1980.

———. *We Who Would Not Kill*. Lyle Stuart, New York, 1958.

Pinkney, Alphonso. *Black Americans*. Prentice-Hall, New York, 1969.

Polenberg, Richard. *One Nation Divisible: Class, Race and Ethnicity in the U.S.* Viking Press, New York, 1980.

"The Politics of Religious Equality." *America*, 108:658, May 11, 1963.

Powledge, Fred. *Free at Last: The Civil Rights Movement and the People Who Made It*. Little, Brown & Company, New York, 1991.

Reed, Linda. *Simple Decency & Common Sense: The Southern Conference Movement, 1938–1963*. Indiana University Press, 1991.

Richardson, Alan. *Religion in Contemporary Debate.* The Westminster Press, Philadelphia, 1966.

Rothschild, Mary Aickin. *A Case of Black and White: Northern Volunteers and the Southern Freedom Summers, 1964–1965.* Greenwood Press, Westport, Connecticut, 1982.

Rowe, Gary Thomas, Jr. *My Undercover Years with the Ku Klux Klan.* Bantam Books, New York, 1976.

Salter, John R., Jr. *Jackson, Mississippi.* Robert E. Krieger Publishing Company, Malabar, Florida, 1987.

Schultz, Debra L. *Going South: Jewish Women in the Civil Rights Movement.* New York University Press, New York, 2001.

Sellers, James. *The South and Christian Ethics.* Association Press, New York, 1962.

Shelton, Robert. *No Direction Home: The Life and Music of Bob Dylan.* DaCapo Press, New York, 1997.

Sherrill, Robert. *Gothic Politics in the Deep South.* Ballantine Books, New York, 1968.

Shirah, Sam. "White Youth Seek Liberation." *The Southern Patriot,* November 1963.

Silberman, Charles E. *Crisis in Black and White.* Random House, New York, 1964.

Silver, James W. *Mississippi: The Closed Society.* Harcourt, Brace & World, New York, 1963.

Sitkoff, Harvard. *The Struggle for Black Equality, 1954–1980.* Hill and Wang, New York, 1981.

Skolnick, Jerome H. *The Politics of Protest.* Ballantine Books, New York, 1969.

Smith, Lillian. *Killers of the Dream,* W. W. Norton & Co., New York, 1949.

Sobel, Lester A., ed. *Civil Rights 1960–66 Interim History.* Facts on File, New York, 1967.

Sosna, Morton. *In Search of the Silent South.* Columbia University Press, New York, 1977.

Spong, John Shelby. *Rescuing the Bible from Fundamentalism.* Harper, San Francisco, 1991.

Sterne, Emma Gelders. *They Took Their Stand.* Crowell, Collier, New York, 1968.

Stoper, Emily. *The Student Non-Violent Coordinating Committee: The Growth of Radicalism in a Civil Rights Organization.* Carlson Publications, Brooklyn, New York, 1989.

Strunk, Orlo, Jr. *The Choice Called Atheism.* Abingdon Press, Nashville, 1968.

Sugarman, Tracy. *Stranger at the Gates: A Summer in Mississippi.* Hill & Wang, New York, 1966.

Thurman, Howard. *The Luminous Darkness: A Personal Interpretation of the Anatomy of Segregation and the Ground of Hope.* Harper & Row, New York, 1965.

Tilson, Everett. *Segregation and the Bible.* Abingdon Press, Nashville, 1958.

Tracy, James. *Direct Action: Radical Pacifism from the Union Eight to the Chicago Seven.* University of Chicago Press, Chicago, 1996.

Traynham, Warner R. *Christian Faith in Black and White: A Primer in Theology from the Black Perspective.* Parameter Press, Wakefield, Massachusetts, 1973.

Tucker, Richard. *The Dragon and the Cross.* Archon Books, Hamden, Connecticut, 1991.

Valenstein, Elliot S. *Great and Desperate Cures: The Rise and Decline of Psychosurgery and Other Radical Treatments for Mental Illness.* Basic Books, New York, 1986.

Vivian, C. T. *Black Power and the American Myth.* Fortress Press, Philadelphia, 1970.

Wade, Wyn Craig. *The Fiery Cross: The Ku Klux Klan in America.* Oxford University Press, New York, 1987.

Wakefield, Dan. *Revolt in the South.* Grove Press, Inc., New York, 1960.

———. "In Hazard." *Commentary,* September 1963.

Walls, David S., and John B. Stephenson, eds. *Appalachia in the Sixties: Decade of Reawakening.* University Press of Kentucky, Lexington, 1972.

Warren, Robert Penn. *Segregation: The Inner Conflict of the South.* Random House, New York, 1956.

Waskow, Arthur. *From Race Riot to Sit-In, 1919 and the 1960s: A Study in the Connections Between Conflict and Violence.* Anchor Books, New York, 1967.

Watters, Pat. *Down to Now: Reflections on the Southern Civil Rights Movement.* Pantheon Books, New York, 1971.

Watters, Pat, and Reece Cleghorn. *Climbing Jacob's Ladder: The Arrival of Negroes in Southern Politics.* Harcourt, Brace and World, New York, 1967.

Weisbrot, Robert. *Freedom Bound: A History of America's Civil Rights Movement.* Penguin Books, New York, 1991.

Weller, Jack E. *Yesterday's People.* University of Kentucky Press, Lexington, Kentucky, 1966.

Williams, Juan. *Eyes on the Prize: America's Civil Rights Years, 1954–1965.* Penguin Books, New York, 1987.

Wilson, Charles R. *Judgement and Grace in Dixie.* University of Georgia Press, Athens, 1995.

Wright, Lawrence. *Saints and Sinners.* Alfred A. Knopf, New York, 1993.

Zinn, Howard. *SNCC: The New Abolitionists.* Beacon Press, Boston, 1964.

———. "The Battle-Scarred Youngsters." *The Nation*, October 5, 1963, 193–97.

Index

Made in the USA
Lexington, KY
03 September 2010